T0047642

NOW THAT

Faith

HAS Come

A STUDY OF GALATIANS

BETH MOORE & MELISSA MOORE

Published by Living Proof Ministries
© 2020 Beth Moore and Melissa Moore

No part of this book may be reproduced or transmitted in any form or by any means, electronic or mechanical, including photocopying and recording, or by any information storage or retrieval system, except as may be expressly permitted in writing by the publisher. Requests for permission should be addressed in writing to 12131 Malcomson Rd, Houston, TX 77070.

Atlas map © Christian Standard Bible® Copyright © 2017 by Holman Bible Publishers

Layout/Design by Cheryl Casey (Cover photo provided by Anastasilia Chepinska unsplash.com)
Editing by Abby Perry

Unless otherwise noted, all Scripture quotations are taken from the Christian Standard Bible®, Copyright © 2017 by Holman Bible Publishers. Used by permission. Christian Standard Bible® and CSB® are federally registered trademarks of Holman Bible Publishers.

Scripture quotations marked (NIV) are taken from the Holy Bible, New International Version®, NIV®. Copyright © 1973, 1978, 1984, 2011 by Biblica, Inc.™ Used by permission of Zondervan. All rights reserved worldwide. www.zondervan.com The "NIV" and "New International Version" are trademarks registered in the United States Patent and Trademark Office by Biblica, Inc.™

Scripture quotations marked (CEB) are taken from the COMMON ENGLISH BIBLE. © Copyright 2011 COMMON ENGLISH BIBLE. All rights reserved. Used by permission. (www.CommonEnglishBible.com).

Scripture quotations marked (ESV) are from the ESV® Bible (The Holy Bible, English Standard Version®), copyright © 2001 by Crossway, a publishing ministry of Good News Publishers. Used by permission. All rights reserved.

Scripture quoted by permission. Quotations designated (NET) are from the NET Bible® copyright ©1996, 2019 by Biblical Studies Press, L.L.C. http://netbible.com All rights reserved.

Scripture quotations marked (NKJV) taken from the New King James Version®. Copyright © 1982 by Thomas Nelson. Used by permission. All rights reserved.

Scripture quotations marked (REB) taken from the Revised English Bible, copyright © Cambridge University Press and Oxford University Press 1989. All rights reserved.

Scripture quotations marked (NLT) are taken from the Holy Bible, New Living Translation, copyright ©1996, 2004, 2015 by Tyndale House Foundation. Used by permission of Tyndale House Publishers, a Division of Tyndale House Ministries, Carol Stream, Illinois 60188. All rights reserved.

Scripture quotations marked (NASB) taken from the New American Standard Bible® (NASB), Copyright © 1960, 1962, 1963, 1968, 1971, 1972, 1973, 1975, 1977, 1995 by The Lockman Foundation. Used by permission. www.Lockman.org

Scripture marked "The Message" taken from The Message. Copyright © 1993, 1994, 1995, 1996, 2000, 2001, 2002. Used by permission of NavPress Publishing Group.

Section marked "Excerpt" or "Appendix" taken from Eugene H. Peterson, *Eat This Book* © 2006. Wm. B. Eerdmans Publishing Company, Grand Rapids, MI. Reprinted by permission of the publisher; all rights reserved.

Credits and permissions are listed under the tab marked "Credits" and are considered a continuation of the copyright page.

To order additional copies of this resource, order online at bethmoore.org; call 1.888.700.1999; or email at lproof@lproof.org.

ISBN 978-1-7358909-0-6

Printed in the United States of America

26   25   24   23   22   21
7   6   5   4   3   2

dedication

With tremendous love, deep gratitude and pure respect,
we dedicate this Bible study series to each of our co-laborers:
Cathy Adams
Danielle Belvin
Dana Haddad
Jenn Hamm
Susan Kirby
Kimberly McMahon
Kimberly Meyer
Sabrina Moore
Natalie Mott
Selena Schorken
Mary Scott
Evangeline Williams
and
Clare Wineman.
We took on the monumental task of publishing
this Bible study series in-house at Living Proof Ministries
and it required every last one of us.
Each set of handprints is on this project
in one way or another.
It was an enormous undertaking for a small ministry.
Now That Faith Has Come: A Study of Galatians
is in your hands by the unfathomable grace
and wonder-working power of God
manifested through a team of women
who just won't quit.

Our special thanks also to Abby Perry,
our world's favorite editor.

With much affection,

Beth and *Melissa*

Beth Moore *Melissa Moore*

INTRODUCTION

We are so pleased to serve you! We have each loved studying Paul's letter to the Galatians and look tremendously forward to walking with you through it. Our participants in several previous studies responded so well to Melissa's supplemental articles that we teamed up and cowrote the six weeks of homework for this series. We divided the study in the following ways so you'll always know which teacher to expect:

BETH: All seven video sessions and
days one, three and five in each week of homework

MELISSA: Days two and four in each week of homework

BETH & MELISSA: Midweek podcasts

So, friends, what you've got in front of you is a two-for-one. If you are unfamiliar with Melissa, she brings a wealth to the mix. She holds an M.A. in Biblical Exegesis (Wheaton College Graduate School, 2007), a Th.M. in Biblical Studies (Columbia Theological Seminary, 2010) and an M.A. in Biblical Languages (Houston Baptist University, 2016). Our earnest hope is that having two different teachers, each with her own writing approach and learning style, will be twice the benefit to you. We have taken every moment of preparation seriously, sought God continually and studied as diligently as we could in order, by His enabling power and grace, to offer sound teaching to you that is true to the text. The joy of our ministry lives is to study the Scriptures and to pore over the sacred pages with you. May God take every second you spend in this series and return it to you in deeper, richer love for Jesus and far greater confidence in His glorious gospel. We count it a privilege to serve you.

TABLE OF CONTENTS

Face the sins.

Taste the grace.

Galatians will be that kind of straightforward journey. It is graphic not only in its confrontation, but in its beauty and gospel clarity. Squinting at a list of transgressions as tall as the tower of Babel, we declare, "Jesus gave Himself for these."

— Beth Moore

GOSPEL

zone one

GOSPEL

GALATIANS 1

———

For am I now trying to persuade people, or God?
Or am I striving to please people? If I were still trying
to please people, I would not be a servant of Christ.

Galatians 1:10

VIDEO GUIDE

THE GOSPEL ZONE

Introduction: Today we embark on a six-week in-depth study of a letter of inestimable impact on the identity-formation and theology of the New Testament church.

This book is the most UNAPOLOGETIC APOLOGETIC of the truth of the gospel in the entirety of Paul's letters.

We'll assign a zone to each chapter based on a principal term found within it:

Read Galatians 1:1–12, giving particular attention to the use of the term we've established as our first zone.

Note the wording in Galatians 1:11: "the gospel preached by me."

According to scholar Richard B. Hays, the Greek transliteration *("to euangelion to euangelisthen hyp' emou")* "is impossible to render exactly into idiomatic English; literally, it means 'the gospel that was _____ by me.'"[1]

Paul's premise for the letter to the Galatians:

The gospel was given by God and _____ by man.

The gospel is to be _____, not _____.

NOTES

_____

_____

_____

_____

_____

_____

_____

_____

_____

_____

_____

_____

_____

_____

_____

_____

[1] Richard B. Hays, "Galatians," in *The New Interpreter's Bible* Vol. XI (Nashville: Abingdon Press, 2000), 211. © 2000 Abingdon Press. Used by permission. All rights reserved.

NOTES

GOSPEL

THE GOSPEL ZONE

day one

To the Churches of Galatia

Welcome to a study of Paul's letter to the Galatians. Melissa and I are ecstatic to have you join us. We've talked about this book of the Bible and all we've reaped from it obsessively for over a year. Nothing could make us happier than to have you jump in the conversation with us. You have six chapters of fire in front of you. The fire will warm you at times and may threaten to scorch you at others, but this much I can promise you: if you're willing to engage, Galatians will mark you. It has indelibly marked Melissa and me. Sometimes, the exact same words or concepts in the letter hit us profoundly. Other times, completely different aspects held us captive. This is the glorious way of God. He speaks through Scripture both to Church and child. He will meet you in those pages. You're not in them alone even if you're taking this series by yourself.

If you've studied the letter before, perhaps you'll discover what I have as I've revisited passages of Scripture—a journey of unforeseen impact can happen with Jesus even while traversing the most familiar terrain. The words have been fixed, static and immovable on the pages of Bibles for millennia, but their timing in our lives and our posture toward them can join together to birth a brand new work. The original context, culture and content haven't changed but, by the power of the Holy Spirit, the words—still warm with the breath of God—change us. Let's welcome that change.

Each lesson will open with the following three instructions meant for interaction with the Scriptures alone before any further comment:

1. Read the text.
2. Write the text.
3. Mark the text.

Read the text: The Christian Standard Bible (CSB) will be home base for us throughout this series but we will regularly quote from other translations. You are welcome to use any formal translation you choose. Electronic Bibles can be extremely useful and, by all means, consult them as you wish, but we encourage you to keep your own hardcopy of the Scriptures wide open in front of you.

Write the text: Write the verses you read from your Bible, always noting the translation, into the space below.

Mark the text: After you've written the segment, underline, circle or mark any word or phrase that stands out to you. You can keep it simple or you can get as creative as you like. The goal is to familiarize yourself with the Scriptures themselves before you read anything else, so mark the text up in a way that helps you get to know it better.

OK, let's get to it! **Read, write and mark Galatians 1:1–5 in the space below.**

_____

_____

_____

_____

_____

_____

_____

_____

_____

_____

_____

_____

After identifying himself as author, what specific claim does Paul make concerning his apostleship in v.1? _____

Paul uses a different phrase in 1 Corinthians 1:1, Ephesians 1:1 and Colossians 1:1 to make a similar point. How does he qualify his apostleship in those three salutations? _____

In short, Paul reminds his readers that he did not call himself nor did any human call him. He was called to be an apostle by God alone. While this certainty of his calling must have caused Paul, conscious of the fact that he would answer directly to God, to feel the weight of immense responsibility, surely it also offered some measure of relief. Paul would face relentless opposition over the course of his ministry. He'd undergo severe trials and intense suffering. But he wouldn't have to wonder if he'd signed himself up for it. He hadn't concocted a calling out of thin air. It had come from the throne of heaven. He was "Paul, an apostle . . ."

Paul is a Greek name meaning "little."[1] The juxtaposition seems especially poignant, "little" Paul crouching low next to the looming term "apostle." Scholar Timothy George expounds on the designation:

> As the noun form of the verb *apostellein*, meaning "to send" or "to dispatch," an apostle is literally an envoy or ambassador, one who has been sent in the service of another. In classical Greek the term was actually used of a naval expedition, perhaps deriving from the *apo* prefix, indicating "to send away from," that is, to send off on a long and arduous mission.[2]

One of a thousand things to appreciate about God is His refusal to pander to the human expectation that He will only pick people who look the part.

> The earliest physical description we have of Paul comes from *The Acts of Paul and Thecla,* a second-century apocryphal writing that describes the apostle as "a man of small stature, with a bald head and crooked legs, in a good state of body, with eyebrows meeting and nose somewhat hooked, full of friendliness; for now he appeared like a man, and now he had the face of an angel." Although written many years after his death, these words may well reflect an authentic tradition about Paul's actual likeness.[3]

[1] Richard N. Longenecker, *Galatians*, Word Biblical Commentary Vol. 41 (Dallas: Thomas Nelson Inc, 1990), 2. Copyright © 1990 by Richard N. Longenecker. Used by permission of Thomas Nelson.
[2] Timothy George, *Galatians*, New American Commentary Vol. 30 (Nashville: B&H, 1994), 78.
[3] George, *Galatians*, 77–78.

Assuming the description is somewhat accurate, have you tended to picture Paul differently? If so, how?

_____

_____

_____

_____

Paul may not have stood particularly tall but he stood unswervingly by his calling as an apostle. As George writes, "[Paul's] right to bear its name would figure prominently in the Galatian letter"[4] bringing much that seemed unremarkable about him to a screeching halt.

In the opening to Galatians, Paul bursts out of the gate preaching the resurrection. You'll see the evidence as you write the remainder of v.1: "by Jesus Christ and God the Father who _____."

He sprints straight to the utter distinctiveness of the gospel: Christ crucified, dead, buried and raised.

If you're familiar with Paul's conversion story (which we will revisit later in the week), you know it's little wonder that Paul would launch his letter with a reference to Jesus raised from the dead. After all, Paul's introduction to Jesus differed dramatically from that of the other apostles. He did not encounter a commoner from a small town in Galilee who claimed to be the Messiah. Instead, he ran headlong into a blinding bolt of lightning and had his ears pierced by the thundering voice of the resurrected Christ. Paul's life was forever changed by the gospel, so he gets right to it in his letter to the Galatians.

Next, Paul assures his recipients that he has company in sending this correspondence that they will quickly find to be confrontational. In several of Paul's epistles, he mentions fellow senders by name like Sosthenes in his first letter to the Corinthians, Silas and Timothy in his letters to the Thessalonians then Timothy alone in 2 Corinthians, Philippians, Colossians and Philemon.

How does his letter to the Galatians differ? (Gal 1:2)

_____

Who are the addressees? The _____ of Galatia.

What does the plural tell you? _____

> Paul, an apostle—not from men or by man, but by Jesus Christ and God the Father who raised him from the dead.
>
> Galatians 1:1

---

[4] George, *Galatians*, 78.

You and I are accustomed to references to "churches" but this is an early Christian document written somewhere between AD 49 and the early to mid-50s, which makes the use of *ekklesia* noteworthy.

> In secular usage the Greek word, *ekklesia*, was usually an informal reference to a political assembly...The use of *ekklesia* in early Christian writings seems to show the early Christians finding and using a distinctive vocabulary in contrast to both the synagogue and Gentile religious gatherings.[5]

The intended receivers are, to be sure, a collective of believers from more than one church. But scholars debate exactly which network of churches Paul is addressing. Some scholars argue the letter's destination was most likely the southern region of Galatia where Paul planted churches during his first missionary journey. Others lean toward the region just further to the north where he traveled on his second and third missionary journeys. The difference has to do with the dating of the letter and, thankfully, not the meaning.

Let's familiarize ourselves with the overall territory. Glance at the upper right of your map in the back of the workbook and you'll find the Roman province of Galatia. List the cities named within the province:

_____   _____

_____   _____

Galatia's populace was a mix of ethnic Galatians who, as descendants of the area's earliest settlers, considered themselves "true Galatians," and multiethnic peoples who, over time, had moved into the land or been absorbed into it through redrawn boundaries. Invaders overtook Galatia for several centuries prior to the early New Testament era and many ethnic Galatians left the cities to the occupying forces and moved to the countryside. Then, in 25 B.C. "Rome made Galatia a province of the empire and extended its borders."[6]

Now, glance at the southwestern border of Galatia on the map. Circle the place-name Phrygia.

During this era, Phrygia was a subregion of Galatia and many of her people were slaves or servants living in cities.[7] You don't want to miss historical facts like these because references to "slave and free" are very significant and

---

[5] Marion L. Soards and Darrell J. Pursiful, *Galatians*, Smyth & Helwys Bible Commentary Series (Macon, GA: Smyth & Helwys Publishing, 2015), 16.
[6] "Galatia," *Holman Illustrated Bible Dictionary* (Nashville: Holman Bible Publishers, 2003).
[7] "Phrygia," *Holman Illustrated Bible Dictionary* (Nashville: Holman Bible Publishers, 2003).

multifaceted in Paul's letter to the Galatians. The unclear matter is this: "It is not known whether he visited Phrygian-dominated cities or the true Galatians in the countryside or whether his letter was addressed to the original territory in the north or to the Roman province with its southern additions."[8]

Let's trace Paul's travels within Galatia in the Book of Acts. In doing so, we'll see that the recipients of his circular letter belonged to a network of Gentile congregations within these areas. Scan Acts 13 and 14, keeping an eye out for names of cities. These locales were in southern Galatia and visited by Paul in his first missionary journey. If you write in your Bible, consider writing a "G" in the margin beside the following cities in these references.

> Acts 13:14—Pisidian Antioch
> Acts 14:1—Iconium
> Acts 14:6—Lystra and Derbe
> Acts 16:6 and Acts 18:23—These final two verses refer to the region further to the north, which Paul visited during his *second* and *third* missionary journeys.

Return to Galatians 1:3. After identifying himself as author and the churches of Galatia as recipients, Paul greets his readers with a pair of words found in the opening of all 13 of his letters: "Grace to you and peace from God our Father and the Lord Jesus Christ." He sandwiches "mercy" between the pair in 1st and 2nd Timothy, but Paul's prayer-wish for divine grace and peace to be with his recipients is found in every letter he wrote.

Grace was a standard word of salutation in ancient Greek letters and peace, in Jewish letters. Paul combines them with full force for the believer in Christ.

> As a matter of fact, "grace and peace" are a succinct summary of the entire Christian message. Grace *(charis)* is closely related to the common Greek word for "hello" *(chaire)*. For Paul, grace was virtually synonymous with Jesus Christ since he nowhere conceived of it as an impersonal force or quantity. Grace is God's unmerited goodwill freely given and decisively effective in the saving work of Jesus Christ. Peace *(eirenē;* cf. Heb. *šālôm)*, on the other hand, denotes a state of wholeness and freedom that the grace of God brings.[9]

In Paul's pairings, grace always appears first. Though it never lacks relevance to the themes of his letters, grace is the driving force of Galatians' every word. You won't get a mere sprinkling of grace here. Prepare to swim in it for the next six weeks.

---

[8] "Galatia," *Holman Illustrated Bible Dictionary* (Nashville: Holman Bible Publishers, 2003).
[9] George, *Galatians.* 85.

Might the prospect of a fresh grace awakening be welcome to you right now? If so, explain.

_____

_____

_____

_____

We get no further than verse 4 before Paul shares, in short-form, the gospel of Jesus Christ. How does he word it? *[O]ur Lord Jesus Christ who gave himself for our sins to rescue us from this present evil age.*

F. F. Bruce writes, "This is probably the earliest written statement in the NT about the significance of the death of Christ. It relates his death to the supersession of the old age by the new."[10]

To His final exhale on the cross, Christ guarded the unalterable truth that no one took His life from Him. He gave it. Jesus did not give His life for an ideology or a movement, a philosophy or even a doctrine. He gave Himself for our sins. Paul's use of the plural (*sins*) rather than the singular (*sin*) connects more swiftly to categories than the general concept of missing the mark, so let's go with it.

Our greeds, lusts, jealousies, rivalries, idolatries. Our selfishness, stubbornness, pettiness, thoughtlessness, arrogance. Our thieveries, adulteries, excesses, abuses, injustices. Our slander, gossip, lying, cheating, our disregard for the poor.

Add a few others:

_____

_____

_____

_____

Face the sins. Taste the grace. Galatians will be that kind of straightforward journey. It is graphic not only in its confrontation, but in its beauty and gospel clarity. Squinting at a list of transgressions as tall as the tower of Babel, we declare, "Jesus gave Himself for these."

[10] F. F. Bruce, *The Epistle to the Galatians*, The New International Greek Testament Commentary (Grand Rapids, MI: Eerdmans, 1982), 77.

One quick scroll through the news doesn't exactly engender the feeling that we've been delivered from the present evil age. What has been a recent reminder to you of this present evil age?

_____

_____

_____

_____

_____

_____

_____

_____

We've been delivered *from* this present evil age but reminders abound that we have not yet been delivered *out* of it. This world, however, has no claim on us. No dominion over us. Its hopelessness is not ours. Its corruption is not ours. Its darkness is not ours. We're still living abroad in a land of temptations, trials and terrors, but our visas *will* expire.

———————

This world has no claim on us.
No dominion over us. Its hopelessness
is not ours. Its corruption is not ours.
Its darkness is not ours.

THE GOSPEL ZONE

day two

A Distorted Gospel

Read, write and mark Galatians 1:6–9.

The reformer Martin Luther cherished Galatians so much that he likened the book to his wife, remarking, "The Epistle to the Galatians is my epistle. To it I am as it were in wedlock. It is my Katherine!"[1]

If I'm honest, Galatians' legendary status—especially among Protestants of the evangelical variety—coupled with a surface level familiarity of the book rendered me disinterested in closely studying it. For years, I avoided Galatians in favor of much less popular books

---

[1] Martin Luther, *Commentary on the Epistle to the Galatians* (1535), trans. Theodore Graebner (n.d.; Project Gutenberg, 2013), 8.

of the Bible. Taking it up has been a revelation, both surprising and gripping. Paul does not waste a dot of ink on his typical warm words of thanksgiving. He is amazed and not in a good way.

"I am amazed that you are so quickly turning away from him who called you by the grace of Christ."

The Galatians, Paul reports, are in the process of *turning away* from God and *turning to* something else.

What is that something else, according to verse 6?

_____

> I am amazed that you are so quickly turning away from him who called you by the grace of Christ and are turning to a different gospel.
>
> Galatians 1:6

As Paul wrote, the Galatians were turning to a *different* gospel. The consequence of this shocking and bewildering turn was that the Galatians were forsaking God. Paul's language here is rock strong, reflected by many major English translations which use the verb "deserting": *I am astonished that you are so quickly deserting the one who called you* (NIV, NRSV, CEB, ESV).

Absorb also the sharpness of Eugene Peterson's translation in The Message, *"how easily you have turned traitor to him who called you by the grace of Christ."* L. Ann Jervis says so well in her commentary on Galatians, "In their turning to a different gospel they are transferring their allegiance away from the one who wanted to deliver them from the present evil age."[2]

Presumably, the Galatians were still embracing a message related to Jesus. But the message was distorted, unrecognizable when compared to the good news that Paul had received and passed on to them. From Paul's perspective the new message they were embracing was hardly good news at all anymore!

We Christians use the phrase "the gospel" a lot—it rolls off the tongue. But, has anyone ever asked you to explain what you actually mean by "the gospel"? It's surprisingly hard! Often the phrases we use most are the ones we understand least.

Give it your best shot here:

_____

_____

_____

_____

[2] L. Ann Jervis, *Galatians,* Understanding the Bible Commentary Series (Grand Rapids, MI: Baker Books, 1999), 36.

Jervis says the phrase "the grace of Christ," which Paul refers to in verse 6, is "the gospel in a nutshell."[3] I like that. Capturing a phrase as pregnant and meaningful as "the gospel" fully and definitively in just a sentence is probably impossible. But, if I was forced, I think I would say that the gospel is the good news that God is redeeming and reconciling the whole world through the life, death and resurrection of his son Jesus the Messiah, who reigns as king forever and will return again. I tend to articulate the gospel around Paul's words in 1 Corinthians 15:1-4.

Write out 1 Corinthians 15:3-4 here:

_____

_____

_____

_____

If we suppose, even for a moment, that the new message the Galatians are embracing is "a different" but equally acceptable alternative to the one Paul received and passed on, the apostle sets the record straight with verse 7. The distorted message does not qualify as the gospel, he says. Verse 7 is the first glimpse we get of the troublemakers in Galatia: *there are some who are troubling you and want to distort the gospel of Christ.* Notice that, from Paul's perspective, these troublemakers are changing and distorting the gospel intentionally. They want to distort it. John Stott sums it up well:

> So the two chief characteristics of the false teachers are that they were troubling the church and changing the gospel. These two go together. To tamper with the gospel is always to trouble the church. You cannot touch the gospel and leave the church untouched, because the church is created and lives by the gospel.[4]

Paul does not name or identify the troublemakers anywhere in Galatians, nor is it clear if he knows them personally, but his antagonism toward them is real. Jervis suggests this "may be either because he does not know their names or because he does not want to dignify them by naming them."[5] Paul makes specific reference to the troublemakers three additional times in Galatians.[6]

> There are some who are troubling you and want to distort the gospel of Christ.
>
> Galatians 1:7b

---

[3] Jervis, *Galatians*, 36.

[4] John R. W. Stott, *The Message of Galatians*, The Bible Speaks Today (Downers Grove, IL: InterVarsity Press, 1968), Kindle edition.

[5] Jervis, *Galatians*, 36.

[6] Gordon Fee, *Galatians*, Pentecostal Commentary Series (Dorset: Deo Publishing, 2007), 24.

Please look up the following verses in their contexts. Record anything of interest to you:

Galatians 4:17–18

_____

_____

_____

Galatians 5:7–12

_____

_____

_____

Galatians 6:12–13

_____

_____

_____

Fascinatingly, ταράσσω, the verbal form of the participle translated in the CSB as "some who are troubling you" (v.7) is the same verb used for the _stirred up_ waters of the pool of Bethesda in John 5:7. Paul's opponents in Galatia are stirring things up for his vulnerable new converts. This verb ταράσσω is also in an extremely relevant passage in Acts 15 relating the events of the Council at Jerusalem.

Read Acts 15:24–25 carefully.

Since we have heard that some without our authorization went out from us and troubled you with their words and unsettled your hearts, we have unanimously decided to select men and send them to you . . .

In that chapter of Acts, some men came down from Judea to Antioch and taught that the new Gentile Christians ought to be circumcised according to the Mosaic Law in order to be saved (Acts 15:1–2). In a word, this was troubling. Paul and Barnabas had an intense argument that resulted in them going up to Jerusalem to resolve the issue with the church leaders stationed there, like Peter and James and the elders (15:2–4). After a lot of debate, the judgment was made that Gentile Christians did not need to be circumcised or keep the Law of Moses!

As James put it, the judgment was made "not to cause difficulties for those among the Gentiles who turn to God" (15:19). So a letter was drafted to Gentile believers to urge them to do a couple of things that basically consisted of the bare minimum, such as abstaining from sexual immorality and food offered to idols. Now, remember, the Gentile believers had already received the Holy Spirit.

In other words, these exhortations weren't about what's required to be saved. These bare minimum requirements for Gentile believers were drafted to honor Moses who had been so significant in the synagogues since ancient times (see Acts 15:19–21). We will revisit this relevant text again, especially when we get into Galatians chapter two.

Let's look at verses 8–9. Understated is not an adjective we have to worry about wearing out on the apostle Paul.

> In verse 8, Paul says, "But even if we or an angel from heaven should preach to you a gospel contrary to what we have preached to you, _____!"

And, just when hearers of the letter might have tilted their heads, thinking they must have misunderstood him, he repeated it.

> "As we have said before, I now say again: If anyone is preaching to you a gospel contrary to what you received, _____!"

What Paul was saying is akin to, "Let them be damned."[7] That he uses a curse formula so early in his letter makes it all the more striking. He no doubt intended for his words to have enough shock value to be taken seriously. Don't miss the fact that he was also invoking that curse not only on an angel from heaven, should one ever distort the gospel, but on himself and his colaborers if they did so.

No angel or apostle has authority over the gospel the Galatians first received. Lives were at stake. Paul intended for his listeners to understand with startling clarity that what they'd received from him was not a gospel but *the* gospel. And this gospel was not the truth because he, Paul, had preached it. This gospel was the truth because the risen Christ, the Son of God, had given it. If Paul circled back around someday with a different twist on the gospel, he wanted them to know that he, too, should be rejected.

[7] James Montgomery Boice, "Galatians," in *The Expositor's Bible Commentary* (Grand Rapids, MI: Zondervan, 1976), 429. Copyright © 1972 by James Montgomery Boice. Used by permission of Zondervan. www.zondervan.com

The curse formula used here at the beginning is given its opposite parallel at the end. Thus, a curse and blessing frame Paul's letter to the Galatians like bookends. As Craig Keener says, "The letter body of Galatians falls between the curse for those who distort the gospel and the blessing for those who adhere to it."[8] Some have seen these frames as possible indicators that Paul is setting life and death before the Galatians in a manner reminiscent of Moses before Israel in the Old Testament book of Deuteronomy (see 30:19).[9]

Please look up Galatians 6:16 and write it below.

_____

_____

_____

_____

_____

God willing, in five or six weeks we will be well on our way to a fuller understanding of the kind of rule or standard upon which Paul pronounces a blessing of peace. By the way, we're so glad you are studying with us! My hope is that, over the coming weeks, some of your assumptions are shattered as mine have been. Maybe yours have more to do with Bible study in general and less about Galatians in particular. In any case, I pray you find that this letter is not tired but fresh and alive, eager to seize your heart and theological imagination.

I pray you find that this letter is not tired but fresh and alive, eager to seize your heart and theological imagination.

[8] Craig S. Keener, *Galatians: A Commentary* (Grand Rapids, MI: Baker Academic, 2019), 576.
[9] Todd A. Wilson, "Under Law," *Journal of Theological Studies* 56 (2005): 362–392.
On page 368: "the epistolary frame of Galatians contains a conditional curse and blessing, which thus gives a further indication of how Paul envisaged the letter to function on the ground in Galatia: as a means of setting forth before the Galatians the promise of 'life and death, blessing and curse' (Deut. 30:19)—contingent, of course, upon a proper response to Paul's person and message as now mediated through his personal dispatch" (cf. 4:20; 6:11).

THE GOSPEL ZONE

day three

A Bondservant to Christ

Read, write and mark Galatians 1:10–12.

_____

_____

_____

_____

_____

_____

_____

_____

_____

_____

Paul almost certainly would have seen the backlash coming. Once he absorbed the full implications of the gospel made known to him by a revelation of Jesus Christ, he surely knew the opposition would be fierce. He could glance over his shoulder at the man he used to be and imagine his reaction to one of his fellow Hebrews claiming to have received such a revelation. Without the Holy Spirit transforming Paul's heart and opening his mind, the mere suggestion that salvation would come by faith in Jesus alone and not a whit by works of the law would have not only seemed heretical, but blasphemous. Our confidence in the legitimacy of the gospel Paul preached is boosted by the sheer fact that, if he were going to make something up, this would not be it.

Based on Paul's questions in v.10, his rivals obviously accused him of offering the Gentiles a bargain. The way they, apparently, saw it, Paul knew that obligating the Gentiles to the law alongside faith in Christ would be a hard sell, so he cut them a deal. His rivals were yet to grasp that Paul was by no means suggesting the Gentiles alone were freed from all obligation to the law. He was insisting upon something far more extreme—that all who believed were freed from the law, Jew and Gentile alike.

The idea behind persuading people in Galatians 1:10 is that of campaigning to curry favor. If you've lived through enough political election cycles, you've probably wondered at times how far into falsehood any given candidate might be willing to go in order to gain your support. Paul was likely thinking, "Brothers, if I was willing to lose the approval of my own people, why on earth would I be driven to gain theirs?"

No matter how many messages we've heard on the perils of seeking human approval, we can't rush past this emphasis in Paul's letter to the Galatians. The concept is too relevant to our present cultural challenges. We could post Galatians 1:10 on social media with absolute earnestness and find ourselves a few hours later looking to see how many people liked it. The craving for human approval long predated us, of course. Mortals have possessed a voracious appetite for one another's praise since life existed outside the garden. Christ confronted the ravenous desire as a towering obstacle to faith and public witness.

Read John 5:37–46 and summarize Jesus' point regarding the praise of people.

_____

_____

_____

John 12:42–43 is such a telling segment. Read it and record what it conveys.

_____

_____

_____

_____

Few of us are naïve enough to think we could attain everyone's approval. As much as we wish everybody liked us, we know any such prospect is unrealistic, particularly in our increasingly polarized society. We, instead, tend to have particular individuals and groups we greatly desire to please.

This question and the next are not meant for small group discussion. They are for you and God to work through together. Your freedom to be forthright and honest with Him will vastly increase the effectiveness of the exercise. Whose approval do you most want to attain or sustain? Record names below of individuals who are at the top of your list but also focus on groups. Leave the space between them for additional writing that will follow the next question.

INDIVIDUALS		GROUPS

Our motivations for wanting to please certain individuals and groups can differ from person to person and crowd to crowd. For example, you might desire to please one person because his or her favor is so pleasurable while desiring to please another because he or she has the power to make your life miserable. Sometimes, both of those extremes are true of the same person. In regard to groups, you might want your extended family's approval for one reason, your faith community's approval for another and social media applause for yet another.

Go back to your previous list on the diagram above and articulate your most authentic reasons for wishing to please each individual or group.

Any chance you've discovered, as I have, that pleasing one individual or group displeases another? If so, offer an example.

_____

_____

_____

_____

_____

On occasion, seeking God's approval can simultaneously land us the approval of our favorite person or group of people. We didn't seek the latter but we somehow ended up with substantial applause. In those seasons, when you appear to have both divine approval and human approval, consider it an anomaly and refuse to be dazzled by it. Having both kinds of approval can seem like the ultimate accomplishment. We can, in fact, reason that it could be God's will for us based on verses like Luke 2:52. This one Scripture is the only description the Bible supplies for the life of Jesus from the time He was twelve years old until He began His public ministry at thirty.

How does Luke 2:52 describe Jesus? _____

_____

The more public Jesus became, however, the more polarizing He became. His approval rating spiked among some segments of people and plunged among others. During the final 24 hours of His life, God's approval was all Jesus had.

Complete this sentence according to Galatians 1:10. If I were still trying to please people, I would not be a _____.

What conclusion might you draw from Paul's statement?

_____

_____

Scholar Thomas R. Schreiner translates the Greek wording in a way that is particularly significant to the content of the remainder of the letter: "For if I were still attempting to please people, I would never have become a slave of Christ."[1]

In a letter that vigorously waves the banner of freedom for all who are in Christ, we discover an unforgettable paradox in an apostle who saw himself as "the least of all the saints" (Eph 3:8). Freedom for Paul was found in being wholly bound to Jesus. He will refer in the closing of the letter to bearing the marks of Jesus, alluding to the permanence of his "slavery" to his master. Such was the depth of Paul's trust in Christ: he knew that being utterly enslaved to His approval alone was the only way for him to be free. We will see more than once how costly Paul's liberation from human approval proved to be.

> For am I now trying to persuade people, or God? Or am I striving to please people?
>
> Galatians 1:10a

[1] Thomas R. Schreiner, *Galatians,* Zondervan Exegetical Commentary on the New Testament (Grand Rapids, MI: Zondervan, 2010), 89. Copyright © 2010 by Thomas R. Schreiner. Used by permission of Zondervan. www.zondervan.com

The loss of approval may simply be disappointing. But, depending upon the depth of relationship, it can also be devastating. An enormous test of faith comes when pleasing God places us in a situation where we will displease our mentors, or spiritual fathers or mothers, whose approval we've long enjoyed. Until now, pleasing God has seemed consistent with pleasing them. Then, suddenly, we face a situation or season when God's will for us and their will for us collide. Perhaps God is telling you to go. They are telling you to stay. Perhaps God is stirring fresh vision in you for the future but it translates to them as criticism of their way of doing it in the past.

Harder still, we may have gotten close enough to see something disturbing that needs confronting but who are we to question our superiors? Our elders? The temptation to please them rather than God can be gigantic because, truth be told, God is more forgiving than man. We figure He'll get over it and they won't. And, after all, we owe them so much. Sound familiar? This we can have etched in concrete: God will test the relationships we have with virtually every person who lords authority over us in a way that vies for His. Some of those relationships will have what it takes to recalibrate and others won't.

Nothing will train us more effectively to stop seeking man's approval than being scalded by the gain and loss of it. If you know this to be true from personal experience, explain how.

_____

_____

At times, God will call upon us to suffer loss in our faithfulness to Him. He rewards obedience but not always in the ways we expect or hope and not always in this lifetime. He is all-wise and still looks out for our greatest eternal good, even when He allows our unwillingness to crater to the pressure of people-pleasing to cost us dearly. Let's also take caution not to get it in our heads that we're not pleasing God unless we're making everybody mad. The goal is pleasing God, not displeasing man.

Let's draw to a close with our eyes on Galatians 1:11–12, which will prepare us for our next lesson. I memorized the letter in the ESV and its wording here impacts me every time I say it. Read it aloud and with some fervor.

For I would have you know, brothers, that the gospel that was preached by me is not man's gospel. For I did not receive it from any man, nor was I taught it, but I received it through a revelation of Jesus Christ.
Galatians 1:11–12 ESV

The goal is pleasing God, not displeasing man.

It's not man's gospel. We don't get to tamper with it or tinker with it, add to it or subtract from it, no matter how good our intentions may be. We embrace the gospel just as it is because it stands alone as the best of all news, particularly for those of us who share the Gentile heritage of the first century Galatian believers.

How did Paul say he received the gospel?

_____

Conclude today's lesson by carefully reading Ephesians 3:1–13, also written by Paul. Record in this space any information that deepens your understanding of the "revelation" Paul references in both letters.

_____

_____

In this space record every piece of information in Ephesians 3:1–13 that encourages or exhilarates you in your own walk of faith.

_____

_____

_____

_____

_____

_____

_____

_____

_____

_____

Revel in the stunning reality that you have been included in such a plan. As alarming as our present era appears, have the courage to thank God for thoughtfully and deliberately assigning you to this generation. You are not here on accident. The difference you have the capacity in Christ to make is no afterthought. People are desperate for the hope of the gospel God is nurturing within you.

THE GOSPEL ZONE

day four

By His Grace

Read, write and mark Galatians 1:13–17.

_____
_____
_____
_____
_____
_____
_____
_____
_____
_____
_____
_____
_____
_____
_____
_____
_____

Verse 13 begins an autobiographical section that is unique in both length and detail among all of Paul's letters. Let's zone in on verse 13.

What did Paul's former way of life in Judaism consist of? Check all the correct options:

☐ He advocated living peacefully with God's church.
☐ He persecuted God's church.
☐ He had never even heard of the church until a revelation of God came to him.
☐ He tried to destroy the church.

We first learn about Paul in the book of Acts at the scene of the stoning of Stephen, the first Christian martyr. On that horrific day when Stephen was dying—breathing his last words in a manner after Jesus' own—Paul "agreed with putting him to death" (Acts 8:1). Luke describes the pre-Christian Paul as a young man (Acts 7:58).

Please read Paul's account of this, according to Luke, in Acts 22:19–20 and record it below:

_____

_____

_____

Paul was no ordinary Jew. "I advanced in Judaism beyond many contemporaries among my people, because I was extremely zealous for the traditions of my ancestors" (Gal 1:14).

Flip over a few books to Philippians and read 3:4–6 to record as many additional details as you can about Paul's life and history:

_____

_____

_____

Paul was not only heavily credentialed in his former way of life, he also aligned himself with some others in the tradition who employed violence against those they deemed severe violators of the Law of Moses. Among the violators were some Jews in Jerusalem who called on the name of the crucified and risen Jesus, such as Stephen.

All of this utterly changed for Paul after he, too, was encountered by Jesus on the Damascus Road. Shortly after Paul was blinded by a light from heaven, the Lord commanded a man named Ananias to place his hands on Paul to restore his sight. Ananias was baffled, responding with reluctance, "Lord, I have heard from many people about this man, how much harm he has done to your saints in Jerusalem. And he has authority here from the chief priests to arrest all who call on your name" (Acts 9:13–14).

The Lord's response to the troubled Ananias was, "Go . . . this man is my chosen instrument," followed by a line that sends chills down my spine every time I think of it: "I will show him how much he must suffer for my name" (Acts 9:16).

In such a dramatic way, Paul experiences both the glories of Christ and the sufferings of Christ—visions in the highest heavens and all kinds of ecstatic experiences, but also imprisoning and beatings. We don't stop often enough to consider the sheer audacity it must have taken for Paul to assert apostolic authority, particularly in light of his past as a persecutor of Christians.

We can see Paul wrestling with this reality in 1 Corinthians 15:9–10. Please look up these two verses and fill in the blanks:

> "For I am the _____ of the apostles, not worthy to be called
> an _____, because I persecuted the church of God.
> But by the _____ of God I am what I am, and his grace toward
> me was not in vain. On the contrary, I worked _____ than
> any of them, yet not I, but the _____ of God that was with me."

As Gordon Fee says, "Paul still thinks of himself and his churches as belonging most truly to the ancient people of God."[1] For instance, he speaks of "my ancestors" or "my fathers," depending on the translation, in Galatians 1:14. Paul considered his faith in Christ and life in the Spirit to be "nothing less than the authentic expression of OT faith in a new era."[2] Paul will teach us more about how that interplay works over the coming chapters. But, even, in the very next verse, Paul uses the familiar language of the prophets Isaiah and Jeremiah to describe his calling.

Please read these lines from Galatians 1:15–16 carefully a few times:

> But when God, who from my mother's womb set me apart and
> called me by his grace, was pleased to reveal his Son in me,
> so that I could preach him among the Gentiles . . .

> But by the grace of God I am what I am, and his grace toward me was not in vain.
>
> 1 Corinthians 15:10a

[1] Gordon Fee, *Galatians*, Pentecostal Commentary Series (Dorset: Deo Publishing, 2007), 40.
[2] Douglas J. Moo, *Galatians*, Baker Exegetical Commentary on the New Testament (Grand Rapids, MI: Baker Academic, 2013), 99.

Now, look up Jeremiah 1:5 and Isaiah 49:1–9 and note any similarities you find noteworthy between Paul and those two prophets.

Jeremiah 1:5

_____

_____

Isaiah 49:1–9

_____

_____

Please read Acts 9:1–7, which records Paul's encounter with Jesus on the Damascus Road. Note every extraordinary aspect of the story.

_____

_____

Scholars of Paul heavily debate how exactly to speak of what happens to Paul after the Damascus Road experience. David deSilva sums up well the varying perspectives:

> Is it more accurate to think about the effects of God's dramatic intervention in Paul's life as a conversion or as a prophetic call? One might argue that this experience was not a conversion, since Paul was still responding to the same God (the God of Judaism and the God of the church). Paul did not leave behind the faith of Abraham in order to embrace the faith of Christ; he saw himself, rather as embracing the fulfillment of what God had promised and been driving toward all along. Against this position, however, Paul's own narrative of his life clearly differentiates a "before" ("formerly"), described as living "in Judaism" (Gal 1:13–14), from a radically new "after," to which that description no longer applies. Paul's response to the Christian movement prior to his encounter with Christ demonstrates that Paul regarded it to be "other" than the religion of his ancestors; the postencounter treatment that Paul received from his former associates, who now persecute *him*, bears witness to the same.[3]

Paul's life as apostle to the Gentiles had continuity with his former life in Judaism but led to discontinuity as well. Understanding this continuity and discontinuity is complex but also one of the things that makes studying Paul rich and interesting.

[3] David A. deSilva, *The Letter to the Galatians*, The New International Commentary on the New Testament (Grand Rapids, MI: Eerdmans, 2018), 145–46.

What, in your opinion, is the best way to speak of the change that Paul undergoes after he is encountered by the risen Lord in Acts 9?

_____

_____

Let's get to our final verses for today, 16b-17: *"I did not immediately consult with anyone. I did not go up to Jerusalem to those who had become apostles before me; instead I went to Arabia and came back to Damascus."*

Remember the opening line of our letter? Glance back at 1:1. There in verse one, Paul asserts and qualifies his apostleship—first, by way of a denial: not from men or by man. David deSilva thinks these two phrases "are mutually reinforcing but not entirely redundant. With the first, Paul denies that human beings are the point of origin of his apostolic mission; with the second, that any human being was instrumental in sending him out on this mission."[4]

Paul's apostolic authority originated and rested in *Jesus Christ and God the Father who raised him from the dead* (Gal 1:1). It was this act wherein the Father raised Jesus Christ that changed absolutely everything for Paul, including—to the dismay of many—his reading of some key Scriptures. Here in today's passage, verses 13-17, Paul is not telling his story of calling and conversion for its sake alone but to reiterate that all this happened separately and independently from other people.

> *I did not go up to Jerusalem to those who had become apostles before me.*
> **Galatians 1:17a**

Paul knew good and well that the first apostles of Jesus were stationed in Jerusalem, but he chose not to travel there first and foremost. He would not venture to Jerusalem for three whole years (v.18). This sends a message in itself, doesn't it?

Maybe it had something to do with Paul's fear of them misunderstanding him after his complicated past with the Jerusalem Christians. But what is even more important for us to acknowledge is that Paul didn't feel the need to consult with anyone—he didn't need to corroborate his revelation from God with theirs. As deSilva explains: "What he understood to be the significance of the Christ event and the nature of the message he was to proclaim (and that specifically to the gentile nations) took shape independently of the Jerusalem-based Jesus movement."[5]

---

[4] deSilva, *The Letter to the Galatians*, 114.
[5] deSilva, *The Letter to the Galatians*, 145.

So, if Paul didn't go to Jerusalem, where did he go before going back to Damascus? See verse 17. _____

What was Paul doing in Arabia?

In the first century, "Arabia" referred to a massive expanse of land composed of "essentially barren, unpopulated desert" as well as cities like Petra, Bozra, and Madaba.[6] Some have supposed that Paul began his missionary activity in Arabia, immediately upon arrival. Others think he fled to the wilderness for prayer and solitude. The only other time "Arabia" is used in the New Testament, however, is here in Galatians, in chapter 4 when Paul speaks of "Mount Sinai in Arabia" (v.25).

The only thing we absolutely know from Paul about Arabia is that it was home to Mount Sinai, the famous mountain of revelation where God gave the Torah to Moses. N. T. Wright makes a fascinating suggestion that Paul was following, at least to some extent, the pattern of Elijah the prophet, who, ignited by zeal of his own against the prophets of Baal, had an altering encounter that caused him to run for his life to the mountain of God.

On the mountain, Elijah experienced God, heard His voice and then returned to the wilderness of Damascus. Sounds familiar, doesn't it? No one can know precisely what Paul was doing in Arabia but this is one possibility. Paul, as Wright suggests:

> might have been doing what a puzzled zealous prophet might be expected to do: going back to the source to resign his commission. Alternately, and perhaps, preferably, he might be conceived of as doing what a puzzled, newly commissioned prophet might do, complaining (like Moses, Jeremiah, and others) that he is not able to undertake the work he has been assigned.[7]

For Paul to flee to the famous place of revelation where God had revealed his law to Moses and whispered softly to the prophet Elijah is a fascinating prospect. What better place to take all of his questions and fears and disorientation? What better place to reconstruct after sudden deconstruction than Mount Sinai? Paul had a lot to reflect on and work out during the at-minimum three-year period before he would make his way up to Jerusalem to meet Peter. But it all began—everything in Paul's world turned totally upside down—on that great day when God revealed His glorious Son.

> But it all began —everything in Paul's world turned totally upside down— on that great day when God revealed His glorious Son.

[6] deSilva, *The Letter to the Galatians,* 157.
[7] N. T. Wright, "Paul, Arabia, and Elijah," *Journal of Biblical Literature* 115/4 (1996): 683–692.

THE GOSPEL ZONE

day five

Shared Histories

Read, write and mark Galatians 1:18–24.

_____

_____

_____

_____

_____

_____

_____

_____

_____

_____

_____

You, student of Scripture, are just about to complete your first week of this Bible study series. I don't mind saying congratulations are already in order. In a world doing its best to rob us of focus, well done! Keep going! Count on Paul's words in 1 Thessalonians 2:13. "This is why we constantly thank God, because when you received the word of God that you heard from us, you welcomed it not as a human message, but as it truly is, the word of God, which also works effectively in you who believe." God's Word is working effectively in you, Believer. Time well spent.

The first question begging for an answer in our text today is this: who is Cephas? Read John 1:42. Record his identity. Cephas is his name in Aramaic.

_____

How long did Paul wait before going to Jerusalem? _____

Why did he go? _____

The ESV employs the words "to visit," the NIV, "to get acquainted with" and the CSB, "to get to know." Each phrase is an English translation of a marvelous Greek verb.

> Then after three years I did go up to Jerusalem to get to know Cephas, and I stayed with him fifteen days.
>
> Galatians 1:18

The Greek verb *(historeō)* is the word from which we get our word "history." It suggests the telling of a story. Paul would have told his story, Peter his. So the two leading apostles—Paul, the apostle to the Gentiles, and Peter, the apostle to the Jews—became acquainted and encouraged each other in their forthcoming work. For the point of Paul's argument, it is important to note that this was a private visit and not one designed to secure the support of any human authorities.[1]

Peter and Paul told their histories with Jesus to one another. "In classical Greek [*historeō*] indicates an interview of someone else."[2] Perhaps they told their stories in response to one another's questions. "Where were you at the time? What was it like? Who else was there? What happened next?" Can you imagine overhearing such a conversation? Had it happened today, this would be the leadership podcast series of the century.

Based on what you already know about Peter and Paul, what are some similarities and distinctions in their histories you imagine they discussed? Give this section some thought.

Distinctions: Similarities:

_____   _____

_____   _____

_____   _____

_____   _____

[1] James Montgomery Boice, "Galatians," in *The Expositor's Bible Commentary* (Grand Rapids, MI: Zondervan, 1976), 435. Copyright © 1972 by James Montgomery Boice. Used by permission of Zondervan. www.zondervan.com

[2] Thomas R. Schreiner, *Galatians*, Zondervan Exegetical Commentary on the New Testament (Grand Rapids, MI: Zondervan, 2010), 109. Copyright © 2010 by Thomas R. Schreiner. Used by permission of Zondervan. www.zondervan.com

On Day Two, Melissa asked you to read 1 Corinthians 15:1–4 and write out verses 3–4 as you considered how to define "gospel" according to the apostle Paul. I'd like for you to return to it and, this time, broaden your reading to the eleventh verse. The details Paul reports concerning the order of the post-resurrection appearances of Christ may well have been told to him first hand by Peter and perhaps even during the visit recalled in Galatians 1:18.

Read 1 Corinthians 15:1–11 and list the order of Christ's post-resurrection appearances.

_____

_____

_____

Which appearance do you find most fascinating and why?

_____

_____

Return to Galatians 1:19. How does Paul identify this particular James?

_____

Luke makes reference to two different men by the name of James in Acts 12. Scan the chapter for context then read the following verses and record what you are told about each James.

Acts 12:1–2

_____

_____

Acts 12:17

_____

_____

> But I didn't see any of the other apostles except James, the Lord's brother.
>
> Galatians 1:19

Both were prominent figures in the early church. James, a son of Zebedee and the brother of John, was among the Twelve. Even more distinctly, he was among the three who Jesus took with Him to the Mount of Transfiguration, into private quarters to raise a child from the dead and further into the Garden of Gethsemane to watch and pray on the night of His arrest. These three—

John, Peter and James—were set apart by Christ as His innermost circle. This James was also the first of the Twelve to be martyred. His execution by Herod Agrippa I in AD 44 is referenced in Acts 12:1–2. His death would have shaken the early church to the core.

James, the half-brother of Jesus, is the one referenced in Acts 12:17. After his conversion—a story I deeply wish we knew—James rose as the overseer of the Jewish Christian community in Jerusalem and was a major player in church formation. He also authored what we know as the book of James. Imagine the breadth of Christ's story that Peter, a prominent disciple, and James, a half-brother, could have filled in for Paul. The thought of them in one another's company over a period of 15 days is profound and appropriately moving, but Paul's purpose in telling the Galatians was not remotely sentimental.

Reread Galatians 1:20. What tells you that more was going on than just Paul sharing adventures from the road?

_____

_____

_____

_____

David A. deSilva translates the Greek with this wording: "Now in regard to the things I am writing to you, look! Before God I swear that I am not lying . . ."[3]

What is at stake to cause Paul to take an oath swearing that he'd seen none of the apostles for at least three years after he encountered Christ then, when he finally went to Jerusalem, having only seen two, and them for a mere 15 days? In Paul's view, nothing less than the veracity of the gospel he preaches.

The apostle intends for the Galatians to understand that the revelation of the gospel he received from Jesus was completely independent of the apostles and, in and of itself, was in no way reliant upon, contested or changed by them. Church formation may have still been under construction at that time but the gospel was not. It had been given in full. Paul went to Jerusalem for communication, not validation. He is not asking for permission to fulfill his calling.

[3] David A. deSilva, *The Letter to the Galatians*, The New International Commentary on the New Testament (Grand Rapids, MI: Eerdmans, 2018), 158.

According to Galatians 1:21, where did Paul go when he departed Jerusalem?

_____

Many years ago, when God first lit the flame in my heart for Bible study, I heard a theologian say that if there were a fifth Gospel, it would be the land. He meant the Holy Land, of course, but that was the day I started wearing out the maps section in the back of my Bible. If we are to journey, so to speak, with the men and women of Scripture, we need to see where we're going not only biblically but geographically.

Look on your map and locate the two regions Paul mentions in Galatians 1:21. What directions on a compass did he go? List the cities on the map in Cilicia:

_____

_____

_____

_____

Describe the level of familiarity the Judean churches in Christ had with Paul at this point according to Galatians 1:22.

_____

_____

_____

_____

A little history on Judea will help us. Judea is a place-name simply meaning "Jewish." The region was originally called "Judah" but began transitioning to the name "Judea" when it was resettled after the Babylonian exile. Judea "varied in size with changing political circumstances, but always included the city of Jerusalem and the territory immediately surrounding it."[4]

Glance back at your map and note the shaded area labeled "Syria." Syria was a Roman province during the time of the empire and, thus, throughout the New Testament era. As you can see, Judea was part of its procurement as were Galilee and Samaria. Notice how far south Judea is in Syria compared to the region of Cilicia and you'll discover what Paul doesn't want the Galatians to miss. He finished up his 15-day visit with Cephas, during which he also saw James, and immediately headed north.

> If there were a fifth Gospel, it would be the land.

[4] "Judea," _Holman Illustrated Bible Dictionary_ (Nashville: Holman Bible Publishers, 2003), 960.

Paul is probably mentioning the Judean churches in Christ to accomplish two purposes:

1. To reiterate his independence from anyone's authority except Christ's.

2. To remind them that his preaching was not disputed or found deficient even by those who were part of the earliest movement of Christianity. On the contrary, the astonishing news was the cause of praise and glory to God.

Reread v.23 and write once more the exact words Paul uses to quote the Judean churches.

_____

_____

_____

"Preaches *(euangelizetai)* the faith he once tried to destroy." *That* is a headline that would leave its readers begging for some history.

Meditate on the words "the faith." Think of any reason or reasons why those two words might be particularly significant, especially in this context, and record them here.

_____

_____

_____

_____

Richard B. Hays' explanation is worth reading, too:

> The Judean churches understood him to be preaching the same "faith" that they shared. All of this is important because it implies that all the recent trouble and conflict had been caused not by a change in Paul's preaching, as the [trouble-causing rivals] alleged, but by a change of mind in the churches of Judea and Jerusalem that has created new pressure for circumcision and Law observance among the Gentiles.[5]

What would have been the advantage of a change of mind? We'll explore the answer to that question throughout our series and discover that the temptation is no less enticing today.

[5] Richard B. Hays, "Galatians," in *The New Interpreter's Bible* Vol. XI (Nashville: Abingdon Press, 2000), 217. ©2000 Abingdon Press. Used by permission. All rights reserved.

...He who formerly persecuted us now preaches the faith he once tried to destroy.

Galatians 1:23b

As we draw to a conclusion, I'd like to circle back to the list of cities you found in Cilicia. You, no doubt, recorded Tarsus. When Paul left Cephas and James in Jerusalem, he followed the arrow on his compass north. He may have traveled west of the Jordan to head to Cilicia, whether by land or sea, but he may just as likely have traveled east by way of Damascus and Antioch, cities of such profound importance in his history with Jesus. One thing we know for certain. Paul journeyed back to his native soil, for at least a time, to a land he knew as well as the back of his hand. That Tarsus would not be on his Cilician itinerary is unthinkable.

The thought of it strikes me tenderly somehow. I imagine Paul traveling that many days and miles, reflecting on his conversations with men of such renown among those "who belonged to the Way" (Acts 9:2). These were men Paul saw as traitors then, after he encountered Christ, men he saw as pillars. Change often inches so slowly; God's hand is indiscernible. Then, all of a sudden, the Spirit of God works like a whirlwind and our minds can't catch up with all that has happened.

This is where I'd like you to reflect as we close: we're not Paul, Cephas or James, but we have our own histories with Jesus. We've experienced the slow and the quick. We've waited and wondered and walked and wandered and run, sometimes to Him, sometimes away from Him. Thank God we couldn't escape Him or we wouldn't be huddled over the Scriptures.

The page before you is an open invitation to write a synopsis of your own history with Jesus. Rather than a testimony of one big life-changing event centered primarily on the dramatic, recollect your wider story and articulate it on the next page. Your history began with Him long before you knew He was there and long before you believed, so start with your childhood. Don't be distracted by trying to write a masterpiece. You're His masterpiece. Just write and, when you're finished, have the courage to let someone else doing this Bible study read it and offer God praise because of you.

When all is said and done and our histories with Jesus are fully written, the most precious gift we will have offered any fellow human will have been a chance to glorify God. We cannot save another. Only God can do that. But we can give another a reason to praise God.

The chief end of man is to glorify God and enjoy Him forever.
Westminster Shorter Catechism

MY HISTORY

FREEDOM

zone two

FREEDOM

GALATIANS 2

For through the law I died to the law, so that I might live for God. I have been crucified with Christ, and I no longer live, but Christ lives in me. The life I now live in the body, I live by faith in the Son of God, who loved me and gave himself for me.

Galatians 2:19–20 NIV

VIDEO GUIDE

THE FREEDOM ZONE

Introduction: Week One behind us, we now transition into the second chapter of Galatians. We're establishing zones to preview the property that you have ahead.

Read Galatians 2:1–5.

There is a phrase in the ESV that will come up in the third chapter of Galatians that I want you to get a jump on. The phrase is "_____". (Galatians 3:2)

Write down the first 7 words of Galatians 5:13 CSB.

_____

_____

Galatians has often been called the _____ of Christian liberty or the

Christian's _____.

In his commentary on Galatians, Dr. Timothy George writes, "The parenthetical paragraph on Titus and the false brothers concludes with the introduction of two concepts that will dominate the remainder of Galatians: _____ and _____."[1]

Paul sees two categories in Galatians:
Freedom and slavery. Here in 2:4–5, 3:28, 4:1–11 and 5:13.

> *Yet because of false brothers secretly brought in—who slipped in to spy out our freedom that we have in Christ Jesus, so that they might bring us into slavery—to them we did not yield in submission even for a moment, so that the truth of the gospel might be preserved for you.*
> **Galatians 2:4–5 ESV**

Series goal:
To know the truth of the gospel well enough to hold tightly to _____,

"not [yielding] in _____ even for a moment" to any _____.

"False brothers" is the English rendering of the Greek word _____,
also used in 2 Corinthians 11:26.

One of the hard lessons all truth-finding Jesus-followers eventually learn:

Measuring _____ by _____ is a colossal _____.

Final thought: _____ _____ can know the _____ for _____.

[1] Timothy George, *Galatians* (Nashville: B&H, 1994), 151.

NOTES

FREEDOM

THE FREEDOM ZONE

day one

When Not to Yield

Read, write and mark Galatians 2:1-5.

_____

_____

_____

_____

_____

_____

_____

_____

_____

_____

_____

_____

_____

If you were able to join us for Session Two, you have already been formally introduced to these passages in reference to our series. We found that Galatians has, for centuries, held its own unique reputation among the New Testament epistles, having been called by some the magna carta (great charter) of Christian liberty, and, by others, Paul's Declaration of Independence. It has been called the freedom manifesto of the Reformation era as well as a mini-version of the Book of Romans.

In 2 Timothy 3:16-17, the apostle Paul writes, "Every scripture is inspired by God and useful for teaching, for reproof, for correction, and for training in righteousness, that the person dedicated to God may be capable and equipped for every good work" (NET). That means all Scripture is transformative. I'd like to suggest, however, that some books of the Bible seem intent on getting to that transformation a little faster. They don't just woo us with the gentle wind of the Spirit. They rattle the windows of our lives with the subtlety of a cyclone. Galatians is among those.

Through the work of the Holy Spirit, the letter we're studying began to change my life in my thirties and, decades later, it still isn't finished. I don't know of anyone who has needed to hear freedom in Jesus preached on a more regular basis than me. Perhaps you feel the same way. Or maybe you're right on the cusp of realizing your need for reminders of freedom—and you just don't know it yet.

Glance back at today's text. How many years passed before Paul returned to Jerusalem? _____

Keep in mind, the chronological itinerary Paul gives to the Galatians is not meant to be a play-by-play of all his travels but points of reference that are pertinent to the matters at hand.

Who accompanied Paul? _____

Both names would have been familiar to the recipients of the letter, particularly that of Barnabas. He'd founded some of the congregations in Galatia with Paul. A little background on Paul's companions will help us formulate an impression of this band of three men in Jerusalem on this occasion.

Read the following verses next to each name and record what is told or inferred about each one.

> All Scripture is inspired by God and is profitable for teaching, for rebuking, for correcting, for training in righteousness, so that the man of God may be complete, equipped for every good work.
>
> 2 Timothy 3:16-17

Barnabas—Acts 4:32–37; 9:26–27; 13:1–3

_____

_____

_____

_____

Titus—Gal 2:3; 2 Cor 8:23; Titus 1:4–5

_____

_____

_____

_____

Mind you, Paul is no stranger to Jerusalem. He would have attended feasts in the Holy City with his family throughout his childhood. According to his testimony in Acts 22:3, Paul also received his education in the Mosaic Law there at the feet of Gamaliel, a highly esteemed Pharisee and member of the Sanhedrin. Since his encounter with Christ on the road to Damascus, however, this was only the second trip Paul had made to Jerusalem. The gap between measured fourteen years.

Paul was a smart man. Perhaps he brought along these particular traveling companions for strategic purposes. Barnabas, an affable encourager, provided a buffer for Paul in the company of those who were apostles before him. Titus, on the other hand, provided Exhibit A of an uncircumcised Gentile Christian. Despite their differences, nothing would have been unusual about the trio making this trip. Barnabas was still Paul's partner in ministry at that time and, as you no doubt noted, Titus was like a son to Paul.

Scholars are divided on whether the trip cited in Galatians 2:1–3 corresponds best to the one recorded by Luke in Acts 11:27–30 or in Acts 15. Let's take a look at both.

Why did Paul and Barnabas go to Jerusalem in Acts 11:27–30?

_____

_____

_____

> I went up according to a revelation and presented to them the gospel I preach among the Gentiles, but privately to those recognized as leaders. I wanted to be sure I was not running, and had not been running, in vain.
>
> Galatians 2:2

On Day Two of Week One, Melissa mentioned the Jerusalem council in Acts 15 and you looked up several passages within the account. She mentioned that we would see the account again this week. Today's text takes us straight to it. The importance of the theological collision described and addressed in the chapter would be hard to overstate. It also has direct bearing on Paul's letter to the Galatians so, though the segment is lengthy, Acts 15 becomes crucial reading to us. For now, read Acts 15:1–31, keeping in mind that Cephas (in Galatians) and Peter and Simeon/Simon (in Acts 15:7, 14) are references to the same apostle.

Who are the major players in the segment?

_____

_____

What point is emphasized in verses 7–8 and 28–29?

_____

_____

_____

How was the letter received?

_____

_____

I love how God is described in Acts 15:8. "And God who knows the heart . . . " You'll recognize the similarity of our English "cardio" in the Greek transliteration "kardiognṓstēs." The noun used in reference to God simply means "heart knower." He knew theirs. He knows ours.

Shift your attention back to Galatians 2:1–5. What piece of information did Paul want to ensure the Galatians knew in v.3?

☐ Titus was forced to be circumcised.

☐ Titus was rejected by those who were circumcised.

☐ Titus wasn't forced to be circumcised.

In Session Two, I introduced the term *pseudadelphoi* which translates "false brothers" in Galatians 2:4. We learned the word can mean either of two things: they were not true brothers/believers at all or they were brothers who believed falsely.

How did they act falsely according to v.4?

_____

_____

Galatians 2:5 articulates our goal for this 6-week series and we will reiterate and further emphasize it here. We established the goal in Session Two based on specific wording in the ESV. As a reminder, here is the translation:

> *Yet because of false brothers secretly brought in—who slipped into spy out our freedom that we have in Christ Jesus, so that they might bring us into slavery—to them we did not yield in submission even for a moment, so that the truth of the gospel might be preserved for you.*
>
> **Galatians 2:4–5 ESV**

Our series goal: *To know the truth of the gospel well enough to hold tightly to freedom, "not [yielding] in submission even for a moment" to any distortion.*

Not even for a moment.

No matter how tempting it is.

No matter who is selling it and how much you respect him/her.

No matter who is trying to enlist you into their camp and how powerful they seem.

No matter how much pressure you are under.

No matter how much easier your life would temporarily be.

No matter who you will make happy.

No matter who you will make mad.

Why?

For Christ's sake: Because Christ gave His life to set you free and it was enormously costly.

For your sake: Because the moment you let go of your right to live out your blood-bought freedom in Christ, you will automatically embrace some form of enslavement. It may be in servitude to legalism or it may be in servitude to licentiousness, but either way is bondage.

For the sake of others: Because all of us were fashioned by God with a deep yearning for freedom. Our liberty in Christ invariably draws the attention of those close by who long to be free. Both legalism and licentiousness give a false impression—bear false witness—of what life is meant to be in Christ Jesus.

We want to come out of this series able to shake our heads *no* at the first whiff of a distorted gospel. We have the right and responsibility to guard our freedom in Christ and, the more we recognize what it looks like, the better equipped we will be to resist a counterfeit.

Below you'll find a few takeaways from today's text in Galatians. If you have an example of either takeaway, write it in the spaces provided underneath.

1. Those who don't exercise their freedom in Christ won't want you to do so either.

_____

_____

_____

_____

_____

_____

_____

2. Some may misread or malign your freedom in Christ as unfaithfulness.

_____

_____

_____

_____

_____

_____

_____

_____

The latter is difficult to stomach and humbling to accept but, if you've experienced it, you've been in good company. No few saints through the centuries have been accused of apostasy for refusing to compromise their freedom in Christ.

> We want to come out of this series able to shake our heads *no* at the first whiff of a distorted gospel.

Sometimes opposition stems strictly from fear. Freedom in Christ scares some people. Those closest to us may fear changes in relational dynamics. To many, change automatically translates as loss. Let there be compassion when this is the case. The good news awaiting us in Galatians is that authentic freedom in Christ is of great gain in relationships because we are released from the bondage of our flesh to bear the fruit of the Spirit. The only relationships that will suffer from our liberty are those that require idolatry.

I'd like to share something in closing. Like anything else, Bible study curriculum can go to extremes. We can make it all about us or nothing at all about us. God gave us the Scriptures so we could know Him by name, by character, by His words and deeds. He gave us the Scriptures so we could come to know His Son and find eternal life in Him. He is the uncontested focus from start to finish. The spotlight never shifts from Him.

But God spilled innumerable bottles of ink on the sacred pages telling us of His history with humankind, of our human fallenness and His divine faithfulness, of His relentless pursuit of relationship, of His glorious plan for redemption and the abundant, fruit-bearing life that is possible in Him for those who believe. We will work diligently to study Galatians in its ancient context with a steady eye on its cause and culture but, if we miss what these six chapters could do in our own hearts and minds, we will leave this series well-informed but not transformed.

These words by John Stott provide helpful language about the task of Bible study.

> I believe we are called to the difficult and even painful task of 'double listening.' That is, we are to listen carefully (although of course with differing degrees of respect) both to the ancient Word and to the modern world, in order to relate the one to the other with a combination of fidelity and sensitivity . . . [and] only if we can develop our capacity for double listening, will we avoid the opposite pitfalls of unfaithfulness and irrelevance, and be able to speak God's Word to God's world with effectiveness today.[1]

Double listening—to Paul's world and our world. Look around with fresh eyes. There's a world out there in desperate need of the truths Galatians tells.

There's a world out there in desperate need of the truths Galatians tells.

[1] John Stott, *The Contemporary Christian: Applying God's Word to Today's World* (Downers Grove, IL: InterVarsity Press, 1992), 13.

NOTES

THE FREEDOM ZONE

day two

Paul and the Pillars

Read, write and mark Galatians 2:6–10.

_____

_____

_____

_____

_____

_____

_____

_____

_____

_____

_____

My friends, we are well into the heart of Galatians. Please come along and look at verse six with me. It's a confusing verse no matter what English version you are using and, in Greek, verse six actually begins one enormous sentence that does not end until verse ten. Take a look at the end of verse six.

When Paul presented his gospel at Jerusalem, what did "those recognized as important" do?

☐ They rejected Paul's gospel outright and threw him out of Jerusalem.
☐ They added nothing to him.
☐ They asked Paul to become a deacon in the Jerusalem church.
☐ They forced Titus to be circumcised.

God does not show favoritism.

Galatians 2:6b

Paul gets sidetracked for a second—stopping to clarify for his readers that he is not awed by the Jerusalem leaders' history or status—but then he gets right back to his bottom line: the leaders added nothing to his gospel when he presented it for them in Jerusalem! L. Ann Jervis states it succinctly, "The gospel of the uncircumcised is a gospel of completeness; it is a gospel to which nothing need be added."[1] The proof that they added nothing to Paul's gospel was that they did not require Titus, a Greek convert, to be circumcised. The example of Titus is crucial for Paul.

In verse 9, Paul will go on to name the Jerusalem leaders explicitly. Go ahead and glance ahead and record their names here:

1. _____ 2. _____

3. _____

Three out of three of these men knew Jesus in the flesh during his earthly ministry. Peter (also called Cephas) and John, a son of Zebedee, together were part of an intimate triad among Jesus' twelve disciples. They witnessed the transfiguration of Jesus and journeyed alone with Jesus into the garden of Gethsemane to pray (or neglect praying) before his death and betrayal (along with James the other son of Zebedee whose death is recorded early in Acts at 12:1–2; see Mark 5:37; 9:2; 13:3; 14:33). And the other man on our list, the legendary leader of the Jerusalem church, James the Just (distinct from James the son of Zebedee), while not a disciple of Jesus during his earthly ministry, was no less than an actual family member of Jesus of Nazareth. It's a confusing coincidence that the man who ended up filling the space of James, the son of Zebedee, in the trio bore precisely the same name.

Elsewhere in the New Testament, Paul refers to himself as the very least of all the saints and apostles (Eph 3:8; 1 Cor 15:9) and in the order of Jesus's resurrection appearances, "one born at the wrong time" (1 Cor 15:8). Paul is not being unnecessarily self-deprecating. He is well aware of the vast ocean of difference between himself and the Jerusalem leaders and how some might perceive his apostolic calling because of it. On the one hand, he has

---

[1] L. Ann Jervis, *Galatians,* Understanding the Bible Commentary Series (Grand Rapids, MI: Baker Books, 1999), 56.

to wrestle with the way his opponents almost certainly capitalize on this discrepancy for their own gain, but on the other, he wears this distinction as a badge that shines with the brightness of God's glorious impartiality.

Paul's relationship to the Jerusalem pillars' authority is complex in this passage. Real ambivalence exists in the way he relates to their authority. It is certainly possible to overdramatize this tension but also unreasonable to deny it. Paul presents his gospel to the leaders "in order to make sure" he "was not running or had not run in vain" (Gal 2:2). This statement is a real acknowledgment of their singular place in the early Christian movement. If they hadn't acknowledged the validity of Paul's message, Paul plainly says he would have considered himself, in some sense, to have been working to no avail. That's no small thing. But, on the other hand, his use of the phrase "those recognized as important" in 2:6 and again "those recognized as pillars" in 2:9 shows a subtle distancing from these same leaders' authority. As Douglas Moo puts it:

> Paul again combines reserve and respect in referring to the Jerusalem apostles. Paul's language does not necessarily question the right of James, Peter, and John to be called 'pillars,' but it also makes clear that Paul will not unequivocally use this language about them—probably because the agitators were putting too much stock in their authority.[2]

I think we experience this tension with authority in the church. No Christian is autonomous; we are all part of the body of Christ. We know how critical it is to respect those in authoritative positions in Christ's church and voluntarily yield under the position God has called them. But it's of no lesser importance that we are unrelenting in our fundamental theological convictions and that we are able to resist or speak up to that same authority when we have reason to believe that a vital part of the gospel is at stake. Most of us probably do one of these things better than the other but, in fact, we are called to do both of them when necessary. God's authority alone is ultimate and Paul's approach in our passage is a reminder of that sobering reality. Charles Cousar observes:

> Paul may at times appear to be an extremely stubborn theologian whose dogmaticism is uncompromising, and yet ironically the truth he struggles for in the early church is one of diversity and mutuality, where Gentiles are not forced to become Jews and vice versa. Being clear about the nature of the gospel does not constrict or confine the church; instead, it removes all the false conditions to unity laid on by years of tradition.[3]

No Christian is autonomous; we are all part of the body of Christ.

---

[2] Douglas J. Moo, *Galatians,* Baker Exegetical Commentary on the New Testament (Grand Rapids, MI: Baker Academic, 2013), 99.

[3] Charles B. Cousar, *Galatians,* Interpretation (Louisville, KY: Westminster John Knox Press, 1982), 41–42.

What comes more naturally to you, respecting authority or resisting authority? Explain your answer with an example from your personal experience.

_____

_____

_____

_____

The language of "pillars" in verse 9 is worth looking into a little bit further. We use similar language in English today when we speak of key members of our society being "pillars of the community" and the like. But something more theologically rich might be going on here in Galatians. In the Greek version(s) of the Old Testament, referred to as the Septuagint, the Greek word used here—στῦλος—is used to refer to the supporting columns of the tabernacle and temple. The language of these three men as "pillars" sketches a mental image of them as the foundational supporting columns of a building in which God's presence resides.

Please look up and read Ephesians 2:19-21 where Paul elaborates on this image and fill in the appropriate blanks:

> **"So then you are no longer foreigners and strangers, but fellow citizens with the saints, and members of God's household, built on the _____ of the _____ and prophets, with Christ Jesus himself as the _____. In him the whole _____, being put together, grows into a holy _____ in the Lord."**

Please read over Galatians 2:7-9 once or twice more and take some time to explain in your own words below the details of the agreement that Paul and the Jerusalem pillars came to:

_____

_____

_____

As Paul presented his gospel along with Barnabas and Titus, the pillars recognized in Paul a ministry that was tantamount in importance to Peter's but with a focus in reach and emphasis in content geared toward the Gentiles. While we note the distinct emphases here, we should take care not to suppose that Paul was prohibited from ministering to Jews and Peter was prohibited from ministering to Gentiles. The New Testament elsewhere tells us a different story; for example, in Acts, we see Paul visiting synagogues upon arrival in numerous cities.

But Paul and the Jerusalem pillars made a general agreement united around one gospel but with different focus groups. Moo explains this in a helpful way when he says, "What he intends, perhaps, is best captured in our modern idea of 'contextualization.' Proclaiming the same gospel to different audiences means inevitably that different emphases will rise to the surface."[4]

Paul says beautifully in verse 9, that when the pillars saw the grace given to him, they offered Barnabas and him the right hand of fellowship. In the book of Acts, it was Paul's report of the signs and wonders God had done among the Gentiles that was a "sign that paralleled him with Peter."[5] The Holy Spirit was at work among both the Jews and the Gentiles, demonstrating that God shows no partiality between them.

The major point Paul has been moving toward since he began telling his story in 2:1 is that he and the Jerusalem pillars are actually in agreement. From the perspective of Paul, it is the false brothers of verse 4 who are out of line and out of graces with the mighty pillars, not Paul. To Paul, the pillars gave the right hand of fellowship, having affirmed the gospel he proclaimed and the work God had done in him for the sake of the Gentiles. Our passage ends at 2:10 with one final and supremely important request from the pillars.

What was that request, according to Galatians 2:10?

_____

> They asked only that we would remember the poor, which I had made every effort to do.
>
> Galatians 2:10

The pillars asked Paul and Barnabas to "remember the poor." From Paul's perspective this was a worthy request he had already been inadvertently fulfilling and one he would heartily continue to work toward fulfilling until his death. Caring for the poor by helping provide for their material needs is an important theme all across Christian scripture including in the Law of Moses, the prophets of Israel, Jesus' own ministry in the four gospels, and it is certainly consistent with what we know of James of Jerusalem from his epistle (James 1:26-27; 2:1-5; 2:15; 5:1).

The pillars' request here in Galatians could be a general request for Paul and Barnabas to remember to care for the poor wherever they went among the Gentiles. Or, it could more specifically allude to what would eventually become the collection for Jerusalem—a substantial financial contribution

---

[4] Douglas J. Moo, _Galatians_, 134.
[5] Craig S. Keener, _Galatians: A Commentary_ (Grand Rapids, MI: Baker Academic, 2019), 127.

raised by Paul and his Gentile churches for the poor particularly in the Jerusalem church. I lean toward thinking it's an allusion to the latter, myself, though I believe the former would also have been implied as a necessity.

Turn to Paul's words to the Corinthian Christians in 1 Corinthians 16:1–4. Describe what you find there below:

_____

_____

_____

Similarly, at the end of Paul's letter to the Roman church, he records that he was on his way to Jerusalem. Why was he going to Jerusalem this time? To serve the church by delivering a financial contribution from Macedonia and Achaia for the poor among the Jerusalem church (see 15:26).

Please look up and carefully read Romans 15:25–29. Explain as best you can Paul's theological reasoning for these Gentile Christians' financial contribution to the saints in Jerusalem.

_____

_____

_____

_____

Back to Galatians for a final minute. Paul has some harsh words for the false brothers who he describes as freedom spies seeking to enslave his Gentile converts. He also has some harsh words for Peter after the episode in Antioch, too, as we will see tomorrow in verse 11. Paul both respects the pillars and refuses to grant them an ultimate authority reserved for Jesus alone, the Cornerstone (Acts 4:11; Eph 2:20).

But, it's really, really important—and frankly pretty moving—to witness Paul at the end of Romans as he works earnestly to fulfill the request of the Jerusalem pillars. There, some years later, he not only deems it important, still, to remember the Jerusalem poor but to teach the church in Rome that the Gentiles are spiritually indebted to their Jewish brothers and sisters. _"Yes . . . indeed they are indebted to them. For if the Gentiles have shared in their spiritual benefits, then they are obligated to minister to them in material needs"_ (Romans 15:27).

That's something to sit with and reflect on for a while.

THE FREEDOM ZONE

day three

Confrontation

Read, write and mark Galatians 2:11–14.

_____

_____

_____

_____

_____

_____

_____

_____

_____

_____

_____

_____

We may be far removed from those first century Jesus-followers and know very little about the dietary differences between Jews and Gentiles but, my guess is, few of us struggle to imagine this scene. How many of us have never suddenly gone cold in our warm fellowship with others when certain people who would disapprove of us entered the picture?

Think creatively for a moment. Fill in the space below with very basic stick figures to illustrate the events Paul narrates in this segment. Don't attempt to be artistic. Just try to get the point across without using words. I'll get you started with the first one.

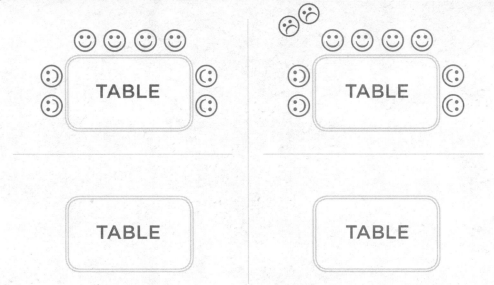

When the "dividing wall of hostility" (Eph 2:14) between Jew and Gentile was torn down by Christ on the cross, one of the last things either group would have expected—or perhaps wanted—was to find themselves, spiritually speaking, standing in one another's kitchens. Many would have preferred that the melting pot stay away from the stove. Second only to the mark of circumcision, the Jewish dietary laws and table practices set them apart dramatically from the Gentiles. One might successfully argue that, indeed, God had given those laws in part to keep them apart.

In Judaism, sharing a table had larger implications than satiating hunger in close proximity. Actions like sharing salt and dipping bread in the same bowl had covenantal overtones to them; therefore, sitting at the same table with Gentiles, let alone eating their food, was an unthinkable reversal. The mindset was deeply ingrained in them to see any such mixing as morally defiling. They were yet to grasp that the new way also had covenantal overtones but they were the tones of a new covenant and not the old. There is nothing like the gospel to challenge our deeply ingrained mindsets.

Leviticus 11:1-23 is the primary section in Scripture specifying prohibited and permitted foods according to the Mosaic Law. Read through the verses to get an idea of the distinctions but, unless you have time for both, save your more careful reading for Acts 10. It is lengthy but fascinating and pertinent to the study of our text today as it revolves around the same person (Cephas/Peter) and the same subject matter.

First, read Acts 10:1–33 and record in each column how God simultaneously works through two different men to accomplish one divine result:

Cornelius	Peter

The NASB identifies Peter's host in Acts 10:32 as "the tanner by the sea." I smile each time I read it, picturing him in swim trunks on a beach towel at the shore. Count this as one of many colorful examples of why the culture in which the passage was penned is key to its interpretation.

Now, read Acts 10:34–43. What had Peter come to understand? (v.34)

_____

Thoroughly familiarizing ourselves with the gospel message according to the apostle Paul is among our chief aims in this 6-week series. Even in our short time together, we've already taken several looks at 1 Corinthians 15:1–4 where Paul recorded matters of "first importance" (ESV).

How does Peter's spontaneous sermon in Acts 10:34–43 hit every matter of first importance in Paul's list?

_____

_____

Wrap up your reading of the chapter with Acts 10:44–48. How does the segment end?

_____

_____

_____

Why all of this backstory? We are now poised to more fully appreciate the scene in Galatians 2:11–14. I'll refer to Cephas as Peter for the remainder of the lesson for simplicity's sake.

Peter and the Gentiles were no longer guests at one another's tables. They were family.

If anyone on earth knew for certain that the old rules of clean and unclean foods no longer applied and that freedom had come to fellowship with the Gentiles, Peter did. God set him up personally, dramatically and unforgettably to receive that fresh revelation. To Paul, Peter's sudden withdrawal from the table with Gentiles wasn't just inappropriate—it was abominable. By his actions, Peter preached a distorted gospel.

Paul's public confrontation of Peter was a turnabout to Peter's equally public retreat from the Gentiles. The whiplash had not gone unnoticed. The CSB wording makes the Greek verb tense more obvious: "For he *regularly* ate with the Gentiles before certain men came from James" (emphasis mine). Peter's freedom in Christ had opened to him an astonishingly new way of living and being. The initial awkwardness had given way to acceptance then, we presume, gladness. Peter and the Gentiles were no longer guests at one another's tables. They were family. So, any reversal of this even for a moment was out of the question to Paul. His silence would be rightly interpreted as more than cowardice or carelessness. It would be complicity.

The year is right around AD 48. The location where this confrontation took place is not incidental to the story. Antioch, in northern Syria, was the Roman Empire's third largest city and among the first places (if not the very first place) where such liberties as Jews and Gentiles sharing a meal were openly practiced. The old labels no longer fit their new identities. Dr. Timothy George writes,

> Obviously a new reality had come into being with this new called-out company of Jews and Gentiles whose identity and self-definition centered neither in their Jewishness nor their Gentile character but rather in their common devotion to the one in whose name they shared a common meal. Thus they were called *Christianoi*, "the folks of Christ," originally perhaps a term of derogation that soon came to be owned with pride by believers everywhere because it was so evidently appropriate.[1]

Do you find anything about the excerpt refreshing? If so, what?

_____

_____

_____

[1] Timothy George, *Galatians* (Nashville: B&H, 1994), 172.

For Peter, Antioch was a long way from home. All was well until, suddenly, home came to Antioch.

Based on what you've already learned about where James served, what do you think Paul means by these certain men "coming from James"?

_____

Look closely at the reason given for Peter's withdrawal from the Gentiles:

"he withdrew and separated himself, because

he _____ **from the circumcision party."**

We wouldn't be out of line to suggest that Peter likely feared the "circumcision party" because they were fearsome. Let's be honest. Sometimes we're scared of certain people because they are, in fact, *scary*. Though his actions were out of place and preached a distorted gospel, Peter couldn't exactly be accused of histrionics. He'd already been beaten and imprisoned in Jerusalem for closely following Jesus and, had an angel not been sent to escort him to safety, he probably would have been beheaded (Acts 12). But fear of physical harm wouldn't have been necessary for Peter to be intimidated by the circumcision party in Antioch.

Our series will offer us several opportunities to reiterate the priority of Paul's resistance to human approval. Factions can become dangerous. Members can be emboldened by one another and the line between differing and bullying completely erased. Sometimes we're afraid of people simply because they are mean-spirited and we dread the social backlash. It takes a strong stomach to come against intimidating personalities, especially those strong-arming in the name of righteousness. Faithfulness to Jesus requires both a sturdy spine and a tender heart. Only the Holy Spirit can accomplish such diversity of characteristics in us. Anticipate further discussion of this in Week Five.

> Faithfulness to Jesus requires both a sturdy spine and a tender heart.

While most of our lives will not be endangered by partisanship, our livelihoods certainly can be. People who can't control us *can* hurt us. Jobs can be lost. Opportunities forfeited. Promotions thwarted. Relationships lost. Reputations ruined. Let's admit, some people are scary to displease but, scary or not, losing club membership is painful. To have never been a part of a certain sect is one thing. Being a part then stepping apart is another matter entirely. Clubs often come with benefits. Leaving them can carry penalties.

To be sure, Judaism had been no mere club to the apostles and other Jews who'd received Christ. Nothing was vaguely compartmentalized about the Jewish faith. For most, it stamped every atom of their existence. Still, factions formed around interpretations and practices were rife in the New Testament era just as they are today in Christianity. In our present text, both are in view. Those of the "circumcision party" were Torah observant Jewish Christians but, as surely as their Jewishness had permeated the way they thought, lived, worked, rested, recreated, drank and ate, their new freedom in Christ was meant to do so through the Spirit.

According to Gal 2:13, what was the ripple effect of Peter's withdrawal?

_____

_____

> But when I saw that they were deviating from the truth of the gospel, I told Cephas in front of everyone, "If you, who are a Jew, live like a Gentile and not like a Jew, how can you compel Gentiles to live like Jews?"
>
> Galatians 2:14

"Even Barnabas ...!" We're meant to sense the shock. Who would be the last person in your life who you'd expect to act hypocritically? "Even _____ ...!" We would do ourselves a service to picture his or her name in the blank because your most respected person has also acted in ways that would disappoint you and perhaps even misrepresent the truth of the gospel. We all have a bent toward hypocrisy and, like Peter, our acts of hypocrisy are often driven by fear.

Can you see where fear has played into an act of hypocrisy in your own life? I can see a connection between the two in mine. If your answer is yes, describe how you think they are tied together in your life.

_____

_____

_____

Take a fresh look at Paul's response to Peter in Galatians 2:14 and rewrite it in your own words.

_____

_____

_____

We need people in our lives with enough nerve to say to us, "You can't do that. You can't live by one standard and hold others to another." What we can assume from Peter's faithful ministry and the words the Holy Spirit later penned through him is that neither Paul nor the circumcision party nor Peter nor the Gentiles won the fight that day. Christ won. And, because Christ won, the church won. The biggest win of our lives is sometimes on the other side of a lost fight.

Hours of rich discussion could spring from our lesson today. Our time is too limited to take advantage of every opportunity to offer personal examples but, as we close, please select one of the two sets of questions below for your response. We're not pretending to be Peter and Cornelius in Acts 10 or Peter, Paul and Barnabas in Galatians 2, but we're also not complete strangers to the concepts.

Option 1: With Acts 10 fresh on your mind, have you ever realized in retrospect that you'd been part of a divine setup when God worked separately but simultaneously on two different sides to prepare each to come together to accomplish His will? If so, tell the story succinctly and think of sharing it with your small group. (Use space on notes page that follows.)

Option 2: With Galatians 2:11-14 fresh on your mind, have you ever been involved in the fallout of two powerful leaders in conflict? If so, when?

What were the immediate and early effects?

_____

_____

_____

_____

_____

_____

If sufficient time has passed, how did the conflict play out as far as you can tell? In other words, was there resolution, dissolution or did it simply fade out of view?

_____

_____

_____

_____

_____

The biggest win of our lives is sometimes on the other side of a lost fight.

NOTES

THE FREEDOM ZONE

day four

Let the Ruins Be

Read, write and mark Galatians 2:15–18.

_____

_____

_____

_____

_____

_____

_____

_____

_____

_____

_____

Verse 15 ushers us right into the middle of Paul's retelling of his response to Peter at Antioch. The verses that follow until the end of chapter two contain some of the most potent contents of the letter. Take a look back at verse 14 just to get your contextual bearings.

Now, who is the "we" in verse 15? _____

The "we" is Paul and Peter and, by implication, other Jews (by birth) who have believed in Jesus, the Messiah. Paul here is setting Jews like himself in distinction with "Gentile sinners," a startling phrase that stops us in our tracks. As J. Louis Martyn explains, "In Jewish tradition Gentiles, not having the Law, are inevitably sinners, who do not hear the call to repentance and thus cannot receive forgiveness."[1]

Since the Gentiles didn't have the Law to reveal to them how to be holy, it's understandable how Jews conceived of them broadly as "sinners." A Jew observing the Law, on the other hand, in Jewish tradition, generally would not be considered a "sinner" but a "transgressor" of the Law or a "lawbreaker" (see 2:18).[2]

Things are about to get pretty theological in this passage, so I want to remind you that the context of Paul's discussion here is a social one: Jews and Gentiles belong at the same table.[3] As I. W. Scott suggests, here Paul places "the situation in Antioch alongside the situation in Galatia, to see the crises as parallel and the true solution as the same in both cases."[4] Not coincidentally, in the gospels, Jesus was also criticized by Jewish legal authorities for eating with "sinners," though the reference is more generally "outcasts" instead of Gentiles (Mark 2:16; Luke 15:1).

What does the table mean to you on a personal level?

_____

_____

_____

What could two very different kinds of people experience by simply eating together?

_____

_____

_____

[1] J. Louis Martyn, Galatians, The Anchor Yale Bible Commentaries (New Haven, CT: Yale University Press, 1997), 248.

[2] Gordon Fee, Galatians, Pentecostal Commentary Series (Dorset: Deo Publishing, 2007), 80.

[3] Charles B. Cousar, Galatians, Interpretation (Louisville, KY: Westminster John Knox Press, 1982), 58.

[4] I. W. Scott, Implicit Epistemology in the Letters of Paul: Story, Experience and the Spirit (Tubingen: Mohr Siebeck, 2006), quoted in Douglas J. Moo, Galatians, Baker Exegetical Commentary on the New Testament; Grand Rapids, MI: Baker Academic, 2013), 154.

A quick word about verse 16. Scholars write entire dissertations on individual words and two-word phrases in this verse. If you find yourself with a lot of questions and confusion, be of good cheer—you are in good company with Paul's most advanced readers. We won't come anywhere near addressing all the exegetical issues in today's reading. This is the kind of passage that warrants filing away and picking up a good commentary later to consult through the more tedious sections.

Read verse 16 and fill in the blanks:

"and _____ because we know that a person is not _____

by the _____ but by _____ in

Jesus Christ, even we ourselves have believed in _____.

This was so that we might be _____ by _____ in

Christ and not by the _____, because by the

_____ no human being will be _____."

It's a mouthful, isn't it?

What do both Paul and Peter know?

☐ A person is justified by faith in the Law.
☐ A person is justified by works of faith.
☐ A person cannot be justified, period.
☐ A person is justified by faith in Jesus Christ.

The book of Acts tells the dramatic stories of both Peter and Paul, describing how they each came to understand, supernaturally, that the God of Israel does not show partiality. The Holy Spirit of God fills both Jew and Gentile alike when they receive the word of the Lord and believe in Jesus, the Messiah (Acts 10:44; 11:15–17; 19:1–7). Peter temporarily digressed from his journey of freedom when he withdrew from meals with Gentiles in Antioch. Likewise, the Galatians are digressing in their journey of freedom by vaguely considering circumcision for their Gentile members. Paul implores them—they must turn back on this road leading nowhere!

We know that the Law of Moses continued to be significant for Jews in the early Christian movement, even after they believed in Jesus. We see this elsewhere even in the New Testament. The issue at hand is not whether *Jewish* Christians ought to keep the Mosaic Law still (an important but entirely different question) but whether *Gentile* Christians ought to start keeping the Law (or at least certain crucial parts of it) now that they believe in the Jewish Messiah.

For Paul, the answer is an absolute "No." But, if Paul is on the right end of the spectrum in his relationship with the Law, other Jewish Christians were more in the middle (James of Jerusalem) and even to the left (Christians from the Pharisee party who wanted Gentiles to keep the Law in Acts 15:5). The diversity of approaches toward the Law is one of my favorite things to pay attention to in the New Testament.

> We know that a person is not justified by the works of the law but by faith in Jesus Christ.
>
> Galatians 2:16a

As Douglas Moo puts it, "In place of the agitators' synthesis of faith in Christ and the law, Paul insists on an antithesis: it is Christ and therefore not the law."[5] While it's quite probable that someone like Jesus' brother James (to be distinguished from the agitator freedom-spies of 2:4), the leader of the Jerusalem church, carried on observing the Law just as he had before he believed in Jesus, Paul did not. His relationship to the Law radically changed after he encountered the risen Christ—maybe to a greater degree than other Jewish Christians because God called him specifically to be apostle to the Gentiles.

What was absolutely unacceptable to Paul for any Jewish Christian, however, was to carry on now like the Law had power to justify people. It was one thing for Jews and Jewish Christians to keep the Law as a continuing expression of piety and heritage, but another to imply that keeping the Law was on equal ground with faith in Jesus. On the contrary, Paul says, no human will be justified by the works of the Law.

What do you think it means to be "justified"? Give it a good shot:

_____

_____

_____

_____

_____

Gordon Fee suggests that being justified means something like being pardoned, not merely acquitted, since being acquitted implies innocence.[6] Being justified means being pardoned with full view of one's guilty status. The result of this pardon includes a "rightstanding with God" through Jesus and the Spirit that makes possible "access into God's presence" and even persists in spite of further sin.[7]

[5] Moo, *Galatians*, 154.
[6] Fee, *Galatians*, 83.
[7] Fee, *Galatians*, 83.

If the Law does not justify, then what does? Faith in Jesus Christ (Gal 2:16). The important Greek word translated "faith" is πίστις. This word is used around twenty two times in Galatians alone and is crucial for Pauline studies. I love Jeanette Hagen Pifer's definition of faith from her close exegesis of these verses in her monograph *Faith as Participation*:

> Our developing definition of faith is: the mode of existence by which the believer participates in the Christ-event and appropriates all the benefits thereof; as such it is necessarily self-negating and thus self-involving in the person and work of Christ ... πίστις depicts the human grasping hold of all that Christ accomplished to justify believers and to enable a continuing manner of living to God. Faith renounces all forms of worth apart from Christ. Faith is an active, self-involving dependence on Christ ... [8]

Scholars and translators struggle both with the best way to render this word πίστις in English and its syntactical relationship to "Jesus Christ" in the Greek phrase πίστεως Ἰησοῦ Χριστοῦ. The CEB and the NET translations, for example, translate the phrase "the faithfulness of Jesus Christ" while the vast majority of the English translations render it with "faith in Jesus Christ." This is a notorious ongoing debate in scholarly circles with significant implications. If you find yourself intrigued and want to read more on these topics, look into Nijay K. Gupta's book *Paul and the Language of Faith*, published by Eerdmans in 2020.

Let's talk about Paul's antithesis. I want to drive home the point that here in Galatians, Paul creates an antithesis between faith in Jesus Christ and a specific kind of works: the works of the Law of Moses (the most relevant is circumcision for the Galatians). In most of our church circles, it is standard to explain the gospel as a message of "salvation by faith and not by works" and then to read this antithesis back into every verse of the Bible, from Genesis to Revelation! I am not saying this antithesis is not found in Scripture. Off the top of my head, it is clearly found in James 2:14–18, though there it is used in a way exactly opposite of our reformation creed.

Explain in your own words the distinction between "works" in general and "works of the Law" in particular. Why might this distinction matter?

_____

_____

_____

[8] Jeanette Hagen Pifer, *Faith as Participation: An Exegetical Study of Some Key Pauline Texts* (Tübingen, Germany: Mohr Seibeck, 2019), 159.

I want to be crystal clear that I don't believe anyone is saved by any work(s) but Jesus' own. But sometimes the faith and works antithesis is lifted so far from its scriptural context that it loses all meaning. Even "faith" can be articulated as mere optimism instead of trust in the person of Jesus. We have to take care to understand the particular idea before we start abstracting it. Maybe we rush to the abstract idea because Galatians feels inaccessible to us if we don't. We, wrongly, have been taught that if we cannot immediately apply a concept to our "everyday lives" then it is not worth the bother to understand it.

Please read the final two verses of our lesson, verses 17–18.

Write down anything that puzzles you about these verses or anything that sticks out to you:

_____

_____

_____

_____

> We, wrongly, have been taught that if we cannot immediately apply a concept to our "everyday lives" then it's not worth the bother to understand it.

When Peter drew away from eating dinner with Gentiles in Antioch, he went back to a former way of life, one in which he was easily distinguishable from Gentile sinners. At times, Peter's old way of life probably felt a lot less confusing than the one he was living now. The problem was, there was no going back. He and Paul had long since made decisions that placed them in a new and undoubtedly uncomfortable solidarity with Gentiles.

Try to think for a moment, from the perspective of the Gentiles in Galatia. What could have been attractive about observing the Torah in specific ways? Use your imagination and give it a try!

_____

_____

_____

_____

_____

_____

In verses 17–18, Paul says that only if they or other Jewish Christians reestablish the Mosaic Law as the standard of behavior for God's people could Christ, in any way, be conceived of as "a promoter of sin."[9] But, Christ is not a promoter of sin! As it actually is, God raised Jesus from the dead and everything has changed because of it, even the role of the Law. Paul, as Moo puts it: "has replaced his attachment to the law with an attachment to Christ."[10] To assert the same former beliefs about the Law—to insist that Gentiles be circumcised—would mean to rebuild something that Paul and Peter tore down for a divine reason. And those reasons are coming tomorrow. You won't want to miss it. It's rich.

As we close down for today, I'd like for you to think broadly about this concept of rebuilding something purposefully torn down. Have you ever deconstructed something major in your life that you later reconstructed, and in doing so, you became less free?

_____

_____

_____

_____

When we first follow Jesus, many of us turn from certain things and rightly leave them behind. But, over time, we come to see that even the church has its idols. And some of those same old things we rightly gave up when trusting Jesus end up having a subtle sanction among church people. Regularly, I look up from my life and realize I've forgotten my belovedness. I realize I'm living in condemnation and have myriad reasons to support my claim. I often call to mind Brennan Manning's words that captivated me years ago: "God loves you unconditionally, as you are and not as you should be, because nobody is as they should be."[11] That line brings me back to what the Psalmist calls "a spacious place."

He brought me out to a spacious place;
he rescued me because he delighted in me.

Psalm 18:19

---

[9] Moo, *Galatians*, 154–55.
[10] Moo, *Galatians*, 155.
[11] Brennan Manning, *All Is Grace: A Ragamuffin Memoir* (Colorado Springs, CO: David C Cook, 2011), Kindle edition, 192.

NOTES

THE FREEDOM ZONE

day five

Crucified with Christ

Read, write and mark Galatians 2:19–21.

_____

_____

_____

_____

_____

_____

_____

_____

_____

_____

At the end of today's lesson, if I have explained this section of Scripture to complete satisfaction and understanding and swept out all the clouds, I will have successfully failed at teaching it. We are eager to avoid heresy but we will not be able to avoid mystery nor do we want to. We could take a scalpel to every syllable, correctly parse every verb and seek the wisdom of a thousand scholars and still not be able to fully grasp everything said in these words.

I love the imagery author Mike Cosper uses to describe what can happen when we go to either of two extremes in our approach to Scripture: picking it apart to suit every cultural whim or forcing it from first to last into a "rigid literalism." Cosper suggests both extremes can have negative effects like these:

> The text has no life of its own. It isn't a living whole—a breathing, fiery creature full of mystery, something to be approached with care and humility; it's a subject to be mastered, a corpse to be dissected. It's placed on a steel table and subjected to a thousand acts of violence. It is split into its component parts, footnoted for historicity, and commented on from every angle. In effect, it becomes hedged behind high walls of specialized knowledge, and most Christians—unless they've spent many hours in classes or in inductive Bible studies—are as frightened to talk about what a text might mean as they are to answer a question in math or science class.[1]

We will not master these verses. We will meditate on them and study them but we will not beat the life out of them, dust off our hands and move to the next set to conquer. By its very nature, Scripture requires breathing room.

First, let's look at Galatians 2:19 and consider what Paul means when he says of himself, "through the law I died to the law." Cross reference Romans 7:4-6 where Paul expounds on the concept and read the portion carefully.

How were we also "put to death in relation to the law"?

_____

Why? _____

How may we serve now according to Romans 7:6?

_____

_____

> For through the law I died to the law, so that I might live for God.
>
> Galatians 2:19

Shift your attention to the second half of Galatians 2:19. Though the CSB wording "that I might live for God" makes more immediate sense, the ESV and NAS wording "that I might live _to_ God" (emphasis mine) come closer to capturing the idea. The phrase "living for God" was worn threadbare in Christian circles during my young faith walk. What became apparent both

---

[1] Mike Cosper, _Recapturing the Wonder: Transcendent Faith in a Disenchanted World_ (Downers Grove, IL: IVP Books, 2017), 15.

from observation and experience was that we could work ourselves to dust living for God without ever particularly involving God.

Living "to God" is directional, not just transactional. It calls for continual involvement in shifting the trajectory from the lateral view to the vertical. Perhaps the idea is easier to picture in Paul's metaphor in Galatians 2 of running his race (cf. 2 Tim 4:7). We are not just running for Jesus but literally to Him. Paul describes a holistic existence in which our entire lives are lived to God. In Christ, we die *to sin, to self, to the world, to the flesh and to the law* that we might live *to* God. Our worshipping is to God. Our working, our befriending, our suffering, our loving, our hoping, our wrestling, our grieving, our feasting, our resting, our dancing, our living and our dying are all to God.

Could a shift in perspective from living "for God" to living "to God" be of any help to you? If so, how?

_____

_____

_____

_____

Galatians 2:20 was my first real acquaintance with Paul's letter to the churches in Galatia. Raised in church, I'd no doubt heard much of the letter but a wide gulf separates a verse passing through our ears and actually abiding in our hearts. I was in my late twenties when I bought a Scripture memory starter kit that contained about six cardstock sheets with select verses printed on small, perforated rectangles. I stacked those cards, bound them with a rubber band I'd pulled off a *Houston Chronicle* and wore them out. Galatians 2:20 was among them and one of the loveliest Scriptures I'd ever heard, even with all its talk of crucifixion. The rhythm, the movement and the way it said so much in so few words seemed equal parts poetry and theology. That verse can woo a soul to the whole letter. My prayer is that it is wooing us even now.

In Galatians 2:20, Paul does not intend to be the solitary owner of the "I" in the passage. He invites us all in. As Richard B. Hays writes, "The 'I' throughout vv.18–21 is a paradigmatic 'I,' rhetorically inviting readers of the letter to join with Paul in these confessional statements."[2]

Let's take this gorgeous verse in segments.

> Living "to God" is directional, not just transactional.

[2] Richard B. Hays, "Galatians," in *The New Interpreter's Bible* Vol. XI (Nashville: Abingdon Press, 2000), 243. © 2000 Abingdon Press. Used by Permission. All rights reserved.

"I have been crucified with Christ." The verb tense conveys an action completed in the past with continuing effects. In other words, "what it has done affects all I now do."

Compare Romans 6:5-7. What reason is given for "our old self" being "crucified with him"? _____

" . . . and I no longer live . . . " Scholar F. F. Bruce viewed the arrangement of the Greek wording with particular significance.[3] While his point isn't evident in all English translations, including the CSB, you can see it in the ESV. Compare the two:

> **" . . . I no longer live . . . " (CSB)**
>
> **"It is no longer I who live . . . " (ESV)**

What is the difference between the two?

_____

_____

_____

Bruce explains the significance:

> But so completely is self dethroned in the new order that in this context Paul will not say ἐγώ ζῶ but 'it is no longer I who live; it is Christ who lives in me' (ζῇ δὲ ἐν ἐμοὶ Χριστός).[4]

In other words, Paul does not say "I live [no longer]" but "no longer I live." The ordering of the "I" (ἐγώ transliterates ego) represents the displacement of the ego as the driving force. Dr. R. N. Longenecker makes a similar point.

> Crucifixion with Christ implies not only death to the jurisdiction of the Mosaic law (v 19), but also death to the jurisdiction of one's own ego. The "I" here is the "flesh" of 5:13-24, which is antagonistic to the Spirit's jurisdiction. So in identifying with Christ's death, both the law and the human ego have ceased to be controlling factors for the direction of the Christian life. Instead, Paul insists, the focus of the believer's attention is to be on the fact that "Christ lives in me."[5]

---

[3] F. F. Bruce, *The Epistle to the Galatians*, The New International Greek Testament Commentary (Grand Rapids, MI: Eerdmans, 1982), 144.

[4] Bruce, *The Epistle to the Galatians*, 144.

[5] Richard N. Longenecker, *Galatians*, Word Biblical Commentary Vol. 41 (Dallas: Thomas Nelson Inc, 1990), 92. © 1990 by Richard N. Longenecker. Used by permission of Thomas Nelson. www.thomasnelson.com

It sounds technical but nothing could be more practical. Imagine if we really did remind our egos when they loom large, "actually, you're not in charge here. You are neither judge nor jury. Get over that offense. Die to that need to be affirmed and approved and exalted in this situation. You don't need to be known by the world. You are known by the one who made the world." When our egos crave to be fed, we can remind them that, in Christ, they are actually dead.

" . . . but Christ lives in me. The life I now live in the body, I live by faith in the Son of God . . ." We naturally think in terms of living then dying but Paul repeatedly reverses the order in his writings. Dying gives way to living. He states this most succinctly in the trustworthy saying in 2 Timothy 2:11.

"For if we _____ with Him, we will also _____ with Him."

2 Corinthians 4:10–11 offers another example. Draw a cross over occurrences of the word death and a rectangle around the words life and live.

> "We always carry the death of Jesus in our body, so that the life of Jesus may also be displayed in our body. For we who live are always being given over to death for Jesus's sake, so that Jesus's life may also be displayed in our mortal flesh."

No greater reality exists within the believer's life than Christ's indwelling Spirit. The natural mind tends to assign existence primarily according to substance but faith is "proof of what is not seen" (Heb 11:1). Second Corinthians 4:16 says, "even though our outer person is being destroyed, our inner person is being renewed day by day." That means nothing happening right around us or even to us is as remarkable as what is happening within us. Nothing we can see with human eyes or hold in our hands is more actual or factual than Christ living in us.

To embrace this truth, we have to embrace quite the mystery, don't we? How does Paul describe this "mystery" in Colossians 1:25–27?

_____

_____

_____

_____

No greater reality exists within the believer's life than Christ's indwelling Spirit.

The finite mind cannot calculate "the glorious wealth of this mystery" (Col 1:27). You see, mystery doesn't diminish reality. As for substance assumed as the truest evidence of existence, Paul says further in Colossians that the observances of religious devotion according to the Mosaic Law are "a shadow of what was to come; the substance is Christ" (Col 2:17). You can put your hand on your chest and feel your heart pumping and yet nothing is more alive in you this moment than the Spirit of Christ. Indeed, nothing is of greater substance. The substance of Christ, unseen and often unfelt, far exceeds the weight of your body on a bathroom scale.

Proceed to the next portion of Galatians 2:20.

" . . . **who loved me and gave himself for me.**" You likely believe, based on John 3:16, that God so loves the world. You almost certainly believe Jesus loved His disciples (John 13:1). You may know to your core that Jesus loves the church and, by that, we mean all who belong to Him (Eph 5:25). Mary and Martha knew Jesus loved their brother Lazarus (John 11:3).

But how easy or difficult is it for you to believe He loves you? Briefly explain why.

_____

_____

_____

_____

_____

_____

_____

Bruce writes,

> While Paul is still using the pronoun "I"/"me" representatively, it is difficult not to recognize the intense personal feeling in his words: it was a source of unending wonder to him "that I, even I, have mercy found" . . . Charles Wesley tells of the part these words played in his own conversion experience: as he studied Luther's commentary on Galatians, he says, he found special blessing in "his conclusion of the second chapter. I laboured, waited, and prayed to feel 'who loved _me_ and gave himself for _me_'" (_Journal_, I [London, 1849], 90).[6]

[6] Bruce, _The Epistle to the Galatians_, 146.

We need not feel it all the time to know it. Those occasions in which God causes us to feel it can sustain us for many days. We need only remember them and steady ourselves to walk by faith and not by sight or feeling. When strain, pain or numbness cause us once again to long for such mercy, to think Jesus would be put off by our laboring, waiting and praying to feel "who loved me and gave himself for me" underestimates His tenderness toward us.

This single section of Galatians 2:20 sums up to perfection what the life of Christ looks like lived out in His followers. It looks like love and self-giving.

How might this summation be helpful in a present challenge you are facing?

_____

_____

_____

_____

_____

_____

_____

"I do not set aside the grace of God, for if righteousness comes through the law, then Christ died for nothing." So exalted was the death of Christ in the mind of Paul, so weighty, so holy, so divinely planned, so complete in purpose and pivotal in history that nothing was more unthinkable than it being in vain. Worthy is the Lamb who was slain.

I have been crucified with Christ, and I no
longer live, but Christ lives in me. The life I now
live in the body, I live by faith in the Son of God,
who loved me and gave himself for me.

Galatians 2:20

NOTES

PROMISE

zone three

PROMISE

GALATIANS 3

For if the inheritance is based on the law, it is no
longer based on the promise; but God has graciously
given it to Abraham through the promise.

Galatians 3:18

VIDEO GUIDE

THE PROMISE ZONE

Introduction: Today we move into our third week of study and the third chapter of Galatians. Within these 29 verses we find a zone-word that carries endless implications.

Read Galatians 3:15–29 and compare Genesis 15:5–21 (Genesis 12:1–3).

1. _____ **Exodus 20 was** _____.

Law in Galatians refers to the Mosaic Law.

Scholar Timothy George wrote in his commentary on Galatians in regard to 3:18: "For Paul it was crucial that this original "covenant of promise" be distinguished from the law of Moses. **The law demands, "_____!" The promise grants, "_____!"**[1]

[1] Timothy George, *Galatians* (Nashville: B&H , 1994), 249–250.

2. Because the promises of God are _____ enough for Him _____ to keep, they require _____ to believe (Isaiah 25:9 NIV).

_____

_____

_____

3. The promise of God to Abraham was a _____of grace.

Listen to the definition of the Greek lexical term for promise:

> Promise: *ἐπαγγελία epaggelía;* Primarily a legal term denoting a summons or promise to do or give something. Used only of the promises of God except in Acts 23:21 where it means order or mandate. The thing promised, a gift graciously given, not a pledge secured by negotiation (Luke 24:49; Acts 2:33; Gal. 3:14; Eph. 1:13; Heb. 9:15). Antonym: *agnóēma* (51), a thing ignored.[2]

Read Galatians 3:18.

Based on a specific original word in Galatians 3:18, commentator Richard B. Hays translates Galatians 3:18b "But God _____ through promise."[3]

That verb is a form of the word "charis" which means grace. (kecharistai)

_____

_____

_____

_____

4. God's commitment to you _____ you.

_____

_____

_____

[2] Spiros Zodhiates, *The Complete Word Study Dictionary: New Testament* (Chattanooga, TN: AMG Publishers), electronic edition.

[3] Richard B. Hays, "Galatians," in *The New Interpreter's Bible* Vol. XI (Nashville: Abingdon Press, 2000) © 2000 Abingdon Press. Used by Permission. All rights reserved.

NOTES

PROMISE

THE PROMISE ZONE

day one

Bewitched

Read, write and mark Galatians 3:1-6.

In the opening of Galatians' third chapter, ink spurts from the pen like a bursting pipe, resulting in a flood of questions.

Count the questions from the segment on the previous page. Total: _____

Complete this abbreviated version of the first question:

"You foolish Galatians! Who has _____?" (v.1)

> You foolish Galatians! Who has cast a spell on you, before whose eyes Jesus Christ was publicly portrayed as crucified?
>
> Galatians 3:1

The Greek verb *(baskaino)* is what scholars call a "hapax legomenon," meaning it is only used once in the New Testament. The CSB translates the verb "cast a spell on you." The ESV employs "bewitched you." We'll begin our exploration of Paul's meaning with an inquiry of our own because, in all probability, we've experienced something similar.

Have you ever felt like an individual or group of people you cared about had been "bewitched" (figuratively or literally)? If so, describe what distinguished the situation from regular, run-of-the-mill persuasion:

_____

_____

_____

Fill in the blank and you'll find a key to help unlock Paul's meaning of bewitched. "You _____ Galatians! Who has cast a spell on you?"

J. M. Boice explains,

> The word used here is not *mōros*, so often used in Christ's parables (Matt 5:22; 7:26; 25:2ff.). *Mōros* refers to one who is mentally deficient or who plays the fool, particularly in the moral or spiritual realm. In Galatians the word is *anoētos* which, quite differently, suggests the actions of one who can think but fails to use his powers of perception . . . They were being intellectually inconsistent, self-contradictory. How can such nonsense be explained?[1]

Explain the difference between mōros and anoētos in your own words:

_____

_____

_____

[1] James Montgomery Boice, "Galatians," in *The Expositor's Bible Commentary* (Grand Rapids, MI: Zondervan, 1976), 453. Copyright © 1976 by James Montgomery Boice. Used by permission of Zondervan. www.zondervan.com

Glance back at the dynamics you listed from a situation where you felt someone was bewitched. Can you see a connection between your description and Boice's distinction of terms? Put more clearly, did your thoughts circle somewhere in this neighborhood? "This is no moron! What on earth is happening here?"

We may not use the word *bewitched* or talk in terms of casting spells but most of us have had thoughts like these: "They're smarter than this. This makes no sense. It's utterly inconsistent. They've somehow been seduced." *Hoodwinked*. The sense is that something sinister is in play. In Eugene Peterson's words recorded in The Message, "Did someone put a hex on you? Have you taken leave of your senses? Something crazy has happened . . . "

In its most literal sense, *baskaino* (translated "bewitched") means "to give someone the evil eye, to cast a spell over, to fascinate in the original sense of holding someone spellbound by an irresistible power."[2] We tend to imagine an evil eye as a look of obvious malice but evil intent can be masked as desire or even concern.

One of the first painful lessons we learn about spiritual warfare from personal experience is that evil doesn't always *look* evil. It can be seductively accommodating and thoughtful.

Read Hebrews 5:13–14. How do these two verses imply that distinguishing between good and evil isn't always easy?

_____

_____

_____

_____

_____

_____

Evil doesn't always *look* evil.

Paul writes to the Galatians, "Who has cast a spell on you, before whose eyes Jesus Christ was publicly portrayed as crucified?" Paul preached the gospel to them so clearly that he claimed it could hardly have been plainer had Jesus been crucified right in front of them. Remember, in Paul's writings, "Christ crucified" is shorthand for the gospel in its entirety.

[2] Timothy George, *Galatians* (Nashville: B&H, 1994), 207.

We come to a crucial introduction in Galatians as we move to verse 2. Fill in this blank:

"I only want to learn this from you: Did you receive the _____ by the works of the law or by believing what you heard?"

Though tarrying 47 verses before appearing in the letter by name, the Spirit's role in Paul's message to the Galatians could not be more significant. Start paying very close attention to every word about the Spirit in the remainder of the letter. If the only information we had about the Holy Spirit were in Galatians, we'd have enough to know who He is, how we received Him and what kind of fruit He bears in the life of the Jesus follower.

You'll notice in Galatians 3:2 that Paul never questions whether the Galatians have received the Holy Spirit. They undoubtedly had. This insight sweeps away doubt as to whether or not we can be in Christ and still develop a disturbingly distorted version of the gospel. Paul doesn't ask the Galatians *if* they had received the Spirit but *how*.

Fill in the blanks with the two options he offered.

Option one: Did you receive the Spirit by . . . ?

_____

Option two: Did you receive the Spirit by . . . ?

_____

Galatians 3:3 poses a crucial question. I don't recall when I first took the verse to heart, but it has been part of my self-examination for many years. By now you could almost certainly recite the immediate context by heart because Paul has repeated it unapologetically since the letter opened: Having come to God by grace through faith in Jesus, how could they shift their reliance now to human efforts?

Perhaps you and I can keep the truth straight in the overarching matter of justification yet we could still rely on our flesh in our living and serving.

Have you, like I, felt called by God to a project, position, process or relationship and launched enthusiastically in the Spirit, through the power of the Spirit and utterly reliant on the Spirit, but, somewhere along the way, started relying on your own flesh?

If so, share the occasion that comes most prominently to mind.

_____

_____

_____

_____

_____

Why do you think we have such a tendency to start with the Spirit but try to sustain it or finish it with the flesh?

_____

_____

_____

_____

_____

Whether consciously or not, sometimes our approach goes something like this: "God, you get me started and I'll take it from there." The issue however, is that what God starts only He can sustain and finish. At first blush, we might argue that we've kept many things going and finished multiple works in the flesh, but, when Jesus said in John 15:5 "without Me you can do nothing," He didn't mean we'd be humanly inept. He meant we'd be unable to do what only He could do.

We can perform great feats in the flesh. People do it all the time. But we who are in Christ are called to works of the Spirit that produce fruit of the Spirit which results in accomplishments by the Spirit that outlast an adrenaline rush and endure for eternity.

Paul captures the consistency between coming to faith and walking in faith most succinctly in Colossians 2:6. What does the verse say?

_____

_____

_____

> What God starts only He can sustain and finish.

The questions in today's text are perfectly ordered. Remember, the Galatians Paul addresses are in Christ. They were not born into faith yesterday. Paul asks this question next:

Did you experience so much for nothing—if in fact it was for nothing?

If you check parallel versions, you will note quite a difference between several formal translations of Galatians 3:4. The ESV, for example, reads, "Did you suffer so many things in vain—if indeed it was in vain?"

The explanation is that the word *paschō*, translated experience in the CSB and *suffer* in the ESV, can mean either one, depending upon the context. Scholars are divided on what the context calls for in this case. Though the letter doesn't specify the suffering of the Galatians, imagining them persecuted for their faith is certainly no reach for this historical timeframe.

Though I learned the verse in the ESV, I've come to lean toward the CSB translation. "Did you experience so much for nothing . . . ?" Note its potential connection to Paul's next question in Galatians 3:5. (Fill in blanks.)

"So then, does God _____ you _____ and

work _____ by your doing the

works of the law? Or is it by believing what you heard?"

Do you find anything about the verse particularly noteworthy? If so, what and why?

_____

_____

_____

Virtually every translation of Galatians 3:5 expresses the present tense of the participles translated *give* and *work* in the CSB. F. F. Bruce offers this commentary:

> The present participles ἐπιχορηγῶν and ἐνεργῶν probably imply that this divine activity still continues: Paul is not simply referring to something which the Galatians had witnessed once for all when first they believed the gospel . . . Paul would not have appealed to mighty works accomplished by the power of the Spirit and experience by the Galatians if in fact they had experienced nothing of the kind . . . Paul knows well

enough that miracles in themselves prove nothing . . . But here he makes an *ad hominem* appeal to the Galatians' experience: their acceptance of the gospel as Paul preached it was in fact followed by miraculous signs, whereas presumably nothing of that sort accompanied the activity of the agitators.[3]

Look up both of these references in Paul's letters to the Corinthians and record any additional insight.

1 Corinthians 2:4–5

_____

_____

_____

2 Corinthians 12:12

_____

_____

_____

> Because our gospel did not come to you in word only, but also in power, in the Holy Spirit, and with full assurance.
>
> 1 Thessalonians 1:5a

According to Galatians 3:5, the miracles God worked among the Galatians were not limited to those He performed through apostles. We can't be certain what kinds of miracles Paul had in mind, but F. F. Bruce suggests some of the spiritual gifts were surely among them.

> . . . it no doubt includes several of the manifestations separately listed in 1 Cor. 12. Even in this wider sense, probably not all the Galatian Christians had been empowered to perform mighty works, but their performance was a feature of their life together, and marked out their churches as communities of the Spirit.[4]

We live in a culture of extremes. Some who profess faith in Christ have left the Scriptures behind to seek the miraculous. Others have left the miraculous behind to seek the Scriptures. The Scriptures cannot replace demonstrations of the Spirit nor can demonstrations of the Spirit replace the Scriptures. The church needs both, just as the Spirit conveys on the sacred pages. Indeed the very gospel we are presently studying is meant to be delivered not only in

[3] F. F. Bruce, *The Epistle to the Galatians,* The New International Greek Testament Commentary (Grand Rapids, MI: Eerdmans, 1982), 151.

[4] Bruce, *The Epistle to the Galatians,* 151.

word, "but also in power, in the Holy Spirit, and with full assurance" (1 Thess 1:5). We who are in Christ are never bereft of the indwelling Spirit but I believe God still often supplies a seeking, needing and believing saint with an abundance of the Spirit. I also believe He still works miracles. To be sure, He does not work all the wonders we seek or even practice the faith to receive and our hearts are bewildered and sometimes grieved. I think, on the other side of this life, however, we will see with eyes immortal He worked more wonders than we knew. Sometimes making it without the miracle is the real miracle.

Our text today concludes in Galatians 3:6 with Paul placarding Scriptures' prime example of a human being, no less flawed than we are, "who

_____, and it was credited _____

for _____".

Prepare to meet this Old Testament figure anew through the fascinating lens of Paul's letter to Galatia.

NOTES

_____

_____

_____

_____

_____

_____

_____

_____

_____

_____

_____

_____

_____

_____

_____

Sometimes making it without the miracle is the real miracle.

THE PROMISE ZONE

day two

Blessed with Abraham

Read, write and mark Galatians 3:7–14.

_____

_____

_____

_____

_____

_____

_____

_____

_____

_____

_____

_____

_____

_____

_____

_____

Paul's agitators were as real as the people you find hard to get along with at your church.

Paul transitions from persuading the Galatians to resist the agitators on the basis of their extraordinary experience of the Holy Spirit to—now, in this new set of verses—persuading them toward the same goal through elaborate exegesis of key Scriptures. He draws primarily from Genesis and Deuteronomy, but you'll find references to Leviticus and Habakkuk as well.

Paul's opponents, the agitators, were grounding their pro-circumcision-for-Gentile-believers argument in something, but what? It's impossible for us to know for certain. However, the attention Paul gives Abraham in chapters 3-4 seems to indicate that the crux had something to do with the patriarch, and, more specifically, the narrative told in Genesis 17.[1]

Please flip to Genesis, in the very front of your Bible, and read 17:1–14.

What, according to Genesis 17:10–11 is the sign of the covenant between God and Abraham (and Abraham's offspring)?

_____

_____

_____

_____

Imagine an argument that the agitators could have been making against Paul and his uncircumcised Gentile congregants. Use the Genesis 17 narrative as your basis. In other words, make your very best argument against Paul.

_____

_____

_____

_____

This exercise wasn't an attempt to play the devil's advocate but, rather, an invitation to stop and reflect on the reality that Paul had actual flesh and blood opponents with fierce convictions, alternate readings of authoritative Scripture, and serious influence over the Galatians. Paul's agitators were as real as the people you find hard to get along with at your church.

[1] Gordon Fee, _Galatians_, Pentecostal Commentary Series (Dorset: Deo Publishing, 2007), 115.

It's also important, from time to time, to remind ourselves that Paul and his first readers had knowledge of details that we, the readers of Galatians almost two millennia later, do not. But, whatever the exact details of the agitators' argument were, we can be pretty confident that they were "using the story of Abraham to contend that unless the Galatians were circumcised they were not true heirs of Abraham."[2] Paul counterargues that Abraham's sons are those who relate to God by faith and not circumcision.

Since you looked carefully at Genesis 17, you probably agree that this was not a simple argument to make, to say the least. As Nijay Gupta puts it, "Paul's appeal to Abraham as a model of faith (without Torah works) would have been ironic. Jewish interpreters in Paul's time came to see Abraham as a kind of prototype of Torah obedience, even though Torah did not come into the picture until Moses (see Jubilees 24.11; 2 Baruch 57.2)."[3]

Paul may well have been the first Jew to separate Abraham's faith and circumcision in this manner; this was just not a popular idea at the time.[4] Paul employs his own choice of various Scripture passages as "an attempt to outflank" the agitators "by showing that Scripture actually supports the inclusion of Gentiles by faith alone, apart from doing any aspect of the Law."[5]

Let's look at how Paul makes his case.

First, turn to Genesis 15 and read v.1–6. Describe the context in just a sentence or two:

_____

_____

_____

_____

What do you think it means, in context, that the LORD "credited" righteousness to Abraham?

_____

_____

_____

> Abram believed the LORD, and he credited it to him as righteousness.
>
> Genesis 15.6

[2] L. Ann Jervis, *Galatians*, Understanding the Bible Commentary Series (Grand Rapids, MI: Baker Books, 1999), 85.

[3] Nijay Gupta, *Paul and the Language of Faith* (Grand Rapids, MI: Eerdmans, 2020), Kindle edition.

[4] Jervis, *Galatians*, 84.

[5] Fee, *Galatians*, 99.

I like how succinctly scholar Douglas Moo explains it: "God graciously viewed Abraham's faith as having in itself fulfilled all that God expected of Abraham in order for him to be in the right before God . . . Just as, then, it was Abraham's faith that led to his being considered 'in the right before God,' so it was the faith of the Galatians that led them to be 'declared right.'"[6]

Let's focus now on verses 8–9 of Galatians 3. Give them a quick read. What is the content of the gospel proclaimed ahead of time to Abraham, according to v.8?

☐ Jesus Christ is Lord.
☐ God in three persons, blessed Trinity.
☐ All the nations would be blessed through Abraham.
☐ The Law will be given to Moses at an opportune time.

The content of the gospel preached way back in the patriarchs' day, according to Paul, is found primarily in Genesis 12:3 (which alludes to Gen 18:18 and Gen 22:18, etc. in the specific phrase "all nations"). Genesis 12:3 falls in the well-known account of God's call to Abram, one of the most important passages in the Old Testament:

> *The Lord said to Abram: Go from your land, your relatives, and your father's house to the land that I will show you. I will make you into a great nation, I will bless you, I will make your name great, and you will be a blessing. I will bless those who bless you, I will curse anyone who treats you with contempt, and all the peoples on earth will be blessed through you.*
> **Genesis 12:1–3**

The gospel that these early Scriptures proclaimed to Abraham was one that proclaimed that the Gentiles would be justified before God by faith, just like he was. Although the name of Jesus is not mentioned here, as Moo says, "God's promises to Abraham . . . are important announcements of the good news that is bound up with Christ."[7]

Curiously, Paul never mentions in Galatians that Abraham and all the sons in his household were ultimately circumcised as a sign of the covenant God made with him (see the end of Genesis 17). For Paul, it doesn't matter. The gospel had already been preached—and the promises concerning the Gentiles had already been made—to Abraham before the covenant of circumcision was established. And before Abraham himself was circumcised, it was his faith that God had reckoned as righteousness (Gen 15:6).

---

[6] Douglas J. Moo, *Galatians*, Baker Exegetical Commentary on the New Testament (Grand Rapids, MI: Baker Academic, 2013), 188.
[7] Moo, *Galatians*, 199.

As Gordon Fee puts it, "For Paul it was in the happy providence of God that in Genesis 15, before the covenant of circumcision, God had already both declared Abraham to be righteous by faith and included Gentiles in the promise made to Abraham. Thus both the language of Scripture and the timing of events are crucial for Paul's argument."[8]

Now, glance back at Galatians 3. Were you struck by the subject—"the Scripture" —Paul presents as the proclaimer of the gospel preached to Abraham in verse 8? I sure was. J. Louis Martyn describes Paul's use of "the Scripture" here beautifully:

> For the first time in the letter Paul uses this term, doing so in an arresting manner, indicating that scripture is not a passive text to be quoted and interpreted by human beings as they will. On the contrary, it is alive, having, as it were, eyes and intelligence and a mouth . . . And gifted with such foresight, it did nothing less than preach the gospel itself ahead of time to the patriarch, telling him that in him, the man of faith, all the Gentiles would one day be blessed.[9]

In verses 10–12, Paul says that those who set out to keep the law are under the "curse" of having to do the entire law. Picking and choosing just one or two or three among 600+ laws was not the way it worked. Deuteronomy 27:26 (in the Greek version of the OT), the quotation Paul cites in verse 10, pronounces a curse on anyone who doesn't fulfill the whole law.

A similar idea is expressed a chapter later in Deuteronomy 28:58–59, only it is even more explicit. Write out those two verses here:

_____

_____

_____

_____

_____

_____

These verses in Deuteronomy were written in order to exhort the people of Israel to keep the entire law and thereby be blessed. Paul does the exact opposite here, so unwavering is he on his God-given mission to reach the Gentiles.

[8] Fee, *Galatians*, 102.
[9] J. Louis Martyn, *Galatians*, The Anchor Yale Bible Commentaries (New Haven, CT: Yale University Press, 1997), 300.

Paul is not, in our passage, saying that people don't have the ability to keep the whole law. The law itself offered provision for transgression, making it possible for adherents to keep the whole law. In fact, in Philippians 3:6, Paul writes that he himself was: *regarding the righteousness that is in the law, blameless.* So, Paul's problem is not with the idea that the law can be kept. His problem is with the idea that the law has the power to justify. Scripture itself indicated that no one is *justified* by the law, because as Habakkuk 2:4b says: *the righteous one will live by his faith.*

Read Galatians 3:13–14 carefully. How did Christ redeem us from the curse of the law?

_____

_____

_____

Please look up Deuteronomy 21:22–23 (CSB) and fill in the proper blanks:

"If anyone is found guilty of an offense deserving the _____

penalty and is _____, and you hang his body on a tree,

you are not to leave his _____ on the tree overnight but

are to _____ him that day, for anyone hung on a _____

is under God's curse. You must not defile the land the LORD your

God is giving you as an inheritance."

This is absolutely stunning to see come together, isn't it? Jesus Christ is hung on a tree under an explicit curse from God's law given to Moses; His holy body a defilement to the land God gave Abraham as an inheritance. The death of Jesus changed everything. Marilyn McCord Adams states this theological idea brilliantly: "If God in Christ crucified becomes curse, the power of curse is cancelled: curse cannot exile us from God any more."[10]

For through the law I died to the law, so that I might live for God. I have been crucified with Christ, and I no longer live, but Christ lives in me. The life I now live in the body, I live by faith in the Son of God, who loved me and gave himself for me. I do not set aside the grace of God, for if righteousness comes through the law, then Christ died for nothing.

Galatians 2:19–21

[10] Marilyn McCord Adams, *Horrendous Evils and the Goodness of God* (Ithaca, NY: Cornell University Press, 1999), 99.

The purpose of Christ's Torah-cursed death was to usher the blessing of Abraham to the Gentiles, so that Jew and Gentile alike would receive the Holy Spirit. The blessing promised to Abraham is associated with and fulfilled by the gift of the Holy Spirit. In some ways, our final verse brings us right back to where we started in day one yesterday, at the beginning of chapter 3. Why would anyone who experienced the miraculous power of life in the Holy Spirit now want to go back in time and take on the entire Law? For Paul, this is an unthinkable move—backsliding in the purest sense of the word.

At times, I find myself pretty sympathetic to what I imagine the agitators' arguments to have been in Galatia. The Torah, after all, takes up a huge chunk of our Bibles and was given to Israel by God. I see why many Jewish Christians wanted to honor it in a meaningful way, even after trusting in Jesus. But what I'm starting to get my head around—even be compelled by—is that Paul was, in some revolutionary ways, already living in a new world. The old categories, even if they were good and beautiful, no longer set the terms for him like they still did for some. God's action in Christ and the blessing of the Spirit did not just lead to a reordering of the former things but had ushered in a new world even within this old one.

Do you see it with me?

But the righteous one will live by his faith.

Habakkuk 2:4b

NOTES

THE PROMISE ZONE

day three

A Human Illustration

Read, write and mark Galatians 3:15–20.

_____

_____

_____

_____

_____

_____

_____

_____

_____

_____

_____

_____

_____

_____

_____

_____

_____

I told Melissa that trying to condense these six verses into one lesson is like trying to catch a whale with a hairnet; however, spending a lifetime diving into Scripture and never finding the ocean floor is precisely what I love about Bible study. The concepts mentioned in today's text are immense, and the technicalities are challenging to navigate, but the overall point is clear.

What is Paul's point?

_____

_____

Paul's introduction to our segment today carries more meaning than we might assume. The CSB translates Galatians 3:15, "Brothers and sisters, I'm using a human illustration." The ESV reads, "To give a human example, brothers . . . "

Spending a lifetime diving into Scripture and never finding the ocean floor is precisely what I love about Bible study.

Paul is doing more than simply introducing an illustration. He is recognizing the limitations of drawing an analogy between human testamentary practices and divine transactions that cannot be fully interpreted in human terms. Unlike the divine reality, a human analogy eventually breaks down but, taken for what it is, an analogy can be a means of learning the unknown through the known.

In order to catch the nuance in a key Greek term, compare these two translations of Galatians 3:15b.

"No one sets aside or makes additions to a validated human will." (CSB)

" . . . even with a man-made covenant, no one annuls it or adds to it once it has been ratified." (ESV)

What differences do you see in the wordings used by the two translations?

_____

_____

The Greek term translated "will" in the CSB and "covenant" in the ESV is "*diathēkē*" (διαθήκη). As you've no doubt already assumed, the Greek word can mean either one. It can be used for a binding agreement between two parties or for a last will and testament that distributes the testator's property to a designated heir following the testator's death. Paul wants the Galatians to grasp the binding nature of God's covenant with Abraham but he combines the concept with a legality most would find more familiar: a last will and testament. To track with Paul's analogy in today's text, we'll need to keep both in view.

Covenant is a central concept in Scripture. It is also a lens through which Scripture comes into focus with a refreshingly recognizable order. Some books ought to be on every believer's shelf and, in my estimation, one of them is Sandra L. Richter's *The Epic of Eden: A Christian Entry into the Old Testament.* In it she writes,

> I stand on the shoulders of many scholars before me when I make the claim that covenant is a major structuring principle of our Scriptures. This is most obvious in the fact that the two divisions of our book are known as the Old and New Covenants. (Although English speakers know their Bibles as the Old and New "Testaments," the actual term behind our English convention is the Greek word *diathēkē*, which is a translation of Hebrew *bᵉrît*, both of which mean "covenant.")[1]

A covenant is an agreement bound by oath between two parties through which promises are made to act according to stipulations. A covenant might take the form of an Ancient Near Eastern suzerainty treaty where a greater party (the suzerain) protects, blesses or provides for a lesser party (the vassal) that, by agreement, stays loyal, serves and obeys. A treaty between nations could be a form of covenant. At times in Scripture the promise-keeping is dependent on specified conditions but covenants could also be made unconditionally.

The Old Testament is organized around 5 central figures with whom God engaged covenantally: Adam, Noah, Abraham, Moses and David.

Adam—(Genesis 1–2) You'll find the Adamic or Edenic Covenant missing from many charts but elements of the suzerain/vassal relationship are very much in play. Add to those the land grant and it earns a solid place on a list. The blessings of the divine suzerain were almost innumerable but He issued only one stipulation: "but you must not eat from the tree of the knowledge of good and evil" (Gen 2:17). They broke the solitary condition of the covenant and were cast from the Garden.

Noah—The Noahic Covenant is announced in Genesis 6:18 but established after the waters subside in Genesis 8:20–9:17.

Read Genesis 6:17–18 and record the nature of the covenant.

_____

_____

_____

[1] Sandra L. Richter, *The Epic of Eden: A Christian Entry into the Old Testament* (Downers Grove, IL: IVP Academic, 2008), 69–70.

Abraham—(Gen 12:1–3; 15:1–21; 17:1–14; 22:15–18) The Abrahamic Covenant carries enormous weight in Paul's letter to the Galatians and certainly in our current passage.

Record the blessing that God promised Abraham as Galatians 3:8 restates it.

_____

_____

We've talked about Abraham's belief credited as righteousness but our present task is to view the relationship between God and Abraham (first called Abram) specifically through the lens of covenant. The ratification ceremony God enacts in Genesis 15 is stunningly visual. The words sketch a scene alive with sounds, scents, flames, darkness, life, death, terror, reassurance and promise.

Read Genesis 15. Use this space to write single key words in order that would help you recount much of the scene if given a glance.

_____

_____

_____

> ### God has no reluctance to reward His people.

The NKJV wording in Genesis 15:1 is sublime.

After these things the word of the Lord came to Abram in a vision, saying, "Do not be afraid, Abram. I _am_ your shield, your exceedingly great reward."

The NIV reads, "Do not be afraid, Abram. I am your shield, your very great reward."

How does the following translation differ from those? "I am your shield; your reward will be very great" (CSB).

_____

_____

God has no reluctance to reward His people. In fact, Hebrews 11:6 says, "Now without faith it is impossible to please God, since the one who draws near to Him must believe that He exists and that _He rewards those who seek Him_" (emphasis mine). How astonishing to think that God is displeased by our unwillingness to believe He is a rewarder of those who seek Him. But what God knows and we discover is that no reward He could ever offer can match the gift of Himself. He is our exceedingly great reward.

What preparations did God assign Abraham in Genesis 15:9–10?

_____

_____

_____

Abraham's level of participation in the actual ceremony is meant to be striking. While God makes His declaration then passes between the severed animals in a theophany of smoke and fire, what is Abraham doing?

_____

In the Ancient Near East, participants walked between parts of slaughtered animals, soles of their feet and hems of their garments soaked in blood, as a way of invoking death upon themselves should they break the terms of the covenant. In this scene, God incapacitates Abraham with a deep sleep then moves between the pieces by Himself. The significance of the covenant being unilateral, God obligating Himself alone, cannot be overemphasized. Terence E. Fretheim writes, "God's personal involvement constitutes the unusual character of the rite. In an act of self-imprecation, God in effect puts the divine life on the line, 'writing' the promise in blood!"[2]

Look back at Galatians 3:16. How does Paul identify Christ in this passage?

_____

The word "offspring" (ESV) or "seed" (CSB) is translated from the Greek noun sperma (σπέρμα). The term is singular but could also be used as a collective noun. Richard N. Longenecker explains, "'Seed' in the Abrahamic promise is a generic singular that was always understood within Judaism to refer to the posterity of Abraham as an entity, excluding only the descendants of Abraham through Ishmael ('for in Isaac shall thy seed be called') and those born of Esau."[3]

Paul's claim in Galatians 3:16? The singular was ultimately and always meant to point to Jesus Christ Himself! What is the equivalent to the land grant in our inheritance according to Hebrews 11:14–16?

_____

_____

> He is our exceedingly great reward.

[2] Terence E. Fretheim, "Genesis," in *The New Interpreter's Bible* Vol. I (Nashville: Abingdon Press, 2015), 446. Copyright © 1994 Abingdon Press. Used by permission. All rights reserved.
[3] Richard N. Longenecker, *Galatians,* Word Biblical Commentary Vol. 41 (Dallas: Thomas Nelson, 1990), 121. Copyright © 1990 by Richard N. Longenecker. Used by permission of Thomas Nelson. www.thomasnelson.com

Marvel over the wonder of what God considers to be His inheritance. The Old and New Testaments are beautifully consistent. What is the LORD's inheritance according to Deuteronomy 32:9?

_____

_____

What about Ephesians 1:18?

_____

_____

> **We may not feel like much of a prize but, God considers us a glorious inheritance.**

We may not feel like much of a prize but, because of Jesus Christ, and together with the saints, God considers us a glorious inheritance of inestimable wealth.

Moses—(Exodus 19–23)

The Mosaic Covenant is best summed in Exodus 19:5–8. Record the essence of it.

_____

_____

_____

_____

_____

_____

_____

_____

_____

_____

Now read Exodus 12:40–42. What is the context?

_____

_____

_____

What is the tie between Exodus 12:40–41 and Galatians 3:15–20?

_____

_____

_____

_____

The reference to 430 years does not present a troublesome discrepancy with Genesis 15:13. "Know this for certain: your offspring will be resident aliens for 400 years in a land that does not belong to them and will be enslaved and oppressed." The thirty years leave room for the sojourning of the patriarchs in Canaan and the transition of their descendants to Egypt.

Having established the order of the inheritance promised to Abraham and the law as delivered to Moses, what is Paul's point in Galatians 3:17?

_____

_____

_____

Now review Galatians 3:19–20 and fill in the following blanks.

According to Paul, the law "was added for the _____ of

_____ until the _____ to _____

the _____ _____ would come."

We know the Seed to whom the promise was made is Christ, but what on earth does Paul mean by saying the law was "added for the sake of transgressions"? Timothy George cross-references the verse with one in Romans, offering a great illustration.

> This meaning is further clarified when we look at the parallel verse in Rom 5:20: "The law was added so that the trespass might increase." In Romans the word for "added" (*pareisēlthen*) means literally "came in by a side road." The main road is the covenant of promise—inviolate, irrevocable. The law has the character of something additional, a side road intended to carry extra traffic and excess baggage and, if we may anticipate Paul's argument, designed not to lead to a separate destination but to point its travelers back to the main road.[4]

[4] Timothy George, *Galatians*, The New American Commentary Vol. 30 (Nashville: B&H, 1994), 253.

What is meant by the law being put into effect through angels is unclear but, fascinatingly, Stephen says something similar just before he is martyred.

What was his wording in Acts 7:53?

_____

_____

Remember, Paul witnessed Stephen's speech and his stoning. The garments of those hurling the rocks were piled at his feet. One or both may have had Deuteronomy 33:2 in mind in reference to the presence of angels when God gave Moses the Law.

> *The Lord came from Sinai*
> *and revealed himself to Israel from Seir.*
> *He appeared in splendor from Mount Paran,*
> *and came forth with ten thousand holy ones.*
> *With his right hand he gave a fiery law to them.*
> **Deuteronomy 33:2 NET**

In our next lesson we'll see Paul expound on the relationship between the law and the promise in equally intriguing terms. The segment to come has particular meaning to us because you will find the title of our series tucked within it. But, before we get there, let's quickly look at our fifth and final figure:

David—(2 Samuel 6) The declaration of the Davidic Covenant comes from the Lord through the prophet Nathan to the man after God's own heart: "The LORD declares to you: The LORD himself will make a house for you . . . Your house and kingdom will endure before me forever, and your throne will be established forever" (2 Samuel 7:11, 16). Both the Abrahamic Covenant and the Davidic Covenant were promises God bound Himself to forever. Where land was given to Abraham, office was given to David.

You have worked hard today. I hope you've discovered some riches. With these two names freshly on your mind I'll ask you for one last action.

Write Matthew 1:1 in this space to conclude.

_____

_____

_____

_____

114 NOW THAT FAITH HAS COME

THE PROMISE ZONE

day four

Faith Has Come

Read, write and mark Galatians 3:21–26.

_____

_____

_____

_____

_____

_____

_____

_____

_____

_____

_____

_____

_____

_____

_____

_____

_____

_____

Our passage begins with an important question—one that Paul knows weighs heavy on the minds of his readers: *Is the law therefore contrary to God's promises?* His answer is an emphatic negative: μὴ γένοιτο. Or, *absolutely not!*

While hardly the most pressing topic at your next dinner party, understanding the relationship between the law of Moses and earliest Christianity is a valuable pursuit, even if tedious and perplexing at times. Frank Thielman describes its importance in a helpful manner:

> What role should the Mosaic Law play in Christian theology and practice? This is one of Christian theology's oldest and most persistent questions. Already in the mid-first century, it vexed the mother church in Jerusalem, its daughter church in Antioch, and Paul's mission to the Gentiles. In the second century, permutations of orthodox Christianity arose that alternately claimed that all believers should live by the Mosaic law and that the Mosaic law was the product of a pettifogging deity of secondary importance.[1]

> ### Is the law therefore contrary to God's promises? Absolutely not!
>
> Galatians 3:21a

I promise, if you hang in there with these verses today and over the next few weeks, you'll gain an enriched understanding of the New Testament. Thielman writes, "Paul has been at the center of the church's debate over the Mosaic Law. The reasons for this are clear. Over 60 percent of the New Testament's nearly two hundred references to the term 'law' *(nomos)* belong to the Pauline letters."[2]

In order to grasp the heart of Paul's theology, we must understand his new relationship to the law that he'd spent much of his former life zealously keeping. Getting to know Galatians through and through won't take us the whole way in this endeavor (Romans, for example, is crucial, as well as the Corinthian letters), but it's a solid start.

In case this is all new to you or, like me, you often need a refresher, "the law" refers to the approximately 613 commands God gave to Israel, primarily through Moses. They are scattered throughout various narratives in the first five books of the Old Testament, most heavily from Exodus 20 to the end of Deuteronomy. "The law" is also referred to—interchangeably—as "the Torah" or "the Mosaic Law" or "the law of Moses."

[1] Frank Thielman, *The Law and the New Testament: The Question of Continuity* (New York: The Crossroad Publishing Company, 1999), 1. Copyright © 1999 by Frank Thielman. Reprinted with the permission of The Permissions Company, LLC on behalf of the Crossroad Publishing Company, Inc. crossroadpublishing.com

[2] Thielman, *The Law and the New Testament: The Question of Continuity,* 7. Copyright © 1999 by Frank Thielman. Reprinted with the permission of The Permissions Company, LLC on behalf of the Crossroad Publishing Company, Inc. crossroadpublishing.com

Sometimes people even refer to the entire five-book collection of Genesis through Deuteronomy as "the Torah." But, of course, those books are much more than long lists of laws. The laws are embedded within the larger telling of Israel's story with her God, the God who delivered her out of slavery in Egypt with a mighty hand and an outstretched arm. The law showed a delivered and chosen people (Israel) how to live "a distinctive way of life" that honored God and would lead to blessing and flourishing.[3] The Psalmist wrote a beautiful poem about it that you've likely read before but, I find, warrants regular rereading:

The law of the LORD is perfect,
reviving the soul;
the testimony of the LORD is sure,
making wise the simple;
the precepts of the LORD are right,
rejoicing the heart;
the commandment of the LORD is pure,
enlightening the eyes;
the fear of the LORD is clean,
enduring forever;
the rules of the LORD are true,
and righteous altogether.
More to be desired are they than gold,
even much fine gold;
sweeter also than honey
and drippings of the honeycomb.
Moreover, by them is your servant warned;
in keeping them there is great reward.

Psalm 19:7–11 ESV

Most of us have only ever been taught a very negative view of Israel's law(s), despite the presence of passages like this one right in our Bibles. In Deuteronomy 4:6–8, Moses conceives of Israel's law as something that would demonstrate to the world wisdom, understanding, and the nearness of God.

Even though Paul's own relationship to law observance changed after he experienced Christ and His call, the law still functioned for Paul as authoritative Scripture. We saw this in action on day two this week when

[3] Carmen Joy Imes, *Bearing God's Name: Why Sinai Still Matters* (Downers Grove, IL: IVP Academic, 2019), 35, Kindle edition.

Paul rooted his argument against the agitators in an elaborate discussion of select verses from the law itself. Paul wrote to the Roman church: "whatever was written in the past was written for our instruction, so that we may have hope through endurance and through the encouragement from the Scriptures" (Rom 15:4 CSB). The same is true for us. Even though we don't keep the law, its words still function as Scripture for us. The tension here is real.

Take a moment to reflect on the tension I have just described between not observing the law, on one hand, but still regarding its words as authoritative Scripture, on the other. Do you have any thoughts you'd like to add or relevant experiences you would like to share? If so, record them below:

_____

_____

_____

_____

_____

_____

_____

_____

_____

_____

_____

> For if the law had been granted with the ability to give life, then righteousness would certainly be on the basis of the law.
>
> Galatians 3:21b

In the second part of Galatians 3:21, Paul says that righteousness would be on the basis of the law if the law had been granted the ability to give what? Write the answer below:

_____

_____

_____

_____

_____

The law, however, had not been granted the ability to give life, according to Paul. Rather, Scripture, again a primary actor in this drama, *imprisoned everything under sin's power* (v.22a). Why did Scripture imprison everything under sin? So *that the promise might be given on the basis of faith in Jesus Christ to those who believe* (v.22b).

Curiously, according to some verses in the law itself, observance of the law's commands would lead precisely to life.

Please look up both of these verses and fill in the blanks:

Leviticus 18:5

"Keep my _____ and _____:

a person will live if he _____ them. I am the LORD."

Deuteronomy 30:11, 14

"This command that I give you today is certainly not too _____

or beyond your _____ . . . But the message is very _____ you,

in your mouth and in your heart, so that you may _____ it."

So, if the law was intended by God to give life to the covenant people, why had it not ultimately been given the ability to do so? The law was meant for good and God's people had the ability to keep it. The law was not given by a sinister god playing a trick on his beloved people. The problem was not God's law but the terrible power of sin and the way sin used the law.

The story of Scripture speaks of Israel's tendency to rebel against the law God gave them, from their fashioning a golden calf in Exodus to resisting the words of the prophets. Scripture bore witness to sin's capacity to take advantage of the greatest gift God gave the people of Israel. And it was, decidedly, a gift. The prophet Ezekiel foresaw the need for the Spirit of God to be within the people of God for them to be able to follow the commandments (36:26–27).

Gentiles before the incarnation of Christ, for their part, did not have the law, and were left aimless without this specific revelation. Thus, Scripture itself imprisoned **everything** under sin. But God was working providentially to bring about the promise, for all. The mystery being revealed in Paul's day was that the promise given to Abraham's ancestors was fulfilled on the basis of faith in Jesus Christ and the gift of the Holy Spirit, for both Jew and Gentile. The law, in the end, could not bring life. Only the Spirit could do that, for Jew and Gentile alike.

> The law, in the end, could not bring life. Only the Spirit could do that, for Jew and Gentile alike.

Think a little about Paul's life, before and after placing his trust in Jesus. How do you think Paul's experience shaped his understanding of the law's inability to bring life?

_____

_____

_____

> But now that faith has come, we are no longer under a guardian.
>
> Galatians 3:25 ESV

The law and the promise are not in contradiction, but they also don't have the same kind of power. James Dunn puts it this way, saying that, according to Paul: "the law through Moses is not such a full expression of God's grace as the promise to Abraham."[4]

In verses 23-24, Paul describes the relationship and function of the law before faith came. His terms paint a pretty bleak portrait. First, the law confined (or imprisoned, depending on the translation) God's people before faith was revealed (v.23). Second, the law acted as a παιδαγωγός (paidagogos). In the ancient world, a παιδαγωγός was someone who had "responsibility for someone who needed guidance"; this person was often a male slave.[5] Dunn says of the παιδαγωγός, "The slave-custodian given charge of the young, to instruct in good manners, and discipline when necessary, was frequently remembered with mixed feelings—as still the case when adults today look back to tutors and teachers of their youth."[6]

The law's role, described by Paul in these fairly negative terms, was limited to a certain time frame referenced several times in chapter 3. The time period was 430 years after Abraham until the moment everything changed: the death and resurrection of Jesus Christ. Bruce W. Longenecker observes just how many temporal indicators are used in Galatians 3-4: "'added . . . until' (3:19); 'before faith came' (3:23); 'until faith should be revealed' (3:23); 'until Christ came' (3:24); 'now that faith has come we are no longer' (3:25); 'as long as' (4:1); 'until' (4:2); 'when' (4:3); 'when the fullness of time came' (4:4)."[7]

The title of our study—Now That Faith Has Come—draws from one of these phrases, as translated by the English Standard Version. "But now that faith has come, we are no longer under a guardian, for in Christ Jesus you are all sons of God, through faith" (verses 25-26). With the cosmos-shifting arrival

---

[4] James D. G. Dunn, The Theology of Paul's Letter to the Galatians (Cambridge: Cambridge University Press, 1993), 90. © 1993 Cambridge University Press. Reproduced with permission of the Licensor through PLSclear.

[5] Walter Bauer, A Greek-English Lexicon of the New Testament and other Early Christian Literature, rev. and ed. Frederick W. Danker, 3rd ed. (Chicago: University of Chicago Press, 2000), 748.

[6] Dunn, The Theology of Paul's Letter to the Galatians (Cambridge: Cambridge University Press, 1993), 90. © 1993 Cambridge University Press. Reproduced with permission of the Licensor through PLSclear.

[7] Bruce W. Longenecker, The Triumph of Abraham's God: The Transformation of Identity in Galatians (Nashville: Abingdon Press, 1998), 118. © 1998 Abingdon Press. Used by permission. All rights reserved.

of faith, those who once lived confined and under the protection of a guardian, are united in Jesus Christ to the Gentiles, who had formerly not even known God. Abraham's descendants, spiritual and physical, have received the promise, God's Spirit.

In her brilliant book *Bearing God's Name: Why Sinai Still Matters*, Carmen Joy Imes touches on so many of the themes from our lesson today:

> At the time of the exodus, the law was considered a gift . . . But it was only ever a means to an end: relationship with Yahweh. In Christ a new pathway to that relationship opened for us, based on his own faithful obedience to the law. To continue to live under the law ourselves, ignoring Jesus' faithfulness, would be a form of slavery not unlike slavery in Egypt . . . He destroyed the dividing wall between Jew and Gentile, making a way for anyone to become part of his family, without circumcision. Laws regarding sacrifice and laws regarding ethnic separation were no longer appropriate. They had become a form of slavery to how things were. The law was never meant to offer salvation. It was merely the means of maintaining what had been given. Redemption was always made possible by God's gracious gift. To reject that gracious gift in Jesus would be a return to Egypt.[8]

Before we conclude, think about your own then and now with God. How did you conceive of "life" before faith came to you?

_____

_____

_____

_____

_____

_____

Describe the kind of "life" that faith in Jesus Christ has given you.

_____

_____

_____

_____

[8] Imes, *Bearing God's Name: Why Sinai Still Matters*, 161.

NOTES

THE PROMISE ZONE

day five

All Are One

Read, write and mark Galatians 3:27–29.

_____

_____

_____

_____

_____

_____

_____

_____

_____

_____

_____

_____

Shore up your courage, students! You have what it takes! Welcome to the longest lesson in our six-week series. All the others have been meticulously constructed within a word count Melissa and I set from the start, but we agreed this one should be an exception. This Scripture segment is essential to the letter and to the community of faith in any era.

The bright side? You're not likely to get bored. My hope is that you'll become too wrapped up in the discussion to mind the length. Let's begin with Galatians 3:27 and what Paul means by baptism. Is he talking about Spirit baptism or water? In Galatians, Paul associates the gift of the Holy Spirit with the beginning of a relationship with Christ (see Gal 3:3, 4:6). Paul, therefore, certainly could mean Spirit baptism in Galatians 3:27 as he does in 1 Corinthians 12:13.

Read the verse and note its strong similarities to today's text. Who receives this Spirit baptism in 1 Corinthians 12:13?

Paul may just as likely refer to the symbolic reenactment of Spirit baptism through water baptism. David deSilva thinks so.

> Paul explicitly reminds the Galatians about what happened to them, in some sense objectively, as they underwent the Christian rite of initiation. The symbolism of baptism by immersion, as it was no doubt most commonly practiced in the early church, is powerful indeed. Paul could liken it to burial, such that one dies with Christ in baptism to one's former life and its connections, and rises to a new life as one emerges from the water (Romans 6:1–14).[1]

I'll sketch a little imagery. Born in the likeness of "the man of dust,"[2] we frail humans step into the water wearing Adam. The water tugs heavy on our garment of sin and death and the weight of our fallenness sinks our shoulders and lowers our chins. We cannot shake this dust off our skin to save our lives. No wind can whisk it away.

But when the Spirit stirs the pool and woos us, no shame can restrain us. We enter the waters of baptism in grave clothes of dust, confessing that we've—all along—been dead men walking. Plunged beneath the waves where mortal lungs can take no breath, we die with Christ and, in that death, we are reborn of the Spirit. The old garment of Adam sinks to the riverbed and we, the newly born, are drenched in grace, swaddled in Christ and emerge from the mud fully clothed, sparkling clean and alive forevermore.

I increasingly suspect that water baptism has lost much of the meaning and wonder it held in the early church. My water baptism was meaningful, but I wish I'd grasped the reenactment.

[1] David A. deSilva, *The Letter to the Galatians*, The New International Commentary on the New Testament (Grand Rapids, MI: Eerdmans, 2018), 337.
[2] See 1 Corinthians 15:47.

If you've been baptized, what was your experience like?

_____

_____

_____

_____

_____

Compare Galatians 3:27–28 to 1 Corinthians 12:13 again. Note how both declare the removal of differentiations in the context of baptism. These declarations may have been part of a baptismal confession in the early church.

Imagine Galatians 3:28 included among the earliest, most foundational truths you learned in Christ and part of a sacred rite initiating you into a new community. What impact might it have?

_____

_____

Numerous scholars suggest the pairings in Galatians 3:28 may have been an intentional reversal of "the three _běrākôt_ ('blessings,' 'benedictions') that appear at the beginning of the Jewish cycle of morning prayers: 'Blessed be He [God] that He did not make me a Gentile; blessed be He that He did not make me a boor [i.e. an ignorant peasant or a slave]; blessed be He that He did not make me a woman.'"[3]

Parallels exist from ancient Greek texts in a similar spirit and so Longenecker concludes, "it may be surmised that in conscious contrast to such Jewish and Greek chauvinistic statements, early Christians saw it as particularly appropriate to give praise in their baptismal confession that through Christ the old racial schisms and cultural divisions had been healed."[4]

[3] _The Authorised Daily Prayer Book of the United Hebrew Congregations of the British Commonwealth of Nations,_ trans. S. Singer, 2nd rev. ed. (London: Eyre & Spottiswoode, 1962), 6–7. These three běrākôt are credited to R. Judah ben Elai (c. 150 A.D.) in t. Ber. 7.18 and j. Ber. 13b, but to R. Meier (his contemporary) in b. Menahi. 43b. Quoted in Richard N. Longenecker, Galatians, Word Biblical Commentary Vol. 41 (Dallas: Thomas Nelson Inc, 1990), 157. Copyright © 1990 by Richard N. Longenecker. Used by permission of Thomas Nelson. www.thomasnelson.com

[4] Richard N. Longenecker, _Galatians_, Word Biblical Commentary Vol. 41 (Dallas: Thomas Nelson Inc, 1990), 157. (Longenecker, page 157: "for example, 'that I was born a human being and not a beast, next, a man and not a woman, thirdly, a Greek and not a barbarian' (attributed to Thales and Socrates in Diogenes Laertius' Vitae Philosophorum 1.33, but to Plato in Plutarch's Marius 46.1 and Lactantius' Divine Institutes 3.19.17)"). Copyright © 1990 by Richard N. Longenecker. Used by permission of Thomas Nelson. www.thomasnelson.com

The common denominator of the three pairs in Galatians 3:28 is uneven distribution of power. They are "pairs of categories that create socioethnic differentiations."[5] Paul's claim inspired by God was revolutionary.

As I pen this lesson, racial tensions in America are at fever pitch. We need God's words desperately. No need to stretch to make the connection to today's text. David deSilva writes,

> To name just the largest of a herd of elephants in the room for American Christianity, Christians of European descent and Christians of African descent often find the history of race relations in America regulating and restricting their relationships to a far greater extent than their mutual experience of being submerged into Christ and adopted into God's one family. Paul's vision challenges us all to work very diligently, and in the Spirit's power, to love one another as sisters and brothers—and address the very real issues that continue to plague race relations in America from that mutual love and commitment—rather than continue to live out the scripts that the broken domination systems of America have written for us over the centuries. "New creation" is indeed waiting to be birthed in this regard.[6]

In your estimation, what are some of the "scripts" we've continued to live out?

_____

_____

_____

_____

_____

_____

With the earth-quaking cross, tectonic plates shifted. In Christ, mountains of superiority are laid low and valleys of inferiority are raised high and the ground levels. The exalted are humbled and the humbled, exalted. Christ alone is supreme and all in Him are of equal esteem. Despite the Bible saying volumes about justice, the question of the day is whether or not it has a place in the gospel. Remember, Paul's letter to the Galatians from first to last is about living "in step with the truth of the gospel" (2:14) or, said another way, being "in step with the Spirit" (5:25).

> ## Christ alone is supreme and all in Him are of equal esteem.

[5] deSilva, *The Letter to the Galatians*, 337.
[6] deSilva, *The Letter to the Galatians*, 341.

Nations are worldly entities with worldly values. Jesus followers, however, are called to an entirely different set of values in which no image-bearer is superior to another. The gospel-preaching, white-skinned church thumbed its nose to justice. I do not say this as an outsider casting stones. This is my heritage.

In late August of 1619 the White Lion docked at Point Comfort in the British colony of Virginia and traded slaves for food. So delicious was the taste of human slavery to colonists, their appetites grew insatiable. By 1662, a court in Virginia ruled all offspring born to female slaves were their owners' property. Babies were torn from their mothers' breasts at will as they or their mothers were sold. And so began two and a half centuries of slavery in North America.

With few exceptions, churchgoers in the south from pew to pulpit robustly embraced what Galatians 3:28 defied. Economy trumped theology. The Bible wasn't just used to excuse inhumane treatment. It was used to bless it. Of course, they had to dodge Galatians 3:28. Preaching the removal of socioethnic disparities would have had radical effects and, from all indications, many knew it.[7]

In the book *Divided by Faith*, authors Michael O. Emerson and Christian Smith write the following in reference to the early provincial period (1700–1739). I know the excerpt is unusually long but it's better than me reading you the whole book, which is what I wish I could do:

> The push to convert slaves was not well received among many masters, or even among non-slave owners. Objections ranged from the older ideas that Africans did not have eternal souls to their inability to learn the Christian faith. But the major objections centered around preserving the social order. If slaves were Christianized, this could mean automatic freedom or slavery revolts.
>
> Originally unwritten was the rule that in accepting Christ and being baptized, the slave was freed not only from sin, but also from slavery. This was rather troublesome to the Anglos who thought about such things, as they felt it impossible to realize their vision without slave labor. The clergy, being part of the same sociocultural environment and eager to see Christianizing take place, quickly stepped in to refute and change this perceived custom. Their strategy was threefold. First, beginning as early as 1664, and increasingly during the first quarter of the eighteenth century, they encouraged several colonial legislatures to declare that slaves remained slaves even when baptized. They also had Anglican Bishop George Berkley

No image-bearer is superior to another.

[7] Eric Mason, *Woke Church: An Urgent Call for Christians in America to Confront Racism and Injustice* (Chicago: Moody Publishers, 2018), 80.

request a formal statement from Britain's Attorney General and Solicitor General . . . Third, clergymen argued that Christian liberty in no way changed temporal bondage. In a widely distributed 1727 letter to American planters, Anglican Bishop Gibson declared that "Christianity, and the embracing of the Gospel, does not make the least Alteration in Civil Relations."[8]

Oh, but it does. As Paul wrote to Philemon concerning the return of Onesimus, the runaway slave, "perhaps this is why he was separated from you for a brief time, so that you might get him back permanently, no longer as a slave, but more than a slave—as a dearly loved brother" (Philemon 15–16a).

Oceans of blood would be required to criminalize slavery. On January 1, 1863, Abraham Lincoln issued the Emancipation Proclamation, and the 13th Amendment passed two years later. Still, the spirit of slavery continued. It simply mutated. History depicts the white church in the American South as among the chiefest of sinners in opposing justice. There were a few exceptions, individuals who rose from the racist rank and file of church or state, unwilling to remain silent and inactive in the face of bigotry.[9]

How do they sound similar to those described in Hebrews 10:33?

_____

_____

_____

Those are old scars, we say, but America is still hemorrhaging from open wounds. In the words of Tony Evans, "The racial problem is the unresolved dilemma of America." My friend Danté Stewart's words ring in my ears. "Why do you hate us?" The blade from white believers cuts to the marrow of Black brothers and sisters because they know we know better. We know Jesus. As Christina Edmondson teaches, "A love of diversity is not the same thing as a love of justice." We can love a colorful Christian community and still prefer the grievous imbalance of power to remain just like it is. This land has yet to see a generation of Jesus followers with guts enough to live the good news Galatians 3:28 preaches.

[8] Michael O. Emerson and Christian Smith, *Divided By Faith: Evangelical Religion and the Problem of Race in America* (Oxford: Oxford University Press, 2000), 22–3, Kindle edition. Copyright © 2001 by Michael O. Emerson and Christian Smith. Used by permission of Oxford University Press. Reproduced with permission of the Licensor through PLSClear.

[9] My friend Dr. Mika Edmondson, both a pastor and an advocate for the marginalized, recently posted the names and pictures of several such individuals if you wish to research their stories: John Laurens from South Carolina, a soldier during the Revolutionary War; George Bourne, a Presbyterian pastor in the 19th century; civil rights activist Juliette Morgan, whose life was marked after attending an interracial prayer meeting; civil rights activist Viola Luzzo who was murdered by the KKK.

Why couldn't it be ours?

The divide is so wide that it feels impossible to cross, but gaping wounds are closed with stitches. You may already be an active agent in this healing work of racial justice or perhaps just beginning.

What is the next stitch for you? What is the next step you could take?

_____

_____

Let's bring our attention to the final pair in Galatians 3:28. Please note a significant word change. Underline each appearance of "or" then circle "and."

> **"There is no Jew or Greek, slave or free, male and female;**
> **since you are all one in Christ Jesus."**

The phrase "male *and* female" (emphasis mine) is meant to ring a Genesis 1:27 bell.

Fill in the blanks:

> **"So God created man in his own image; he created him in the image of**
> **God; he created them _____."**

To confirm the direct connection to the creation narrative, read Galatians 6:15 and write it here.

_____

_____

_____

_____

Compare 2 Cor 5:17–18, also written by Paul, and record any added insight.

_____

_____

_____

The phrase "no male and female" in Gal 3:28 (ESV) is the gospel declaration that the old codes rendering males superior and females inferior are utterly removed in Christ. In the New Covenant of Christ's blood, the new community transcends all the old ethnic and social differences. The 3:28 declaration wasn't out of the blue. Repeatedly in the Gospels we can see Jesus reorienting perspectives on women. One of the least familiar but most powerful glimpses is found in Luke 11:27. Jesus is in the throes of an iconic sermon when a woman yells from the crowd. Complete her sentence.

"Blessed is the . . .

_____

_____

Awkward, isn't it? How does Jesus respond?

_____

_____

Jesus continually pushed back against the social codes, which He knew better than anyone. He entered a world where a woman's role was entirely within the home. Divine blessing looked one way to a woman: childbearing. Centuries of women hoped for the grand prize: to be chosen by God to bring forth the Messiah. The role had been filled by Mary. The Messiah had come and in His palm He held radically reordered priorities. The people most blessed by God would be the ones who heard His word and did His will. Childbearing was not rendered *un*important. One thing was simply declared *more* important.

The reordering of priorities was not futuristic. It was immediate. Luke 8 unfolds with women in the company of Jesus and the Twelve, traveling from town to town as he preached the good news. Astoundingly, these women bankrolled the road trip.

How does Luke 10:38–42 paint a picture of reordered priorities for women?

_____

_____

_____

_____

Following His resurrection, Jesus revealed Himself first to women then sent them to tell the men the good news. He shoved hard against the code that rendered women unreliable witnesses by making them the first eyewitnesses of the most glorious event in history.

How does Acts 1:12–14 show these reordered priorities in practice?

_____

_____

To borrow from the concept Paul uses in Galatians, the household codes found in the epistles don't annul priorities reset by Christ.[10] The top priority for every female Jesus-follower is still to hear and do the will of God, whether her hearing and doing is within the walls of home or without. Students of the whole counsel of God don't have the luxury of holding the Scriptures without tension. Tension is built into it. The way we've historically tried to remove the tension is by cutting and pasting, constructing systematic theologies that ignore or explain away other texts. But "All Scripture is inspired by God" including 1 Timothy 2:12 *and* Acts 2:17, including 1 Corinthians 11:5 *and* 1 Corinthians 14:34.

If the texts are unfamiliar to you, read them and feel the tension.

_____

_____

Rather than grapple, we often take the easy way out, making doctrines of proof texts we defend with quips like, "God said it. I believe it. That settles it!" But what if that's not all God said? Keep studying, student of Scripture, and never forget that a disciple is a learner above all else. You know you've stopped learning the moment you've figured it all out. Embrace the tension.

———————————————

Postscript: We have been given the most beautiful gift. In his marvelous work, *Eat This Book*, pastor and author Eugene Peterson tells the fascinating story of what caused him to first translate a book of the Bible into contemporary English. That book was Galatians. The audience was his own church. The circumstances were reminiscent of ours. Peterson believed Galatians spoke directly to those challenges. I found the story so thoroughly compelling and relevant to this lesson that we contacted the publisher of *Eat This Book*, asking if we might include any of the 7-page segment where Peterson shares it. Stunningly, they granted us permission to include the entire portion. So, with deepest gratitude to Tom Devries, subsidiary rights manager at Wm. B. Eerdman's Publishing Company, and Andrea Heinecke at Alive Literary Agency, I invite you to read what planted a seed in one man's heart that would grow into *The Message: The Bible in Contemporary Language*. You are going to love it.

[10] The household codes are found in Eph 5:22ff, Col 3:18ff, and 1 Pet 3:1ff.

EXCERPT FROM:

Eat This Book: A Conversation in the Art of Spiritual Reading

By Eugene Peterson pp. 130–136

Translation into American

Two thousand years later I found myself in the company of translators, but without any self-awareness that I was a translator. I was a pastor in America. My work involved calling the two to three hundred people who make up my congregation to worship and serving them the Eucharist. I preached sermons and taught Bible studies, I prayed with and for them, I visited the sick and cared for souls, I baptized and confirmed, I married and buried. We were all fluent in American English. Who needed a translator with these people and under these circumstances?

And yet I often found myself identifying with Ezra's thirteen Levites in post-exilic Jerusalem. George Steiner in his wide-ranging treatment of translation, *After Babel*, convinces that translation *within* a language (intralingual) is on a continuum with translation *between* languages (interlingual).[11] I was most conscious of being in the company of the Levites when I was in the pulpit, attempting to make the Scriptures understandable in the colloquial language of the day. Just as the Levites assisted Ezra in Judah by "giving the sense" for understanding the Bible in those post-exilic days of a rapidly disintegrating biblical culture, I was doing something very similar as a pastor in postmodern American, for neither was my congregation familiar with their past, with their Scriptures, their biblically formed identity. In parallel with the Levites using vernacular Aramaic, most of my "translation" was also oral, giving the interpretation, the "understanding," of the Scriptures as they were read out in the sanctuary to my assembled congregation, and also providing an occasional American equivalent to an unfamiliar idiom or metaphor.

And then something happened that without my being aware of its significance at the time put me in the company of translators. It took place in the early 1980s in our small town twenty miles from the city of Baltimore. A financial downturn had raised anxieties among many in the mostly middle-class congregation. Race riots flaring up in many of the cities of America including nearby Baltimore exacerbated the anxiety. The entire community in which I lived and worked was suddenly security conscious. Neighbors were double-locking their doors and installing alarm systems. Men and women who had never held a gun were buying guns. Racial fears developed into racial slurs. Paranoia infected the small talk I would overhear on street corners

[11] George Steiner, *After Babel* (New York: Oxford University Press, 1975).

and in barbershops. To my dismay, all of this seeped into my congregation without encountering any resistance.

My dismay soon turned to anger. How could this congregation of Christians so unthinkingly absorb the world's fearful anxiety and hateful distrust—and so easily? Overnight, it seemed, they had turned their homes into armed camps. They were living defensively, guardedly, timidly. And they were Christians! I had been their pastor for twenty years, preaching the good news that Jesus had overcome the world, defining their neighbor with Jesus' story of the good Samaritan, defending them against the status quo with Jesus' story of the cautious servant who buried his talent. I had led them in Bible studies that I had supposed were grounding them in the freedom for which Christ had set us free, keeping their feet firmly in, "but not of," the world around us for which Christ died. And here they were, before my eyes, paralyzed by fear and "anxious for the morrow."

As my anger and dismay subsided, I began plotting a pastoral strategy that I hoped would recover their identity as a free people in Christ, a people not "conformed to the world" but living robustly and spontaneously in the Spirit. Galatians seemed a good place to start. I was angry and this was Paul's angriest letter, provoked by a report that Christian congregations that Paul had formed a few years before had abandoned the life of freedom for the security system of the old Jewish codes. I thought it was Galatians-time from my congregation. The secure and cautious conditions of suburbia had softened and blurred the sharp edges of the gospel and left them undefended against the anxieties of the day. I thought that the parallel between our congregations, Paul's in Galatia and mine in Maryland, was exquisitely serendipitous, and I was going to make the most it.

But I also knew that this was going to take awhile. I decided that I would teach an adult class on Galatians for a year and follow that up by a year of preaching through Galatians. I was going to soak them in Galatians. They were going to have Galatians coming out their pores. After two years they wouldn't know whether they were living in Galatia or America. But they were going to know something about freedom, the freedom for which Christ set them free.

I announced an adult class for the study of Galatians to the congregation. Our adult church-school class met in the basement of our educational wing on Sunday mornings, bare cement block walls, folding chairs, a horseshoe arrangement of vinyl-surfaced tables, an easel of newsprint—our suburban Presbyterian equivalent of the catacombs. I had always loved the intimacy and leisure of these gatherings, the immersion in Scripture, the experiences of surprise and recognition—God's word!—and the ambience of honesty and revelation that always seemed to develop. As we set ourselves in the arena of God's revelation, moments always seemed to occur when first one, then another, would become capable of revealing herself, himself, cautiously edging out from behind the disguises and make-up by which we all attempt to make ourselves respectable and acceptable in the world.

On the Sunday set for the beginning of the study, fourteen men and women showed up, my usual take from our congregation. My routine was to arrive early, brew an urn of coffee, prepare hot water for tea, put out the condiments and Styrofoam cups, spread Bibles out on the tables. Small talk consumed the first few minutes as we got our coffee and took our places around the tables. I always felt that for the first ten minutes or so the Bibles on the table were competing for attention with the liturgical act of stirring cream and sugar into the coffee cups; most Sundays the Bible would eventually pull out in front, but on this particular Sunday those white Styrofoam cups seemed to be winning. Here I was laying the groundwork for a major renewal of Spirit-torched imagination in my congregation. Galatians, Paul's angry, passionate, fiery letter that rescued his congregation from their regression to culture slavery, was on the table and nobody was getting it. Sweetly smiling, they were giving more attention to stirring sugar into those Styrofoam cups than to the Spirit words that pulsed in Paul's metaphors and syntax. It was obvious that they weren't getting it. And I was offended, mightily offended.

I don't know why I was particularly struck that day, for it happens all the time: parents with children, friends with friends, pastors with parishioners, teachers with students, coaches with players. We get hold of something that turns life inside out—a truth-probing idea, a blaze of beauty, a passionate love—and urgently press our discovery on another person. After a short time of polite listening, the person, obviously bored, either wanders away or changes the subject, not unlike those times as an adolescent when we fell totally in love with another and couldn't wait to tell our best friend. Whereupon our friend said, "I don't know what you see in him, in her." Here we have just discovered this extravagantly beautiful person, every sentence coming from his lips a melody, every step she takes a figure in a dance, and our friend, our best friend, says, "I don't know what you see in her."

That is how I felt that Sunday morning in that Presbyterian basement room in Maryland. They were reading sentences that charted a revolution—and stirring sugar into their coffee.

Later in the afternoon, I told my wife of the sputtery morning launch of the

Galatians study. Frustrated and fuming I said, "I know what I'm going to do; I'm going to teach them Greek—if they read it in Greek, those sweet smiles will vanish soon enough. If they read it in Greek, Paul's somersaulting, cartwheeling, freedom-trumpeting Greek, they'll get it." She gave me one of her sweet smiles and said, "I can't think of a better way to empty out the classroom."

The smile did it. I abandoned the Greek project. What I did instead was spend the week doodling with Paul's Greek, trying to turn it into how I thought it sounded in American English. I tried to imagine Paul as pastor to these people who were letting their hard-won freedom in Christ slip through their fingers. How would he write to them in the language they used when they weren't in church? I had no plan, no program, nothing ambitious like Greek. I just wanted them to hear it the way I heard it, the way the Galatians heard it, the way Luther heard it, the way so many men and women through our Christian centuries have heard it and found themselves set free by and for God.

The next Sunday I brewed the coffee and heated the water for tea as I always did, but I omitted the Bibles. Instead of Bibles I had fourteen copies of my doodles—one page double-spaced, about 250 words—spread out on the tables. And I read:

I, Paul, and my companions in faith here, send greetings to the Galatian churches. My authority for writing to you does not come from any popular vote of the people, nor does it come through the appointment of some human higher-up. It comes directly from Jesus the Messiah and God the Father, who raised him from the dead. I'm God-commissioned. So I greet you with the great words, grace and peace! We know the meaning of those words because Jesus Christ rescued us from this evil world we're in by offering himself as a sacrifice for our sins. God's plan is that we all experience that rescue. Glory to God forever! Oh, yes!

I can't believe your fickleness—how easily you have turned traitor to him who called you by the grace of Christ by embracing a variant message! It is not a minor variation, you know; it is completely other, an alien message, a no-message, a lie about God. Those who are provoking this agitation among you are turning the Message of Christ on its head. Let me be blunt: If one of us— even an angel from heaven!—were to preach something other than what we preached originally, let him be cursed. I said it once; I'll say it again: If anyone, regardless of reputation or credentials, preaches something other than what you received originally, let him be cursed.

And so it continued. We went over the pages week after week, trying to get Paul's Greek into the American that they spoke when they weren't in church, the words and phrases they used when they were at work on the job, at home playing with their children, out on the street. Every week I brought in another page. We tested the metaphors and phrasings against American English, suggested emendations, threw out clichés, all the time trying to preserve the sharp edge of Paul's language in our vernacular.

After the second week of using this new format, as I was cleaning and straightening up the room, I noticed that all the Styrofoam coffee cups were half-full of cold coffee. I knew I had them. I've never taken so much satisfaction in cleaning up after guests—pouring all that cold coffee into the sink and pitching their cups into the waste can!

We pored over a freshly xeroxed copy of the translated text every Sunday morning through that autumn, winter, and spring. In nine months we had completed Galatians. Without knowing what we were doing, or the impact it would make on our culture, we had joined the company of translators, "God's secretaries."[12] The next autumn I set out on a nine-month course of preaching this same Galatians text to the worshiping congregation. The following summer I started writing, hoping to make a book of these two years of Galatians conversations and prayer, worship and teaching, pastor-and-congregation collaboration in listening to the Spirit's great freedom text, recovering and submitting ourselves and our culture to God's shaping word.

Several years after the book was published,[13] I received a letter from an editor. "Do you remember that book you wrote on Galatians? Well, I photocopied the translation portions, taped them together and have been carrying them around ever since, reading them over and over and reading them to my friends. All of us are getting really tired of Galatians. Why don't you translate the whole New Testament?"

I protested that it was impossible; I was a pastor – it had taken me two years to translate one of the smaller New Testament books. And besides, weren't there enough translations and paraphrases already? In the most recent definitive history of the Bible in English, David Daniell calculates that over twelve hundred new translations into English of the Bible, or parts of

---

[12] The title of Adam Nicolson's book on the work of the company of translators, the fifty or so scholars and pastors, who translated the King James Bible in the seven years 1604 to 1611 (New York: HarperCollins, 2003).

[13] *Traveling Light: Modern Meditations on St. Paul's Letter of Freedom* (Colorado Springs: Helmers and Howard, 1988; first published as *Traveling Light: Reflections on the Free Life*, by InterVarsity Press, 1982).

it, were made from the original Hebrew and Greek between 1945 and 1990. Thirty-five were fresh translations of the whole Bible, and eighty were fresh translations of the New Testament alone. His comment, "these are huge figures," is a huge understatement.[14]

My editor persisted. After a couple of years of letters and telephone conversations, it seemed "good to the Holy Spirit and to us" (editor and publisher, my wife and me) that this was the work set before us. I resigned from my congregation (after twenty-nine years) and set to work translating the biblical text into an American English vernacular.

When I sat down with the Hebrew and Greek text to translate them into American for the congregation beyond my congregation, it didn't seem all that different from what I had been doing for thirty-five years as a pastor, a life ordained by my church to bring the word of God in Scripture and sacrament to the people whom I had been called to assist and guide into a life of worshiping God the Father, following Jesus the Son, and receiving the Holy Spirit in all the details involved in raising families and working for a living, living a joyful and responsible life in the American neighborhood. I was always aware as a pastor that I was required to be neighborhood-specific. Generalities and "big" truth would not do. My neighborhood was American; in *The Message* the language was necessarily American. I set to work. It would take me 10 years.

[14] David Daniell, *The Bible in English: Its History and Influence* (New Haven: Yale University Press, 2003), pp. 764–65.

Eugene H. Peterson, *Eat This Book: A Conversation in the Art of Spiritual Reading* © 2006. Wm. B. Eerdmans Publishing Company, Grand Rapids, MI. Reprinted by permission of the publisher; all rights reserved.

Turns out, these days, that most things
are more complex than we once believed.
Yet the truth remains—

*Nothing at all
is impossible with
this God who has
encountered us.*

— Melissa Moore

zone four

CHILDREN

GALATIANS 4

———

When the time came to completion, God sent his Son,
born of a woman, born under the law, to redeem those
under the law, so that we might receive adoption as sons.
And because you are sons, God sent the Spirit of his
Son into our hearts, crying, "Abba, Father!"

Galatians 4:4–6

VIDEO GUIDE

THE CHILDREN ZONE

Introduction: We've officially arrived at the halfway point in our study of Paul's revolutionary letter to the Galatians. Today we begin our preoccupations with one of the most fascinating chapters of the book.

Read Galatians 4:1–7, 19–20, 27–28.

4:1 **"child"**—He is a *nēpios*, literally an "infant," In the NT, there is as wide range for the use of the word child. Obviously in reference to actual children but also in comparisons of adults to children.

(1 Cor 3:1; 13:11; Eph 4:14)
1 Cor. 3:1–3a
Luke 10:17–21
Matthew 18:1–4

There's a very big difference between CHILDISH and CHILDLIKE.

Consider an excerpt by Bible commentator Dr. Timothy George in two parts, starting here and picking up again under our second point.

> The word *Abba* is a term of familial _____ that can still be heard through the Middle East as a word of address used by young children to greet their father. *Abba* is an Aramaic expression that may have derived originally from the first syllables uttered by an infant (cf. the corresponding *'immā*, "mother"). However, we _____ this word when we refer to it as mere baby talk and translate it into English as "daddy." The word *Abba* appears in certain legal texts of the Mishna as a designation used by grown children in claiming the _____ of their deceased father.[1]

Read Mark 14:32-36.

1. No other   compares to _____ Father.

John 5:17-18

John 20:17

2. No other _____ compares to this exclamation.

Read Galatians 4:6 again. "Abba Father!"

Continuing with the excerpt written by Dr. Timothy George, "As a word of address *Abba* is not so much associated with infancy as it is with _____. It is a cry of the heart, not a word spoken calmly with personal _____ and _____, but a word we 'call' or 'cry out' *(krazō)*."[2]

[1] Timothy George, *Galatians* (Nashville: B&H, 1994), 307.
[2] George, *Galatians*, 307.

NOTES

CHILDREN

WEEK FOUR

THE CHILDREN ZONE

day one

Full-grown Freedom

Read, write and mark Galatians 4:1–4.

_____

_____

_____

_____

_____

_____

_____

_____

_____

_____

_____

I like to claim that my longtime friend Susan once said that I'm only happy when I'm learning. "I did not," she corrects. "I said you are *happiest* when you are learning." I like the story better my way because, even as it makes Susan sound delightfully straightforward, it is the truth if I've ever heard it.

I love research so much that I tend to get bored and dispirited between Bible study projects. For anyone who loves the process of discovery, the Bible is a goldmine. The topics and themes are endless. The breadth alone could keep a student occupied for a lifetime. Add to it the depth and you've found a tome with square footage too vast to measure. The number of books written about this one book would challenge the girth of the Library of Congress.

This is a long-winded way of telling you that I learned something new that I'm thrilled to get to share with you today. Let's work our way there together.

The chapter break between Galatians 3 and 4 is unfortunate because Galatians 4:1 flows directly from the preceding verse.

What does Galatians 3:29 say we are if we belong to Christ?

_____

_____

As we study the inspired writings of Paul, particularly in Galatians, we have to be students on the move, ready to shift from metaphor to metaphor or, more challenging still, from *this* to *that* aspect of a continuing metaphor without confusing them or forcing them to function simultaneously. Loosen up, is what I'm saying, and let Paul be Paul. (Later in the chapter, don't say I didn't warn you.)

What is the general analogy Paul draws in our text today?

_____

_____

_____

When Paul says of the young master that "he is no different from a slave," Paul exaggerates as a rhetorical device for the benefit of the metaphor. A world of difference existed then, as it has throughout history, between

And if you belong to Christ, then you are Abraham's seed, heirs according to the promise.

Galatians 3:29

slaves and most heirs of minor age. Paul means that the minor could no more take authority over his inheritance than could a slave. Neither the underage heir nor the slave is his own master. Of even greater significance to the letter's developments in the next chapter is this: neither the child-heir nor the slave is free. Dr. F. F. Bruce writes of our present text,

> Paul takes up a different analogy from those used in 3:22–26 to set forth the contrast between the previous period of spiritual immaturity and the new life of full-grown freedom, bringing it up to date by including the theme of inheritance, introduced in 3:29. The law has been compared to a prison-warden and as a slave-attendant; now its role is compared to that of the guardians and trustees appointed to take care of a minor and his property.[1]

The new life of full-grown freedom. I love the sound of that. Do you? Or does it frighten you a little? If it does, what scares you about it?

_____

_____

_____

_____

I long to know what *full-grown freedom* looks like and how it is lived out. The hope of this discovery is among numerous reasons we're neck-deep in this study. To borrow Paul's own words in Romans 5:5, "this hope will not disappoint us."

We don't know which legal practice Paul had in mind in the opening of Galatians 4. In Judaism, a boy entered manhood and became a "son of the law" shortly after turning 12.[2] Under Greek law, the male heir could not take authority over an inheritance until around 18. Under Roman law, the heir took full control of the estate at age 25; however, individual provinces within the empire could exercise a certain amount of flexibility, which would empower a father to set the date.

Since the child-heir illustrated in verses 1–2 has guardians and trustees and is called "owner of everything," Paul may have in mind the surviving heir of a deceased father, in which case the ownership has been designated through

> This hope will not disappoint us, because God's love has been poured out in our hearts through the Holy Spirit who was given to us.
>
> Romans 5:5

[1] F. F. Bruce, *The Epistle to the Galatians: A Commentary on the Greek Text* (Grand Rapids, MI: Eerdmans, 1982), 192.
[2] A. T. Robertson, *Word Pictures in the New Testament* (Nashville, TN: Broadman Press, 1933), Logos Bible software edition.

a last will and testament but the parent died while the child was underage. If this is Paul's meaning, the analogy only goes far enough to depict the law as a guardian but stops short of the father's death since God, in fact, *is* the father.

Paul's opening illustration depicts the people of God as the descendants of Abraham who'd been heirs for centuries but remained underage and unable to receive their inheritance. Their full rights as inheritors would not be issued until Christ came, bringing the plan—and the heirs themselves—to adulthood. In the meantime, God, their Father, gave them the law to serve as a guardian and trustee until the time designated by His own design. Galatians 4:1–7 is God's story of redeemed humanity's coming of age. It's a timeline drawn with language.

In v.3, Paul further develops the analogy to include the Galatians and, ultimately, us along with them. What does Paul specifically say we were in slavery under "when we were children"?

_____

_____

_____

_____

The CSB and NKJV read "the elements of the world."
The NIV says "the elemental spiritual forces of the world."
The ESV uses "the elementary principles of the world."

We've come to the material that held new discoveries for me. I was quite familiar with the phrase "elementary principles of the world" (ESV) because it appears not only here, but also twice in Colossians.

Look up Colossians 2:8 and 2:20 and record any clues the two verses lend toward defining what Paul means by the phrase.

Colossians 2:8

_____

_____

_____

_____

_____

_____

> In the same way we also, when we were children, were in slavery under the elements of the world.
>
> Galatians 4:3

Colossians 2:20

_____

_____

_____

_____

_____

"When we were children" (Gal 4:3) refers to the pre-Christian condition. Before Christ came and, subsequently, before we came to Christ, we humans were enslaved under the "stoicheia" (Gk στοιχεῖα) of the world. According to Paul's analogy, this enslavement occurred whether converts were "under the law" (in other words, Jewish-Christians) or under godless or pagan influences (Gentile-Christians). The former were people of the covenants, of course, but they were still minors in Paul's analogy and, therefore, unable to enjoy the full-grown freedom of heirs come-of-age.

Picture "stoicheia" like the letters of the alphabet. Words are built from them that can then be constructed into sentences and further into paragraphs. Think of your elementary school experience and learning the basics. My granddaughter, Willa, is learning to draw the letters of her name and stick figures for people. Sometimes her "W" is turned upside down. She still sees a "W", but we who are grown see an "M." She is a child, still under the elemental principles of the world. Make sense?

In the first century when Paul wrote to the Galatians, "stoicheia" was primarily used in extra-biblical literature to describe the basic elements used to compose the natural world. People have traditionally understood these elements to be earth, air, fire and water. Here, we will look to David deSilva, whose exposition brings the concept to life. We'll take the excerpt in three parts so we can absorb it as we go.

> In Paul's usage here, they are the basic, fundamental principles upon which social reality (the "world" of human systems, interaction, and activity) is constructed and by which it is governed. They are, especially, the categories (like those listed but swept aside in Gal 3:28) that divide, order, and create hierarchy within social reality, as well as the rationales that undergird the same.[3]

[3] David A. deSilva, _The Letter to the Galatians_, The New International Commentary on the New Testament (Grand Rapids, MI: Eerdmans, 2018), 347.
[4] deSilva, _The Letter to the Galatians_, 347.

Glance back at Gal 3:28 and remind yourself of the divisions it lists. What were those three social divides?

1. _____

2. _____

3. _____

Now, back to the excerpt expounding on "stoicheia" from deSilva:

> They are the rules and values that each child, born into and confronted with the society that had long since taken shape on the basis of such rules and values, must inevitably internalize, accept, and live by. They are the individual parts of "the way the world works," to which each child must adapt himself or herself, by which each child must be willingly constrained as his or her mind, practices, and life trajectory are shaped thereby.[4]

Are you tracking with the line of reasoning? I could hardly stop thinking about these last two sentences.

> The *stoicheia* are happiest (if the conceit be allowed that impersonal forces can be happy) when this child arrives at his or her grave without having questioned them. This is the slavery in which every person is born, and which most never recognize as such.[5]

We find ourselves, now, staring into the face of a disorienting truth—we can be enslaved all of our lives without ever realizing our pitiable estate.

Enslavement was the only world we knew until the Spirit moved us to ask questions. To offer an illustration, I look back now on the days when I thought I couldn't question my husband about our spending even though I helped earn our living. The concept of marital submission I had absorbed was so convoluted in my mind that I thought divine blessing was almost entirely dependent upon what kind of wife I was. Submission meant accepting virtually anything or losing the favor of God. In my mind, it was make-Keith-happy or make-God-mad.

Well, for one thing, Keith had endured such childhood trauma, he wasn't happy in his own heart. I couldn't have made him happy if my life depended on it. I love my husband. We've been married almost 42 years, but we've become vastly healthier since my faith-world grew and I saw godly marriages (not free of opposition, of course, but) free of oppression. You see, the

We find ourselves, now, staring into the face of the disorienting truth—we can be enslaved all of our lives without ever realizing our pitiable estate.

[5] deSilva, *The Letter to the Galatians*, 347.

"elemental principles of the world" aren't limited to the secular world. They are also present and powerful in any religious world.

OK, your turn. Describe a way you've been enslaved under the elementary principles of the world.

_____

_____

_____

_____

Let's conclude with our sights set on Galatians 4:4–5. On Day Four of last week, Melissa pointed out the remarkable references to time in Galatians. Concepts of *before* and *after* stamp the entire letter. Words like "then" and "when" are spiritual markers in these chapters.

The most important reference to time is found in Galatians 4:4. What is it?

_____

_____

_____

The opening words of the Bible burst at the seams with meaning: "In the beginning." God—Three-in-One, Father, Son and Holy Spirit, each shown in Scripture to have been active in creation—had no beginning and have no end. We might say time was the first thing God created. "In the beginning" marks the initial tick-tock of the divine clock. That clock began ticking rhythmically and deliberately toward the first advent of Christ and ticks now toward the second. Nothing was haphazard about the moment of His birth. A segment of time allotted by God had been filling up for millennia and, when finally full, "God sent His Son."

What comfort can be found in verses 2 and 4 about God's relationship to time even now?

_____

_____

_____

_____

_____

What does Galatians 4:4 suggest about God's patience?

_____

_____

_____

_____

As our lesson draws to a finish, glance ahead at the gorgeous words of Galatians 4:5 and allow God to stir your heart and mind toward our next segment. You have a Redeemer. He is the One who created all things with the sound of His voice, who owns the cattle on a thousand hills, from whom the lightning comes and to whom the lightning reports.

He who saw us bruised purple and bloodied by the chains that bound us bought us from our taskmasters. Most of us dared to hope no higher than the thought that perhaps we'd been transferred to a gentler, kinder slave-master whose bonds weighed less heavily on our wrists. Who could have imagined that, when we got home, He'd show us to the room of a royal heir?

NOTES

_____

_____

_____

_____

_____

_____

_____

_____

_____

_____

_____

_____

THE CHILDREN ZONE

day two

Because You Are Sons

Read, write and mark Galatians 4:5–11.

_____

_____

_____

_____

_____

_____

_____

_____

_____

_____

_____

_____

_____

_____

Our passage begins right in the middle of a rich section. Go ahead and read verses 4–5 again. Paul describes the mission God initiated when he sent his Son to redeem the child heir still under guardianship, so that "we might receive adoption as sons." Who exactly is included in the "we"? Paul could either be referring particularly to Jews who trust in Jesus or all Christians. I oscillate but tend toward the latter interpretation 51% of the time.

The term translated "adoption as sons" is υἱοθεσία in Greek. Erin M. Heim describes the meaning of adoption in the ancient world in her monograph *Adoption in Galatians and Romans:*

> Roughly then, the various literary sources … illuminate … that adoption was considered a means of installing a son (and rarely a daughter) in a family (not of his birth) by means of a legal decree, and that this relationship mirrored, to some extent, the relationship between a natural father and son. In both Greek and Roman sources where the legal practice of adoption is in view there is a strong connection between adoption and inheritance, and the purpose of adoption was to secure a suitable heir to take over the father's name, cult, and estate.[1]

Compare and contrast the practice of ancient adoption as explained in this paragraph with what you know about modern adoption.

_____

_____

_____

_____

_____

You might notice in some English translations of Galatians 4:5 that "sons" is translated as "children" (NLT, NRSV). But, in this particular case the gender-specific translation (ESV, CSB) is preferable because, in the ancient world, families primarily adopted sons, not daughters. Sons, not daughters, had status. And yet, Paul says that God adopted us, both men and women, *as sons.* Carolyn Custis James captures how, surprisingly, this particular example of non-inclusive language has a delightful spin:

> Given the fact that in the first century patriarchal culture sons were prized above daughters—who didn't inherit, didn't show up in genealogies, and

> But when the fullness of time had come, God sent forth his Son, born of woman, born under the law, to redeem those who were under the law, so that we might receive adoption as sons.
>
> Galatians 4:4–5 ESV

---

[1] Erin M. Heim, *Adoption in Galatians and Romans: Contemporary Metaphor Theories and the Pauline Huiothesia Metaphors* (Leiden; Boston: Brill, 2017), 146.

were married off to build another man's family—the fact that Paul is telling a mixed audience that they are "all sons" is not diminishing women in the least. To the contrary, Paul's words are elevating them to the same high status in God's family as their brothers. Paul is telling women, Gentiles, and slaves that, in God's family, they are all sons![2]

Now, I totally track with Gentiles being adopted into God's family in Christ, but it's taken me time to get my head around how Paul could conceive of Jews only just now being adopted into God's family, in Christ. This language originally surprised me because Israel had been established in the Old Testament as God's son since long before Paul wrote to the Galatians. To name just a few verses that testify to this: *When Israel was a child, I loved him, and out of Egypt I called my son* (Hosea 11:1-2). Or: *This is what the LORD says: Israel is my firstborn son* (Exodus 4:22).

While the concept of sonship is distinct from adoption, Paul actually uses the precise language of adoption to refer to non-Christian Jews in Romans 9.

In Romans 9:4-5 Paul lists the amazing benefits that belong to Jews. What are they?

_____

_____

_____

_____

_____

_____

_____

_____

> They are Israelites, and to them belong the adoption, the glory, the covenants, the giving of the law, the temple service, and the promises.
>
> Romans 9:4

The word "adoption" listed in that context is the same word ἡ υἱοθεσία that we find in Galatians 4:5. I have puzzled for many days over how to make sense of the distinction between the sonship Jews had already enjoyed for many centuries prior and the "adoption as sons" Paul says they receive now that faith has come. I can't tidy it all up but I've realized that two things are key: the metaphor Paul uses and the uniqueness of Jesus the Son.

[2] Carolyn Custis James, "Lost in Translation," HuffPost Blog, September 19, 2016, accessed July 6, 2020, https://www.huffpost.com/entry/lost-in-translation_5_b_12019892. For more by this author, consult her blog www.carolyncustisjames.com. See also *Half the Church* and *Malestrom,* both volumes published by Zondervan.

First, in terms of the metaphor, the missing link may be the relationship between adoption and inheritance in the ancient context. If Paul considers Jews to be adopted as sons already, perhaps he can still speak of them "receiving adoption" in Christ, like Gentile Christians, because it's not until Christ that they experience the full rights of adoption. An already-but-not-yet element could exist here implicitly, as it explicitly does in Romans 8:23, where Paul says that though Christians have the Spirit as firstfruits, we groan eagerly waiting for our *adoption*.

Second, Paul may be distinguishing between the sonship of Jesus and the sonship of everyone else. Richard Hays puts it like this, "In contrast to God's own Son, all other human beings, including Jewish believers, enter God's family only by adoption."[3]

In verse 6, Paul then switches pronouns, declaring to the Galatians: *"because **you** are sons, God sent the Spirit of his Son into **our** hearts."* The Greek verb ἐξαποστέλλω used for "sent" is used only twice by Paul, here and two verses earlier in 4:4, which creates a vivid parallel between God's dispatch of the Son and God's dispatch of the Son's Spirit. The word often captures sending off or away in an official sense, like a mission (see Acts 7:12, 9:30, 17:14, 22:21). We tend to think of the incarnation of Jesus in more concrete terms than the sending of the Spirit, but the sending of the Spirit is just as real and missional.

Since faith has come, the Gentiles who trust in Jesus are sons of God. As a result, God sent forth Jesus' Spirit into the hearts of all who trusted him, Jew and Gentile alike. J. Louis Martyn calls this "the invasion of the heart."[4] I like that.

How is God's sending of Jesus' Spirit into the human heart significant to you personally? Reflect below:

_____

_____

_____

_____

The combination of heart and spirit recalls Ezekiel's prophecy of Israel's restoration: *"I will give you a new heart and put a new spirit within you . . . I will place my Spirit within you"* (Ezek 36:26–27). The prophet Ezekiel

---

[3] Richard B. Hays, "Galatians," in *The New Interpreter's Bible* Vol. XI (Nashville: Abingdon Press, 2000), 284.

[4] J. Louis Martyn, *Galatians,* The Anchor Yale Bible Commentaries (New Haven, CT: Yale University Press, 1997), 391.

even mentions a sprinkling of clean water on Israel (36:25). It's probably not a coincidence that Paul has just alluded to baptism a few verses earlier in Galatians 3:27–28. Indeed, some scholars think the ritual of baptism is still in view here at 4:6.[5]

A theme we find often in Paul's letters, especially Romans, is the uniqueness of Israel and Gentile dependence on Israel for salvation. The mutuality between Jews and Gentiles that Paul envisions in Galatians is striking. *Interdependence* is the word John W. Taylor uses:

> Paul's interpretation of the Abrahamic covenant makes the eschatological blessing of Jews and Gentiles mutually necessary and interdependent. One will not happen without the other. The idea that the blessing of Gentiles would result from the eschatological fulfillment of divine promises to Israel is common . . . Even more strikingly . . . Jewish believers receive the Spirit because of this same blessing of the Gentiles (3:13–14; 4:6). Thus Gentile inclusion in Christ, Paul claims, far from being subsidiary or secondary, is necessary for the full eschatological blessing of Jews.[6]

The last two words of Galatians 4:6 tell us what Jesus' Spirit cries out. Please write it here: _____

"Abba" is an Aramaic word transliterated (not translated) in most translations because no one knows what it means but it is likely a term of endearment. Some have suggested translating it as "Daddy" or "Papa," but others think those terms miss the mark. I, for one, find it awkward when people pray to "Daddy-God," but I'm also not the least cynical girl on the block. To each her own?

In the New Testament, "Abba" occurs three times (here, Rom 8:15, Mark 14:36), each instance followed by ὁ πατήρ, the Greek word for "Father." Determining the exact meaning of "Abba" is less important to me than exploring the context in which Jesus himself uttered it.

Please carefully read Mark 14:32–38. Describe the context in which Jesus utters "Abba, Father":

_____

_____

_____

_____

---

[5] J. Louis Martyn, *Galatians*, 391.

[6] John W. Taylor, "The Eschatological Interdependence of Jews and Gentiles in Galatians," *Tyndale Bulletin* 63.2 (2012): 291–316.

God sent the Spirit of Jesus into our hearts crying out the same address Jesus used in the garden of Gethsemane. We never see Jesus more grieved. The text says he was "grieved to the point of death." His closest friends asleep, opposite of the alertness he'd asked of them, Jesus calls on "Abba." In the most tender request I can imagine, he asks his Father to please make it all stop somehow yet still submits to his plan, whatever it is. When the Spirit of the crucified and risen Son cries out to the Father inside of us, we are profoundly united to God in a way none of us can fathom.

> When the Spirit of the crucified and risen Son cries out to the Father inside of us, we are profoundly united to God in a way none of us can fathom.

Jesus brings everyone into greater relationship to and intimacy with God. In the metaphor Paul has sketched, Jews are imagined as child heirs under *external* guidance. The sending of the Son ushers them into a new era of maturity and prophetic fulfillment in which their status as sons is further realized. They're no longer *under* anything but are guided *internally* from the heart by the Spirit. And to Gentiles, visualized as slaves in Paul's metaphor, well, verse 7 tells us the rest of the story: "you are no longer a slave but a son, and if a son, then God has made you an heir."

In verses 8–9 Paul reminds the Galatians of their former lives: they were enslaved to things "that by nature are not gods" (v.8). One of my favorite parts of this passage is in verse 9 when Paul corrects himself mid-sentence.

Read Galatians 4:9. Explain how Paul clarifies himself:

_____

_____

_____

_____

This small correction says so much, doesn't it? The Galatians' transformation rests in God's action of knowing them; it has nothing to do with their own arrival at the knowledge of God.

What are the two questions Paul asks the Galatians in 4:9? Mark below.

☐ Why do you neglect the law?
☐ How can you turn back again to the weak and worthless elements?
☐ Why aren't you observing the Sabbath?
☐ Do you want to be enslaved to the weak and worthless elements all over again?

If God has made Gentiles sons and heirs through faith, and the heirs in God's family are now in the era of fullness, Gentile Christians have no business walking in the opposite direction or winding back the salvation-historical clock counter to the direction of the Spirit. But, friends, this is precisely what the Galatians are in the process of doing, as verses 9–10 explicitly show us.

In verse 10, Paul tells the Galatians, "You are observing special days, months, seasons, and years." What do you think Paul is referring to here? Take any kind of guess:

_____

_____

To my mind, there is no doubt that Paul is referring to Jewish observances, whether the Sabbath, various festival days, and so on. We might expect Paul to be more specific, but I think Douglas Moo is right on when he says Paul may "choose a rather vague way of referring to the Jewish observances to tie them as closely as possible to the 'elements' and perhaps also the religious observances in the Galatians' pagan past."[7] In effect, Paul says to these Gentile Christians that, if they add on The Law now, it's no better than backsliding to their godless past. It's either Jesus or The Elements of the World.

Verse 11 is the perfect line to sit with until next time, since it passionately encapsulates all that's at stake for Paul and his Galatians:

I am fearful for you, that perhaps my labor for you has been wasted.

[7] Douglas J. Moo, *Galatians,* Baker Exegetical Commentary on the New Testament (Grand Rapids, MI: Baker Academic, 2013), 278.

NOTES

THE CHILDREN ZONE

day three

My Little Children

Read, write and mark Galatians 4:12–20.

_____

_____

_____

_____

_____

_____

_____

_____

_____

_____

_____

_____

_____

In our passages today, Paul fights for his relationship with the Galatians. If Paul believed in a good fight of faith (and he did), then the gospel was a literal free-for-all. We've all been involved in vicious fights in which parties seemed intent on destroying one another, to be sure. However, not all conflict is destructive. At times, conflict is necessary for healing.[1] A vital question in any conflict is whether we're fighting against relationship or for it.

"I beg you, brothers and sisters," Paul implores the Galatians.

When you've fought hardest for a relationship, you've probably used the words "I beg you." I certainly have. What were the circumstances the last time you pleaded with someone for the sake of your relationship?

_____

_____

_____

_____

_____

Paul begs the Galatians to become like him because he also had become like them. He had formerly believed that a Gentile must become like a Jew to receive the promises. Jesus thoroughly upended that belief. So rigorously had Jesus overturned Paul's conviction, this self-described "Hebrew born of Hebrews; regarding the law, a Pharisee . . . regarding the righteousness that is in the law, blameless" (Phil 3:5–6) experienced his own emancipation.

As a result, Paul had come to live in numerous ways like a Gentile. Paul wanted the Galatians to answer the question, "how could you become like the old me when the new me had become like you?" The irony baffled him.

When pleading with someone for the sake of a relationship, we naturally bring up our history with them. In verses 13–15, Paul does exactly that. The Galatians hadn't originally been on his travel itinerary. So why had he come to them?

_____

_____

_____

_____

[1] It's necessary for me to say here that I do not recommend conflict in abusive situations. If you are in an abusive or unsafe relationship, please seek help immediately to safely distance yourself from harm.

The CSB words Paul's condition as "a weakness of the flesh" while the ESV calls it "a bodily ailment." The nature of the physical malady is unclear but we can draw two conclusions about it:

1. The ailment burdened caregiver and receiver alike. Perhaps Paul had been badly beaten, stoned or flogged. He may have contracted an illness demanding much of his custodians, both physically and psychologically. The most common theories suggest malaria, epilepsy or ophthalmia.

2. The ailment was somehow repugnant because Paul commended the Galatians for not recoiling from him. "You did not scorn or despise me" (ESV). According to Richard B. Hays, "The second verb in v.14a, ἐκπτύω (ekptyo), refers literally to the act of spitting at someone."[2] If meant literally, the term likely references the ancient practice of spitting to ward off an evil eye or evil spirits.[3] If meant figuratively, it signifies a salivating repulsion that could result from the seeing and smelling infected flesh or malfunctioning bodies.

Has there been a time you had to overcome a natural inclination to recoil in order to care for someone with a physical ailment or, perhaps the reverse, when you feared others would recoil as they cared for you in yours? If so, what got you through it?

_____

_____

_____

_____

_____

How does Paul describe the Galatians' reception of him?

_____

_____

_____

_____

_____

[2] Richard B. Hays, "Galatians," in *The New Interpreter's Bible* Vol. XI (Nashville: Abingdon Press, 2000), 294.

[3] Hays, "Galatians," 294.

Love is the overcoming factor for most of us in caring for someone with an ailment that assaults the senses but, remember, Paul was a stranger to the Galatians. Their embrace is impressive. "Where, then, is your blessing?" In other words, what happened to the people who blessed me with such tender care in my raw estate?

What does Paul say they would have done if possible?

_____

_____

> So then, have I become your enemy because I told you the truth?
>
> Galatians 4:16

This verse lends significant support to the idea that Paul's ailment involved his eyes. Some scholars insist "torn out your eyes" could have been a figure of speech indicating nothing about Paul's eyes but that doesn't explain what he writes toward the end in Galatians 6:11. What makes the possibility hard to dismiss?

_____

_____

_____

In an epistle heavily stocked with questions, Galatians 4:16 is among the most potent of Paul's inquiries. What is it?

_____

_____

Fighting for relationship often involves taking the risk of telling someone a hard truth. As tempting as it is to posture ourselves as the victims, thinking who turned against us because we told them the truth, the opposite question is the more compelling and offers the only scenario we can control: Who became our enemy for telling us the truth? Maybe we don't think of them as enemies but, if our hearts slammed shut toward them, the difference is trifling. In high likelihood, the truth they told us set us free in some significant way but the wound was so severe that we were reluctant to tell them.

Does this point resonate? If so, how?

_____

_____

_____

_____

What Paul says about his rivals in Galatians 4:17 is telling. The ESV reads, "They make much of you, but for no good purpose. They want to shut you out, that you may make much of them."

Has anyone made much of you for an impure purpose? If so, how?

_____

_____

_____

Note the next verse: "It is always good to be made much of for a good purpose" (ESV). Some occasions call for making much of one another: birthdays, anniversaries, long-term goals met, test scores improved, rounds of chemotherapy completed, doors of opportunity opened and so forth. But human nature unabated is self-serving and we often make much of others so they will make much of us. Inordinate attention is agenda-driven. In these verses we get a glimpse into the hearts of Paul's rivals: they craved the attention Paul had gotten. Don't think jealousy can't drive human doctrines.

The remainder of our lesson will surround one of the most eye-widening segments in Galatians: the unfiltered, God-breathed maternal imagery Paul uses in verses 19–20.

List every peculiarity and unexpected twist or turn in Paul's metaphor.

_____

_____

_____

_____

Fittingly, Paul viewed his role toward the churches he'd founded and the people he'd mentored as not only pastoral but parental.

Record how he distinguishes his relationship to believers in Corinth and in Thessalonica.

1 Corinthians 4:14–15

_____

_____

_____

_____

> Don't think jealousy can't drive human doctrines.

1 Thessalonians 2:11–12

_____

_____

_____

_____

We could find other verses where Paul expresses himself similarly. For a male leader in a community to extend his role beyond the strictly professional to the paternal is heartwarming and significant but not uncommon. What Paul does in Galatians 4, however, is extraordinary by any measure and it's not the only time he uses the imagery.

Back up a few sentences in 1 Thessalonians 2 and read verses 7–8. How does Paul describe the approach Silvanus, Timothy and he took in regard to the believers in Thessalonica?

_____

_____

_____

_____

_____

Paul uses the metaphor correspondingly in 1 Corinthians 3:1-2, chiding the church for having remained spiritual infants whom he still fed milk when, by then, they should have been ready to eat solids. That Paul would characterize his parental role in the churches as paternal sometimes and as maternal other times is refreshing. Though the roles are equally important, they are not identical, nor does Paul use them interchangeably.

New Testament scholar Beverly Roberts Gaventa's depth of research on Paul's use of maternal metaphors is unsurpassed. She draws the following distinction:

> Maternal imagery appears in contexts referring to the ongoing nature of the relationship between Paul and the congregations he founded; paternal imagery, by contrast, regularly refers to the initial stage of Christian preaching and conversion.[4]

[4] Beverly Roberts Gaventa, _Our Mother Saint Paul_ (Louisville: Westminster John Knox, 2007), 6.

The one exception to this distinction occurs in 1 Thessalonians 2:11–12. In these verses, the nuances of spiritual parenting bear striking resemblance to the One whose image Paul bore. God uses maternal metaphors to describe His tender love and care for His people in numerous Scriptures including Deuteronomy 32:11–12, 18; Hosea 11:3–4; Isaiah 42:14 and 66:13. Jesus does something similar in Matthew 23:37.

Pick one of the aforementioned verses and describe the maternal aspect.

_____

_____

_____

_____

Numbers 11:12 is particularly delightful unless you're Moses. How did he apparently feel about having to mother the Israelites?

_____

_____

_____

As it turns out, a godly leader serving in a parental role that bears both paternal and maternal aspects isn't all that peculiar. Galatians 4:18–20, on the other hand, is brilliantly peculiar. Remember when I said on Day One that, if we're going to study the metaphors of Paul, we better be students on the move? The first unexpected feature of a Pauline metaphor, of course, is Paul casting himself as a mother. But now that we've seen biblical precedent, it seems less unusual. The second feature is Paul likening himself to a woman in excruciating labor. He has suffered many things but nine centimeters is not among them. Still, we can deeply appreciate the parallel because we've each had relationships almost as painful as childbirth.

The third metaphorical feature is where the real anomalies begin. In the metaphor, Paul not only depicts himself as a woman in labor but as a mother giving birth to the Galatians a *second time*. Galatians 4:19 (ESV) reads, "my little children, for whom I am again in the anguish of childbirth."

My firstborn required 14 stitches to birth. I'm unspeakably thankful to have her, but I don't want to birth her again. Yet even this anomaly—the idea of birthing the same person or people again—does not prepare us for what comes next in Paul's metaphor. Just when we expect Paul to birth the Galatians a second time then proceed to raise them up in the likeness of Christ, we are redirected.

The image before us is Paul remaining in labor—not until the Galatians are fully formed in him but until Christ is fully formed in the Galatians.

Don't you love studying the Bible? What does Paul have in mind by the words "until Christ is formed in you"? Each time I recite the passage, another segment written by Paul pops in my mind. I may be drawing a connection where one doesn't exist, but I'll offer it as food for thought.

> And [Jesus] gave the apostles, the prophets, the evangelists,
> the shepherds and teachers,[12] to equip the saints for the work
> of ministry, for building up the body of Christ,[13] until we all attain
> to the unity of the faith and of the knowledge of the Son of God,
> to mature manhood, to the measure of the stature of the fullness
> of Christ,[14] so that we may no longer be children . . .[15] Rather . . . we
> are to grow up in every way into him who is the head, into Christ.
>
> **Ephesians 4:11–13, 14a, 15 ESV**

Meditate on the words "until we all attain . . . to mature manhood, to the measure of the stature of the fullness of Christ." The context is *growing up* "in every way into him who is the head, into Christ." The imagery in Ephesians is a reversal of what we've read in Galatians, but I think they convey a similar idea. If we were to see the segment in Ephesians in pictures only, we'd imagine Jesus standing tall before us in His full stature and ourselves as communities of faith, growing in Him from infancy and toddlerhood into childhood, adolescence and adulthood until we're standing straight up into the full measure of His stature. Simply put, our objective on this side of eternity is to become grownups in Christ until the body is fully formed under the Head.

Take this same idea back to Galatians 4. Paul is in the throes of labor, gestating the Galatians *within him* until they've allowed the full measure of formation in Christ to grow *within them.* Side by side, the passages in Galatians and Ephesians convey the image of Christ fully formed in us (Galatians) and us being fully formed in Christ (Ephesians). The concept is mysterious but consistent throughout the New Testament: we are in Christ and Christ is in us.

If we find ourselves yearning for simpler images, perhaps we can understand the Galatians' predicament. Pictures are easier to define when they are colored within the lines. But, when the Word became flesh and dwelt among us, was crucified for our sins, died and was buried and, on the third day, rose again, all those tidy lines broke wide open. A whole new order burst from the seams like new wine from old wineskins. And everything in reach splashed red.

We are in Christ and Christ is in us.

THE CHILDREN ZONE

day four

The Jerusalem Above is Free

Read, write and mark Galatians 4:21–27.

_____

_____

_____

_____

_____

_____

_____

_____

_____

_____

_____

_____

_____

_____

_____

Today's passage has eluded me for my entire Scripture-reading life. It's not one you can breeze by and pick up the gist. A lot of great tools exist to help us study the Bible, but time and attentiveness will always be most important. Today, I am filled with thanks for the pure time to tarry in these verses alongside each of you. May God give us understanding and may we be faithful with our attention. Thank you for being here in this moment.

Let's begin already. In our first verse, Paul poses a question to a certain group of people. How does he describe these people, according to verse 21?

_____

_____

The agitators are not the only threat to Paul. At least some of the Galatians _want_ to take on the law or, at least, significant parts of the law. Persuasion is falling upon eager ears. Paul is working against both the agitators' persuasion and the actual desires of some of his people.

What question does Paul ask in verse 21?

_____

_____

_____

Twice in our passage, Paul uses the phrase "for it is written" (γέγραπται γὰρ). Please browse through our passage again and identify the two verses where he uses this formula:

_____

Compare and contrast how Paul uses "for it is written" in v.22 with the way he uses it in v.27: (Hint: what is the difference between the content he introduces in each of these verses?)

_____

_____

_____

_____

_____

_____

_____

Paul typically uses "for it is written" to introduce an Old Testament quotation. We see him do this in verse 27 where he introduces a near word-for-word quotation from Isaiah. But, quite distinctly, in verse 22 he introduces a summary of a narrative from Genesis.[1]

This isn't the first Genesis narrative we've studied that provided the basis of Paul's argumentation in Galatians. Think back to Galatians 3:7–4:7 and mark the other one we have already studied at length:

☐ Abel   ☐ Aaron   ☐ Abraham   ☐ Joseph

Earlier in 3:7–4:7, as Doug Moo puts it, Paul was concerned with "paternity."[2] Now, in our present verses, he is concerned with "maternity."[3] The narrative Paul retells here is broadly taken from Genesis 16–21 and has to do with Abraham's two sons, Ishmael and Isaac, by Hagar and Sarah.

Please take a few minutes to read our passage (Galatians 4:21–27) once more. List every detail in the text associated with each of the two sons of Abraham. (The list won't be exactly equal.) I have filled out one detail for you.

ABRAHAM'S TWO SONS	
Ishmael—Genesis 16:15	**Isaac**—Genesis 21:2
Born by a slave (Hagar)	Born by a free woman (Sarah)

[1] Douglas J. Moo, *Galatians,* Baker Exegetical Commentary on the New Testament (Grand Rapids, MI: Baker Academic, 2013), 297–298.

[2] Douglas J. Moo, *Galatians,* 298.

[3] Ibid.

Paul says the son (Ishmael, alluded to but not named) born by the slave-woman, Hagar, was born as a result of "the flesh," while Isaac (named once in v.28) was born by the free-woman (Sarah, alluded to but not named) "through promise."

What does it mean, that Ishmael was born "by the flesh" and Isaac "through promise"? Take a few minutes to read all of Genesis 16:1–15. It's crucial. I know this may seem extreme but check the box when you're done reading:

☐ Yes, I read Genesis 16:1–15.

> The LORD came to Sarah as he had said, and the LORD did for Sarah what he had promised.
>
> Genesis 21:1

Sarai (renamed Sarah a chapter later by God) owned an Egyptian slave, Hagar. Although God had promised Abram (renamed Abraham a chapter later by God) that He would make him into a great nation, Sarai still had not borne a child. Sarai, panicking and seeking to resolve the matter on her own terms, builds a family by force through Hagar (16:2). This is every bit the nightmare that you suspect. We know this wasn't consensual sex because Hagar was a slave and because, when Hagar realized she was pregnant, she had nothing but contempt for Sarai (16:4). Further, Sarai says: "I put my slave in your arms" (16:5). The whole thing was a mess. For Paul to conclude Ishmael was conceived "by the flesh" is a real understatement!

Note that the text explicitly records Abraham having sex with Hagar in 16:4. Now, look at something interesting with me. In Genesis 18, the LORD visits near Abraham and Sarah's tent to inform Abraham that Sarah will have a son. Abraham is a hundred years old and Sarah herself is ninety, far past the childbearing age.

Now, you'll spend a lot more time in Genesis 21 tomorrow with Mom, but, for now, read and write out Genesis 21:1–3:

_____

_____

_____

_____

_____

"The LORD came to Sarah . . . the LORD did for Sarah what he had promised. Sarah became pregnant . . . " (21:1–2a).

No mention at all of Abraham and Sarah having sex. Remarkable! I'm certainly not implying Abraham and Sarah didn't have sex, by the way, but only that the narrator of Genesis places the emphasis on the miraculous element of the conception.

No wonder Paul chose this text. The LORD alone was responsible for Isaac's birth; the LORD alone was fulfilling his promise, despite all that had gone on "in the flesh," if you will. In fact, Abraham had wished that the LORD would simply accept Ishmael for the promised covenant line. But the LORD, based on the promise formerly made, refused, even though He vowed to bless Ishmael (Gen 17:15–22).

In verse 24, Paul plainly tells us that the things he is speaking of are an allegory (the CSB and NIV render ἀλληγορέω with the term "figuratively" and the NLT with "an illustration" but there is good reason to consider what Paul is doing here as allegorical interpretation).[4] Paul will now add to the Genesis framing some corresponding realities in his own time. He says the two women, Hagar and Sarah, are two covenants. Hagar is the covenant from Mount Sinai (made with Moses), bearing children into slavery. A surprising claim, since it would have been standard for Jews to suppose exactly the reverse: Ishmael as representing Gentiles and Isaac as representing Jews.[5]

Before going further, I want to acknowledge something that might feel uncomfortable for some of you. In Galatians, Paul asks his readers to identify with Sarah, who is, at best, unlikable in the scenes from Genesis 16. At worst, she's an abusive slave-master (see Gen 16:6b). It's important to understand that Paul asks us to identify with Sarah because of what she symbolizes and because of God's faithfulness to His promise, not because of her high moral virtue.

> Paul asks us to identify with Sarah because of what she symbolizes and because of God's faithfulness to His promise, not because of her high moral virtue.

As Nyasha Junior puts it in her excellent book *Reimagining Hagar*: "In Galatians, the two women and the details of their relationship with each other and with Abraham fade into the background . . . He is not interested in the women as multi-faceted characters but as symbols of opposing covenants."[6] It's also important to know that some Christians through the ages, like John Chrysostom in the fourth century, have seen in Hagar "a model of faithfulness in affliction."[7] While I don't want to get too sidetracked since our primary aim is to understand Galatians, I do want us to note that Galatians is not the only word on Hagar in the canon. Hagar's story with God should be taken seriously and on its own terms.

---

[4] See the discussion in Richard N. Longenecker, *Galatians*, Word Biblical Commentary Vol. 41 (Grand Rapids: Zondervan, 1990), 209–210.

[5] For example, the early Jewish text *Jubilees* 16:17–18.

[6] Nyasha Junior, *Reimagining Hagar: Blackness and Bible* (Oxford: Oxford University Press, 2019), 27.

[7] Andrea D. Saner, "Of Bottles and Wells: Hagar's Christian Legacy" in *Journal of Theological Interpretation* 11.2 (2017): 199–215.

Did you notice that Paul never names the second covenant? Richard B. Hays in *Echoes of Scripture in the Letters of Paul* gives good advice for how to think about it:

> The "two covenants" of Gal 4:24 are not the old covenant at Sinai and the new covenant in Christ. Rather, the contrast is drawn between the old covenant at Sinai and the older covenant with Abraham, which turns out in Paul's rereading to find its true meaning in Christ. In Paul's scheme, the freedom and inheritance rights of the Gentile Christian communities are not novelties but older truths that were always implicit in Isaac, in the promise to Abraham . . .[8]

Personally, I don't have a problem relating the second covenant with the "new covenant," so long as this new thing in Jesus is linked back to the ancient Abrahamic promise.

Paul says that Hagar "represents Mount Sinai in Arabia and corresponds to the present Jerusalem" (v.25). What role has Jerusalem played so far in Galatians? (Hint: glance over 1:13–2:10.)

_____

_____

What do you think Paul means in 4:25 by the "present Jerusalem"?

_____

_____

"Present Jerusalem" could refer generally to the Judaism of Paul's time, "a Judaism that continues to rely on the law and ignore or not give adequate place to Christ."[9] It could also include a more specific reference to the agitators, who are insisting on too prominent a role for the Mosaic Law in this Gentile Christian community. Either way, Paul associates the Sinai covenant and, hence, the Mosaic Law and "everything it entailed: circumcision, Sabbath observance, and animal sacrifices" with Hagar.[10] If we consider what L. Ann Jervis says that "for Jews the word covenant was almost synonymous with circumcision," Paul's argument for a covenant that doesn't require circumcision is nothing short of audacious.[11]

[8] Richard Hays, *Echoes of Scripture in the Letters of Paul* (New Haven: Yale University Press, 1989), 114–115.

[9] Douglas J. Moo, *Galatians*, 304.

[10] Brant Pitre, Michael Barber, and John A. Kincaid, *Paul, A New Covenant Jew: Rethinking Pauline Theology* (Grand Rapids, MI: Eerdmans, 2019), 50.

[11] L. Ann Jervis, *Galatians*, Understanding the Bible Commentary Series (Grand Rapids, MI: Baker Books, 1999), 124.

Let's look at our final two verses: 26-27.

"But the Jerusalem above is free, and she is our mother."

Stick with me. Hagar and Sarah are two Jerusalems: one is "present" and one is "above." Paul surely has in mind a heavenly Jerusalem here, not unlike the one in Revelation: *"He then carried me away in the Spirit to a great, high mountain and showed me the holy city, Jerusalem, coming down out of heaven from God, arrayed with God's glory"* (Rev 21:10-11a). Paul urges his Galatians to identify with Sarah's covenant, linked to the heavenly Jerusalem, above and free. In *Paul, A New Covenant Jew: Rethinking Pauline Theology*, the three authors provide a summary of the implications of our text for thinking about Paul's relationship to Judaism:

> Paul, precisely as a Jew, understands himself and his audience to be children of the heavenly—not the earthly Jerusalem. As Paul puts it elsewhere, their "citizenship is in heaven." Because of this they are no longer "under the law." The reason Paul can both praise the torah as being given by God and also declare that Christ will be of "no advantage" to those who seek circumcision is that to do so is to abandon the freedom of the new covenant Jerusalem in heaven for the slavery of the old covenant Jerusalem on earth.[12]

Verse 27 brings us to the end of our lesson with a quotation from Isaiah 54:1, a prophetic passage that speaks of Israel's future restoration after exile. In what seems at first to be a real exegetical leap, Paul casts Sarah as the "childless woman" and Hagar as "the woman who has a husband." The key to understanding Paul's move is to recall that in Genesis 16:3, the text, rather surprisingly, explicitly refers to Hagar as Abraham's wife, even though she remains subservient to Abraham and Sarah in the subsequent narratives.[13] Hagar was the only one of the two women who could conceive a son, in the flesh.

Turns out, these days, that most things are more complex than we once believed. Yet the truth remains—nothing at all is impossible with this God who has encountered us. Burst into song, children of childless Sarah, for your God brings abundance from desolation. Rejoice over the God in whom Abraham, your ancestor in the spirit, first believed: "the God who gives life to the dead and calls things into existence that do not exist" (Rom 4:17b).

> Burst into song, children of childless Sarah, for your God brings abundance from desolation.

[12] Pitre, Barber, and Kincaid, *Paul, A New Covenant Jew: Rethinking Pauline Theology*, 50.
[13] Douglas J. Moo, *Galatians*, 306-307.

NOTES

THE CHILDREN ZONE

day five

Children of Promise

Read, write and mark Galatians 4:28–31.

_____

_____

_____

_____

_____

_____

_____

_____

Have you ever felt like something was wrong with your bloodline? Like your DNA is defective? Like your family has malfunctioned for so many generations that defeat was written into your destiny before you took your first breath? I have.

I'm awed by those who come from a stable, godly heritage where people were safe and what they seemed; where religion wasn't a smoke screen; where kids got to be kids because adults acted like adults; where good decisions could not be guaranteed but the tools to make them were deliberately passed down. People like my husband, Keith, and me seem hewn from a different rock. Dug from a different quarry. God's grace nevertheless abounds. To our relief, our daughters exceeded us in character and consistency in young adulthood and did not fall into some of our patterns. But, they won't mind me saying that, for each of us, life is a daily battle. We work hard to make it.

These thoughts have a place as we begin today's lesson. We're wise to examine our hearts to discover what we believe to be our most consequential present reality: genetics, generational influence or the gospel of Jesus.

Our text unfolds with these words: "Now you too, brothers and sisters,

like _____, are children of _____."

(Fill in the blanks according to Gal 4:28.)

> Now you too,
> brothers and sisters,
> like Isaac, are
> children of promise.
>
> Galatians 4:28

Today's Scripture segment could serve as *Exhibit A* for how heavily interpretation depends upon context. Based on Galatians 4:28–31 alone, we could wrongly assume the two categories represented by Hagar and Sarah are, respectively, persecutors and the persecuted or, worse yet, Jews and Gentiles. The categories Paul presents in his allegory, simply put, are these:

1. the enslaved (symbolized by Hagar)

2. the free (symbolized by Sarah)

Peruse Galatians 4:21–5:1 carefully, watching for every occurrence of the word "free" or "freedom." The 12 verses will include the segment in your previous lesson with Melissa, today's segment and one of the verses from your next segment in Week Five on Day One. List every person or place Paul associates with freedom.

_____

_____

_____

_____

In the Galatians allegory, Ishmael, Abraham's son by Hagar, represents those who are enslaved by the elementary principles of the world. Isaac, on the other hand, represents those who abide in the God-given freedom of Christ's gospel rather than by "everything written in the book of the law" (Gal 3:10). As we've said often and at Paul's behest, Galatian believers were included among the children of "promise" not as an afterthought but as part of the plan from the very start when God promised Abraham "all the nations will be blessed through you" (3:8).

In the Galatians' case, those categorized under Hagar are attempting to influence Gentile Christians to adhere to the Law of Moses but, keep in mind, it could have been any number of things. Worldly wisdom and impressive speech posed greater risks to freedom for believers in Corinth. Gnosticism sought to take new converts captive in Colossae. Deserting sound faith and being sucked into controversies were prominent captors in Second Timothy. Anything out of step with the truth of the gospel (2:14) puts freedom at risk. The "son of the slave" in the Galatians 4 allegory corresponds with those "who are troubling you and want to distort the gospel of Christ" in Galatians 1:7 as well as those in Galatians 2:4 who try to drag back into slavery believers who have been freed in Christ.

The original story where the "slave woman and her son" were "cast out" is essential to our lesson today. Read Genesis 21:1–21.

Which verse in Genesis 21 does Paul quote in Galatians 4:30?

_____

Whose words were they? _____

To what does Paul attribute those words in Galatians 4:30?

_____

What is your gut-level reaction to the story told in Genesis 21:1–21?

_____

_____

_____

If the scene in the Wilderness of Beer-sheba breaks your heart as it does mine, do you find any consolation in it? If so, what?

_____

_____

_____

The Genesis narrative supplies only one catalyst for Sarah's abrupt insistence on Hagar and Ishmael's exit. According to Genesis 21:9, what had Ishmael done?

_____

_____

The ESV reads "laughing." The NIV and CSB use "mocking." The Hebrew performs a fascinating play on words. "The Piel participle used here is from the same root as the name 'Isaac.'"[1] Ishmael, you might say, is isaac-ing at Isaac.

I have to work hard not to find Sarah uncharitable and unfair in Genesis 21 even with the following explanation. At the same time, we can all testify from personal experience that laughing is not always an expression of lightheartedness or good will.

> In the Piel stem the verb means "to jest; to make sport of; to play with," not simply "to laugh," which is the meaning of the verb in the Qal stem. What exactly Ishmael was doing is not clear. Interpreters have generally concluded that the boy was either (1) mocking Isaac (cf. NASB, NIV, NLT) or (2) merely playing with Isaac as if on equal footing (cf. NAB, NRSV). In either case Sarah saw it as a threat. The same participial form was used in Gen 19:14 . . .[2]

Turn back a page or two to Genesis 19:14. The word will be translated as "joking" or "jesting" or something similar. Who and what does it involve?

_____

_____

_____

_____

The Hebrew word also occurs in Genesis 39:14, 17–18 when Joseph ran from Potiphar's wife after she attempted to seduce him. To revise the scene as though Joseph was a predator, she claimed, "the Hebrew slave you brought to us came _to make a fool of me_" (emphasis mine). These additional uses of the word translated "laughing," "mocking" or "playing" in Genesis 21:9 don't tell us all we want to know but they do offer alternative ways to imagine the scene. Perhaps Sarah thought Ishmael didn't take Isaac's position as Abraham's heir seriously and she feared that Ishmael would end up trying to make a fool of her son. Whatever the reason, Sarah perceived Ishmael as a threat to Isaac. I'm not sure a mother can always explain to an observer's satisfaction why she deems someone a threat to her child's wellbeing.

Scripture only offers us bits and pieces into what was surely a most complicated day-in/day-out coexistence between Sarah, Hagar and Ishmael,

[1] W. Hall Harris, ed. _The NET Bible Notes._ 1st ed. (Richardson: Biblical Studies Press, 2005).
[2] W. Hall Harris, ed. _The NET Bible Notes._ 1st ed.

who was a teenager by that time, on the threshold of manhood. His beard was probably just beginning to come in. This was no longer a toddler playing with toys. This was the boy who had received the covenantal sign of circumcision on the same day under the same sun as his father, Abraham (Gen 17:26). Their wound was their bond. The blood dripping from that blade carried her husband's DNA. Sarah also knew Abraham loved Ishmael and wanted him there. This, perhaps above all things, posed the largest threat to her.

Rivals and rivalries are in the constant foreground in Paul's letter to the Galatians. As Hagar was a rival to Sarah and as Ishmael was a rival to Isaac, each threatening the inheritance, so also the troublemakers in Galatians were rivals to Paul, threatening the inheritance.

Galatians 4:29 leaves us with a glaring question. How did Ishmael "persecute" Isaac *and* in such a way to correlate to the persecution of Paul and the Galatians? Any thoughts?

_____

_____

_____

_____

Several possibilities are plausible:

1. Ishmael persecuted Isaac in ways not communicated in the narrative. Remember, everything God tells us is true but it is also true that God does not tell us everything.

2. Ishmael's descendants persecuted Isaac's descendants.

Our confidence can come from this: Paul knew of what he spoke. No other references he made to persecutions in his writings are considered hyperbole or overstatement. He was relentlessly dogged throughout much of his ministry. His persecutors at times were Jewish, at other times Jewish Christians and, still other times, Gentile non-Christians. It would be Rome who'd finally take his head, not Jerusalem.

The fourth chapter of Galatians concludes with these words: "Therefore, brothers and sisters, we are not children of a slave but of the free woman" (4:31). The word "we" is key. It locks out all notions that God switched the Jews for the Gentiles in the lineage of faith. "We" refers to Paul, a Jewish Christian, and the Galatians who were primarily Gentile Christians. Even so, Paul wraps up his allegory audaciously, clearly and shockingly in terms of the parties involved in the Galatian troubles. He files the Law-observant agitators under Hagar and Ishmael and places the Gentile believers in Galatia squarely under Sarah as descendants of Abraham. As Clark H. Pinnock puts it, "The religion of promise and the religion of works cannot co-exist. God will not divide His blessing between them."[3]

You see, tracing family lines and bloodlines can get a little disorienting. Who are we, really? Whose blood runs through our veins? How much will history determine our destiny? Where do we come from and where are we going? Is there really any such thing as starting over? Looming over all our existential questions sits the eternal, unshakable throne of the One who *is* and *was* and *is to come*. He has never made a promise He won't keep; therefore, all that we who pursue Him perceive as disorientation is, in fact, *reorientation*.

We'll take a reorienting glance at Isaiah 51:1–4 to conclude today's lesson. Isn't it beautiful? What part of it do you like best?

_____

_____

_____

_____

_____

> He has never made a promise He won't keep.

Take note of the portion that says, "Look to the rock from which you were cut, and to the quarry from which you were dug. Look to Abraham your father." You may feel as I have: hewn from a different rock than those with a godly heritage who seem so often to get things right. But you're not. As it turns out, we of faith are all dug from the same quarry, chips off the same old block. We were all preplanned as distinct parts of the same messy, miraculous line. We're a mixed bag and always were. Ours are humble beginnings in Sarah and Abraham. They, too, had decidedly malfunctioned. And yet, they kept believing God. Same with Isaac. Same with Jacob. Same with Moses. Same with David. Same with Peter. Same with Paul.

We are not, some, the blemished, and, some, the blessed. We're all blemished and all blessed. We are people of faith. Children of the free woman. Heirs of the promises. Covenant sons and daughters. Saved by the Son of God.

[3] Clark H. Pinnock, *Truth on Fire: The Message of Galatians* (Eugene, OR: Wipf and Stock, 1998), 48.

SPIRIT

zone five

SPIRIT

GALATIANS 5

You who are trying to be justified by the law are alienated from Christ; you have fallen from grace. For we eagerly await through the Spirit, by faith, the hope of righteousness. For in Christ Jesus neither circumcision nor uncircumcision accomplishes anything; what matters is faith working through love.

Galatians 5:4–6

VIDEO GUIDE

THE SPIRIT ZONE

Introduction: Today we set our sights on Galatians 5, the chapter for which the letter is perhaps most well known and loved.

Read Galatians 3:1–3; 5:13–26.

The divergence Galatians demonstrates between living by the Spirit and living by the law is the furthest thing from subtle. A few differences:

1. There's no slipping into _____ **by simply sticking to** _____.

Recall Galatians 3:10 ESV.

> "For all who rely on works of the law are under a curse; for it is written, 'Cursed be everyone who does not _____ by all _____ written in the Book of the _____, and do them.'"

Set it beside Christ's words in John 15:9. _____ in my love (John 15:4).

In reference to Galatians 5:13–14, David A. deSilva offers this contrast:

> It might seem strange that Paul would refer positively to a commandment of Torah in Galatians, having gone to such pains to demonstrate that Torah had a limited role for a limited time in God's purposes for God's people . . . Paul observes an important distinction in this regard: Torah is not something to be "done" by _____ (contrast Gal 5:3), but _____ is "fulfilled" by Christians.[1]

2. What the Law could only _____ **us to do, the Spirit can** _____
us to do.

Compare Colossians 2:16–23.

3. The Spirit doesn't just _____ **what we do. He changes who** _____
(1 Corinthians 5:7).

[1] David A. deSilva, *The Letter to the Galatians,* The New International Commentary on the New Testament (Grand Rapids, MI: Eerdmans, 2018), 450.

SPIRIT

WEEK FIVE

THE SPIRIT ZONE

day one

Stand Firm Then

Read, write and mark Galatians 5:1–6.

_____

_____

_____

_____

_____

_____

_____

_____

_____

_____

How a single verse of Scripture can redirect a whole life is a divine mystery. Galatians 5:1 was such a verse for me. I was in my late thirties, many years into ministry. I'd written several well-received Bible studies and was thoroughly immersed in church culture. In the psalmist's words, the "ropes of Sheol" had also entangled me no few times in my life and I was presently choking.

I'd known the kindness of the Lord. I'd sensed His nearness innumerable times. Scripture was alive to me and serving deeply satisfied me. I had people in my life whom I loved, and they loved me. But I could never shake the feeling of tangling with a gorilla of some sort that was trying to tear me limb from limb. I'd go back and forth between thinking the gorilla was a predator in my life, the devil himself or the troubled girl in my mirror. A Frankensteinian fusion of all three, I lost as many battles to it as I won.

My path-altering moment in Galatians 5:1 broke the exegetical rules. I couldn't have told you the context. I didn't know a single technical difference between a Galatian and an Ephesian. My aim was to look up the fruit of the Spirit in v.22. I ran into v.1 accidentally.

It is for freedom that Christ has set us free. (NIV)

The only explanation for just the right verse at just the right time is God's sovereignty. To wrap language around the Spirit's conviction—the verse hit me as if Jesus were saying these words:

> I gave my life for more than this. I set you free so that you could actually be free, not so you could live your whole life in varying forms of bondage.

I had the journey of my life ahead. It would include some of the hardest days I'd face and, doubtlessly, the fiercest battles. Gorillas don't like to let go. My best days were also ahead, however, and the effects of the journey that began with Galatians 5:1 continue to accompany me even now. My life is not easy. I still have spiritual warfare. I win battles and lose battles and obstacles loom large, but the oxygen supply to the gorilla that had chased me for a lifetime got all but choked off. My hope is that Galatians 5:1 may be the right verse at the right time for someone today just like it was for me all those years ago.

Every commentary I picked up gave prominence to Galatians 5:1. J. M. Boice writes, "Paul interjects a verse that is at once a summary of all that has gone before and a transition to what follows. It is, in fact, the key verse of the entire Epistle."[1] Scot McKnight spotlights 5:1 as Paul's thesis in Galatians.[2] In his comments regarding the human dimensions of freedom in Christ, McKnight makes this observation:

> [W]e need to observe in Paul that "being free" is personal and existential

The only explanation for just the right verse at just the right time is God's sovereignty.

[1] James Montgomery Boice, "Galatians," in *The Expositor's Bible Commentary* (Grand Rapids, MI: Zondervan, 1976), 486. Copyright © 1972 by James Montgomery Boice. Used by permission of Zondervan. www.zondervan.com

[2] Scot McKnight, *Galatians*, NIV Application Commentary (Grand Rapids, MI: Zondervan, 1995), 243. Copyright © 1995 by Scot McKnight. Used by permission of Zondervan. www.zondervan.com

in the sense of being liberated to be what God wants us to be and to do what God wants us to do . . . In general, we might say that "being free" is the liberation of a person's spirit from everything that shackles it to sin and ugliness; "being free" is the liberation of a person's spirit to do what God wants, to be what God wants, and to enjoy the life God gives us on this earth.[3]

Whatever obstructs our freedom in Christ qualifies as a yoke of bondage. These verses help shape an understanding of emancipation in the life of faith.

Record all insights into the antitheses of slavery and liberty.

John 8:30–31, 36

_____

_____

Romans 6:12

_____

2 Corinthians 3:17

_____

First Corinthians 6:12 is an important go-to verse for freedom. Paul writes,

"Everything is permissible for me," but not everything is beneficial.
"Everything is permissible for me," but I will not be mastered by anything.

Paul brilliantly quotes a common saying of the day to the Corinthians in order to add a caveat: just because one can doesn't mean one should. For example, a loved one has been battered and bruised by a yoke of severe alcoholism throughout her adult life. As she enters her sixth year of sobriety, she knows that, according to the Bible, having a glass of wine is not a sin but, for her, it is a nod to madness. Wine is permissible but, for her, it is not beneficial.

Once anything has held habitual mastery over us, a boundary is a crucial means to liberty. In order to flourish in freedom, we may have to step away from a friendship, relationship, a particular church or circle of people resistant enough to wholeness that, although our involvement may be biblically "permissible," for us it is not beneficial.

[3] McKnight, *Galatians*, 245.

> Whatever obstructs our freedom in Christ qualifies as a yoke of bondage.

Have you experienced this dynamic? If so, expound.

_____

_____

_____

In Galatians 5:1b, Paul writes, "Don't submit _____ to a yoke of slavery." Write in the missing word in the blank.

We can, unfortunately, go back under the same old yokes we once escaped. Or, we could simply trade the old yokes for new ones. For these reasons, freedom in Christ needs to be internalized, renewing our minds and reshaping our understandings, and not just externalized through behavior modification. If we've never let the Holy Spirit tend to our emptiness, for example, we will be subject to one addiction after another trying to fill the chasm. If we don't know the grace of God, our value to Him and how loved we are by Him, we will live at the fractured mercy of our vulnerabilities, setting ourselves up over and over to be mistreated or to mistreat.

Let's move forward now to Galatians 5:2–4. How does the attempt to be justified by works of the law profoundly underestimate Christ's work on the cross?

_____

_____

Let the implications of Galatians 5:3 sink into your mind. "I testify to every man who gets himself circumcised that he is obligated to do the entire law." Try to fathom turning to a system requiring temple sacrifices and fellowship offerings after Jesus gave his life on the cross.

If it were us, where would we draw the line? If one law is good (circumcision in this case), wouldn't two be better? And, if abiding by two works of the law would earn us a more righteous standing before God, what divine favor might come with three? What kind of trap could you imagine yourself getting into?

_____

_____

Two of the most unsettling prospects in Paul's writings are found in Galatians 5:4: "you are severed from Christ" (ESV) and "you have fallen away from grace" (ESV). Paul intends these statements to be scorching hot—putting out the fire would be a mistake, but so would assigning faulty meaning to Paul's words. Paul is not saying that any man who gets circumcised is cut off from Christ. He is saying that any man who gets circumcised *in order to be justified* is severed from Christ and has fallen away from grace.

Though the prospects in Galatians 5:4 are jolting, they are completely consistent with the apostle's arguments from the beginning. The issue is what an individual's faith rests upon for righteous standing before God resulting in eternal salvation.

For many who are in Christ, Galatians 5:4 begs the million-dollar question: Can we lose our salvation? How would you answer the question?

_____

_____

Based on numerous passages, I believe the answer is, emphatically, no. If we did nothing to earn salvation, what can we do to lose it? In John 10:28, Jesus claims that those to whom He gives eternal life can never be snatched out of his hand. He did indeed say in Matthew 24:10 that "many will fall away" but "falling away" seems to reference those who crowded around Him, not those who were "in Him." We can be "around Christ" in worship and prayer gatherings, church services, Bible studies and Christian events for a lifetime and not be "in Christ."

I ordinarily lean on the words of the apostle John in 1 John 2:19 for the best way to explain how people who seemed to have walked with Christ can then walk away. Restate John's explanation in your own words.

_____

_____

Several passages in the New Testament stop me short of smugness in my belief that, once gained, salvation can't be lost. I appreciate Scot McKnight sharing his view in this regard:

> I believe the overall teaching of the New Testament assumes that Christians will persevere; there are numerous utterances of the assurance that they can have of their final destiny. But I am also of the view that there are enough "terrifying" passages to make one think apostasy is a real possibility and that in the case of apostasy one can "forfeit one's salvation." I wish, however, to make a theological and a pastoral remark. Theologically, I believe the only sin that can sever a Christian's relationship

to God through Christ is the sin of apostasy. Apostasy is a violent act on the part of a fading Christian who denounces his or her relationship to Christ and refuses to submit to God's will. Such an act is not haphazard or unconscious; it is intentional and known, and the one who makes such a decision vaunts in it. Pastorally speaking, I am fully persuaded that the person who wonders if he or she has committed this sin has not committed it. The one who has apostatized knows it and proudly glories in it.[4]

Take a fresh look at Galatians 5:5.

If we've already been declared righteous by Christ, why would Paul say we "eagerly await . . . the hope of righteousness"? His reference here is eschatological, looking toward the future when all righteousness will be wholly realized. The righteousness we've fully received will one day be fully revealed. In the Bible, hoping is not mere wishing. It is eager expectation, chin-up anticipation, that God will keep His word. This is the "now and not yet" we often hear referenced. That which is fully true of us will finally be fully seen by us.

These thoughts bring us to our final verse in today's segment and one of the most gorgeous summations of the gospel life offered in Scripture. According to Galatians 5:6, what matters?

_____

We are people who try to make sense of things on a planet where little seems to make sense. We take God at His word, knowing He promised to work everything together for good but we might go years, maybe the rest of our lives, without seeing irrefutable evidence of good coming from that horrible situation or soul-crushing loss. Circumstances can be confounding. Relationships can get so complicated and convoluted—we might never know this side of the veil what was actually going on. Each of us will have moments when much seems futile, when our time and effort appears utterly wasted on something that came to nothing. But I suspect, in all these things, God is trying to show us what matters.

One thing matters above all. It's what matters in your everyday walk, in your efforts, in your work, in your relationships, in your successes and failures, in your mishaps, in your wasted time and in your well-used time.

Faith working through love.

There's no outgrowing it or outdoing it. To this we give our lives.

> In the Bible, hoping is not mere wishing. It is eager expectation, chin-up anticipation, that God will keep His word.

[4] McKnight, _Galatians_, 250.

THE SPIRIT ZONE

day two

The Offense of the Cross

Read, write and mark Galatians 5:7–12.

_____

_____

_____

_____

_____

_____

_____

_____

_____

_____

I ran track back in middle school. Of the three sports I competed in, track was my least favorite by a long shot. I did it solely to be with my friends and to appease coaches. Along with some other field events, I ran the mile relay. I feel nervous just thinking about it: the sound of the whistles, the spiky shoes, the smell of the warm rubber track.

"You were running well."

What happened to break the Galatians' good stride? The NIV captures the picture Paul is drawing: *"You were running a good race. Who cut in on you to keep you from obeying the truth?"*

In my mind, when I read this verse, I am halfway through my lap on the mile relay. I'm one of the lead runners rounding the bend only to be suddenly tripped by another runner who has barreled through my lane on the final sprint.

Paul asks the Galatians a question he already knows the answer to: who cut you off? The answer is: the same ones who have "cast a spell" on the Galatians, according to 3:1. The guilty party is the group we have been calling "the agitators" (see also 5:12). We mentioned early on in this study that Paul never names "the agitators" explicitly.

The agitators' persuasion may sound compelling—it may even derive its key points from beloved Scriptures—but "the persuasion" is not in keeping with the miracle God has performed in Jesus, and right before the Galatians' eyes, no less (3:1). Because of Jesus, Gentiles can know and live in the nearness and favor of God without observing the signs that so importantly distinguished the people of Israel.

Paul wants the Galatians to know—without any doubt—that the persuasion tripping them up does not come from God, no matter how pious and reverent it may fall on their ears. We've seen a very similar phrase to "the one who calls you" already in Galatians. Look back at 1:6.

What is the exact phrase there?

_____

_____

_____

Describe the context that similar phrase falls in at 1:6.

_____

_____

"A little leaven leavens the whole batch of dough" (v.9). Paul uses "yeast as a symbol for evil's powerful corrupting capacity."[1] Perhaps this is a reference to the small number of agitators and how corrupting their presence is to the entirety of the Galatian church members, despite how few the agitators are

> You were running a good race. Who cut in on you to keep you from obeying the truth?
>
> Galatians 5:7 NIV

[1] L. Ann Jervis, *Galatians*, Understanding the Bible Commentary Series (Grand Rapids, MI: Baker Books, 1999), 135.

in number. Or, maybe Paul is implying that a seemingly small addition (like requiring circumcision for Gentile converts) to the good news they received contained in it an immense capacity to render their theology powerless. Whatever the precise nuance may be, this metaphor is strong.

Have you ever seen *a little leaven leaven a whole batch* in the way Paul is using the figure of speech? I know I have. It's breathtaking.

Take a minute to share an example from your own experience.

_____

_____

_____

Please read Gal 5:7–10 again in the CSB, noting any occurrence of "persuaded" or "persuasion":

> *You were running well. Who prevented you from being persuaded regarding the truth? This persuasion does not come from the one who calls you. A little leaven leavens the whole batch of dough. I myself am persuaded in the Lord you will not accept any other view. But whoever it is that is confusing you will pay the penalty.*

So, let's get this all straight. The Galatians are not "persuaded" about the true thing. The "persuasion" of the agitators is not from the God who called the Galatians in the first place. And, as for Paul, he is "persuaded" that the Galatians will view things from his perspective in the end. This is the first vaguely optimistic thing Paul has said about the Galatians. Mostly, he has been appalled and terrified at how dangerously close the Galatians are coming to tossing the glorious gospel of grace out the window.

The end of verse 10 may give us the idea that Paul is referring only to one person: *"But whoever it is that is confusing you will pay the penalty."*

But, likely there is a group of agitators, even if only a small one. Paul has already referred to "some who are troubling you and want to distort the gospel of Christ" in chapter one (v.7). And again, at the end of our passage today, he will say "those who are disturbing you" (v.12). It may be that one person in particular is most responsible or that Paul has a specific leader in mind. In any case, these references to the agitators invited Galatian readers to start looking around them and identifying specific people, even if Paul never named them.

Before we move to verse 11, it's worth noting that the Greek word rendered "penalty" is κρίμα which often simply means "judgment." I think "penalty" is too weak a word for what Paul is getting at here. Paul is plainly saying that whoever is responsible for the confusion and troublemaking among his churches will bear God's judgment, because they have persuasively pedaled a message that did not originate with God.

Galatians 5:11 is a fascinating verse. Please write out the rhetorical question Paul asks in this verse:

"Now brothers and sisters, if I still preach circumcision . . . "

_____

_____

_____

A lot is going on here! It seems the agitators had communicated to the Galatians that, while Paul had not advocated for the circumcision of Gentile men coming to know God in Galatia, he had done so in some other context. This discrepancy would have left some of the Galatians feeling confused or even misled.

Some interpreters have suggested that this is simply a reference back to Paul's life before Jesus as a Pharisee; perhaps he had advocated for circumcision of Gentile converts to Judaism back in the days when he was so zealous for his ancestors' traditions (1:13–14). I lean more toward thinking the agitators are using some piece of information from Paul's more recent Christian experience against him. A few scholars have even argued that, at some earlier point during his Gentile mission, Paul had still been pro-circumcision for Gentile converts but adapted his view over time. I think we find enough information in Acts to imagine how something like this could have happened.

Take a few minutes to read Acts 16:1–4. Describe Timothy's ancestry according to verse 1.

_____

_____

According to verse 3, why did Paul have Timothy circumcised?

_____

_____

NOW THAT FAITH HAS COME

Timothy represents a different situation than Titus. Remember Titus back in Galatians 2:3? Titus was a really important example for Paul. When he took Titus to Jerusalem before the leaders there, Titus "was not forced to be circumcised though he was a Greek" (ESV). But, Timothy was different. Timothy had a mixed ancestry (both his mom and grandmother were Jewish while his father was Greek) which would have made his situation all around more sensitive. So, while Paul was straightforward about not having a Greek circumcised, he took a different approach when a man who had a mixed ancestry was going on mission with him. These two examples show how Paul could exhibit sensitivity toward Gentiles when he felt he needed to and Jews when he felt he needed to.

All of this **brings** us to another relevant text. Please turn to 1 Corinthians 9:19–23 and fill in the appropriate blanks.

"Although I am free from all and not anyone's slave, I have made myself a slave to everyone, In order to _____ more people. To the Jews I became like a Jew, to win Jews; to those under the _____, like one under the law—though I myself am not under the _____—to win those under the law. To those who are without the law, like one without the law—though I am not without God's law but under the law of _____ —to win those without the _____. To the weak I became weak, in order to win the weak. I have become all things to all _____, so that I may by every _____ means save some. Now I do all this because of the gospel, so that I may share in the _____."

The approach Paul spells out here in 1 Corinthians 9 sheds some light on how he could find himself in a situation like the one he is in with the agitators. It's not too much of a jump to imagine that they might try to use one of Paul's more ambiguous choices in the past to their advantage. The rest of the verse contains Paul's defense against the agitators: if he was preaching circumcision for his Gentile converts, he wouldn't still be being persecuted. Why would his stance on circumcision provoke persecution? Craig Keener notes,

. . . nationalism was on the rise in Judea in the 40s and 50s of the first century, probably, generating an increase of nationalism among Jesus's Judean followers as well. When less nationalist Jewish believers welcomed Gentiles without circumcision, they appeared to water down a heritage for which Jews had suffered and died.[2]

[2] Craig S. Keener, *Galatians: A Commentary* (Grand Rapids, MI: Baker Academic, 2019), 470.

The cross's offense is that it puts to an end life as Paul had known it. His former value systems, epitomized by the Jewish law (and, in particular, circumcision in Galatians), no longer held the same meaning. Paul couldn't carry on like righteousness was derived from the law because, in that case, the crucifixion of Jesus would be rendered pointless. And the crucifixion of Jesus was the only thing Paul was willing to boast about anymore.

> The crucifixion of Jesus was the only thing Paul was willing to boast about anymore.

It's not every day that we get to study a passage ending with the biblical writer wishing his opponents would be castrated! But thanks to our delightful apostle, here we are. *"I wish those who are disturbing you might also let themselves be mutilated"* (v.13). L. Ann Jervis captures it this way, "Paul expresses the outrageous risk that the rival evangelists would let the knife slip on themselves. It is a darkly brilliant sentiment, showing that just as the result of his gospel is freedom, the result of his opponents' is the worst form of impotence."[3]

According to Jewish law in Deuteronomy 23:1, *"no man . . . whose penis has been cut off may enter the LORD's assembly."* Keener expresses the significance here and demonstrates in English the vivid wordplay that is evident in Paul's Greek: "Advocates of cutting the Galatians' organs have cut in on them; Paul wishes they would instead cut themselves off, mutilating themselves in a manner that would disqualify them as they have disqualified others."[4]

This is about as angry as we see Paul in his letters. I laughed out loud when I read scholar Richard Longenecker's comment that, "Indeed, it is the crudest and rudest of all Paul's extant statements."[5] Indeed it is. If Paul had ever been ambiguous about circumcision for Gentile converts in his past, he is a long, long way from there now.

[3] Jervis, *Galatians*, 137.

[4] Keener, *Galatians: A Commentary*, 477.

[5] Richard N. Longenecker, *Galatians*, Word Biblical Commentary Vol. 41 (Grand Rapids, MI: Zondervan, 1990), 234, Accordance Bible Software.

THE SPIRIT ZONE

day three

Serve One Another

Read, write and mark Galatians 5:13–15.

_____

_____

_____

_____

_____

_____

_____

_____

The writer of Hebrews tells us "the word of God is living and active" (4:12 ESV). The belief of countless generations that certain portions in Scripture were written precisely about or for their time is an enduring witness of those very qualities. For example, how many generations of Christians since the ascension of Jesus do you suppose believed they were living in the final days before His return? We'll read a quote by a theologian of a previous century and realize, wide-eyed, that he or she was as convinced the globe was on the brink of disaster as we are now. What generation of Bible enthusiasts hasn't tried to match the symbolism in Revelation to their times? Recognizing the propensity to see our own generation as the one in the spotlight, I still can't imagine a time when the words of Paul you've just recorded could've had more relevance.

We continually behold our culture's completely inverted notion of God-given liberty. List several examples of skewed interpretations of freedom whether from personal experience or current events.

_____

_____

_____

_____

Most people interpret the concept of freedom as freedom to serve ourselves. Understandably, then, their motto becomes "Don't tell me what to do." If anything that is good for our neighbor is an infringement upon our personal rights, we who have been indoctrinated by a worldly view of freedom suddenly start seeing our neighbor as our enemy. But, in the New Testament, we run headlong into a jarring truth: the world's idea of liberty is the uncomfortable antithesis of Christ's.

According to Galatians 5:13–14, what does freedom look like?

_____

_____

Today's text signals an important shift in Paul's letter to the Galatians. Thus far we've watched the apostle aggressively build his case *for* the pure, unadulterated gospel of Jesus and *against* every gospel distortion, drawing numerous rhetorical devices from his linguistic arsenal. Paul now propels his argument forward to explicit action. He will show that liberty from the law does not mean that we who follow Jesus are freed from all moral obligations "[b]ut henceforth the obligations of moral conduct are fostered not by the dictates of the law but by the operation of the free Spirit."[1]

If I had a way to build blinking lights and a bullhorn into a page of Bible study, you'd have a set right here. Today and again in Day Five, we will encounter a pivotal concept for the Christ-follower: life in the Spirit. Bruce's quotation above affirms the tectonic shift that took place when God sent the promised Holy Spirit to abide within believers.

We will see how the Spirit bears fruit on Day Five, but today let's circle around how the Spirit leads. The Mosaic Law had been a tangible compass guiding the believing community for centuries. With the coming of the Holy Spirit,

[1] F. F. Bruce, *The Epistle to the Galatians: A Commentary on the Greek Text*, The New International Greek Testament Commentary (Grand Rapids, MI: Eerdmans, 1982), 239.

the compass shifted, in certain respects, from tangible codes that could be held in human hands to Christ's own Spirit hidden in their hearts (Gal 4:6). For the sake of illustration, picture the directions on the compass—not as N-E-S-W for North, East, South and West but—as R-E-S-V for Relational, Ethical, Situational and Vocational (any kind of service to God). Divine "direction" includes understanding. Paul says in Ephesians 5:17 to "understand what the Lord's will is." As we increasingly understand His will, we are meant to move in the direction of that understanding.

Relational | Ethical | Situational | Vocational

The Holy Spirit is infinitely more to us than an internal compass, of course. We speak of no mere mechanism, but of the living, life-bringing, gift-giving Spirit of God who not only leads us but also empowers us to go where we're led. The Spirit not only convicts us of sin but supplies us the unction to repent. The Spirit not only reminds us what Jesus has taught but unlocks our understanding to receive it.

Many of us hoped every trek, turn and tenet involved in the walk of faith would always be obvious, but how oxymoronic would it be for walking "by faith" to be a tight series of footprints pressed in concrete from here to there? We who want to live obedient lives often find security in a binary existence of matters black and white. We're befuddled to learn how much in life involves wide swathes of gray. The big and beautiful irony, should we stick around long enough to see it, is how much color can come bubbling out of gray.

The same Holy Spirit who inspired individuals to pen the black ink on the white pages of the Bibles we're studying also guides us in the gray. Just as Christ alone can open our minds to understand the Scriptures, His Spirit alone can navigate us through the unknown. Despite ample emphasis on discipleship in many of our traditions, the body of Christ remains largely untaught regarding life in the Spirit. Jesus taught the fundamentals of the role of the Spirit in the lives of followers in the farewell discourse in John 14–17. Then Paul was inspired to write expansively about life in the Spirit in his letters, effectively shaping New Testament pneumatology more than any other inspired writer. Some Christian traditions are more squeamish about the Holy Spirit than others, but much of our discomfort stems from knowing we can't very well control what we cannot see.

We come by our hesitation honestly in regard to the Spirit's leadership because we want directions etched in stone (whether or not we follow them). Directions abound in the New Testament but fewer than we might request. For example, Jesus said in the great commission, "Go!" but only His Spirit can lead us where we're meant to "go."

Both Peter and Paul say that every believer receives spiritual gifts but that the Spirit alone can convey which are ours and how to use them. What specific direction are you presently seeking but struggling to find in the Scriptures?

_____

_____

_____

_____

_____

_____

We want the details. God wants our trust. We want to know exactly where we're going. God wants us to walk with Him and find out. We want the mechanical. He wants the relational. We want this God-and-human symbiosis to work like a car. "God, you gas it up. I'll drive it."

The paradoxical thing about humans who have been created to crave freedom is that we find a certain amount of security in rules even when we break them. For us, however, Christ's Spirit is the internal ruler. "And let the peace of Christ . . . rule your hearts." (Col 3:15) The rules of engagement? Be led by the Spirit, filled with the Spirit, live in the Spirit, walk in the Spirit and keep in step with the Spirit.

We want the details. God wants our trust.

In today's text, the Spirit through Paul essentially responds, "You want the Law? I'll give you a Law. The whole thing is fulfilled in one statement: Love your neighbor as yourself." If the original audience of the letter was much like us, I can picture my own face in the scene. The room would go silent as the words sank in, then we'd all erupt in a mighty roar, "Give us another Law! Any other law!"

The command to love our neighbor trips a switch on our fears. If we're looking out for our neighbor, who is looking out for us? Well, God is. If we don't police our fellow believers, who will? Well, God will. Life in the Spirit doesn't cancel out community or accountability nor does it close its eyes to carnality. It doesn't mean we don't confront one another or endure conflict if such is required to restore peace. Remember, Paul spoke of rebuking Cephas in Galatians 2. His other letters are replete with instructions regarding ways to serve one another that require straightforward speech.

What three things does Paul tell Timothy to do with patience and instruction in 2 Timothy 4:2?

1. _____

2. _____

3. _____

The leadership of the Spirit does, however, mean that a massive layoff occurred in the religious police department. All leaders lead by walking in the Spirit themselves and poring over Scripture, not by sheriffing to make sure everybody obeys the laws. In the remaining sections of Galatians 5, Paul describes what operating *apart* from the Spirit and *in* the Spirit looks like. We'll study those descriptions on Days Four and Five.

Glance now at Romans 13:8–10 where you'll find Paul again summarizing the law. List every added insight.

_____

_____

_____

_____

_____

_____

The command to love our neighbor trips a switch on our fears.

F. F. Bruce is masterful in his comments on our present text in Galatians. Take in every syllable.

> Many of Paul's friends would have assured him that the tendency to misuse the freedom of the Spirit as an excuse for enthusiastic licence could be checked only by a stiff dose of law. But Paul could not agree: the principle of law was so completely opposed to spiritual freedom that it could never be enlisted in defence of that freedom: nothing was more certainly calculated to kill true freedom. The freedom of the Spirit was the antidote alike to legal bondage and unrestrained licence.

> The danger of unrestrained licence is touched on but briefly in the letter to the Galatians: it was danger from the opposite extreme that currently presented the greater threat to them. But how seriously Paul warned against the tendency to pervert gospel liberty into unrestrained licence may be seen in his Corinthian correspondence. The particular "work of the flesh" to which the Galatians were chiefly prone at this time seems to have been quarrelsomeness (v.15) . . . The ethical emphases of the law could be effectively satisfied not through submission to the law but through "walking in the Spirit" (v.16). The law belongs to existence in the flesh, and stimulates the very sins that it forbids (3:19).[2]

What part of the excerpt stands out most to you and why?

_____

_____

_____

Let's conclude now with Galatians 5:15. List places you've seen Christians biting and devouring one another.

_____

_____

Have you ever been involved in what Paul describes? _____

I have. To quote Solomon in Proverbs 10:19, "when there are many words, sin is unavoidable." Some of us use more words than we can dole out wisely. But the more timid individual who is less prone to go face-to-face in

[2] F. F. Bruce, *The Epistle to the Galatians,* The New International Greek Testament Commentary (Grand Rapids, MI: Eerdmans, 1982), 240.

a destructive exchange of words with someone isn't automatically exempt from the Galatians 5:15 scene. She may just be hidden from view, gnawing her victim from the back, hence the word "backbiting." Proverbs 10:18 says, "The one who conceals hatred has lying lips, and whoever spreads slander is a fool." Backbiting only serves to add a layer of deceit to the sin of slander.

Can you remember a time when you knew, if the biting and devouring didn't stop, you and the other person(s) would consume each other? If so, expound.

_____

_____

_____

_____

_____

_____

_____

_____

_____

I'm about to state the obvious but the most obvious truths of the gospel often seem to be the very ones missing in cultural Christianity. Where biting and devouring abound, the Spirit is quenched. Biting and devouring erupt from the same inverted notion of freedom we talked about earlier. Egocentrism sharpens the teeth like a honing steel sharpens a knife. Since egotism protects and projects itself, it is soothed by exposing and rejecting the other, particularly the perceived rival.

To borrow Paul's words in Ephesians 4:20, "But that is not the way [we] learned Christ!"

Through love, serve one another.

NOTES

THE SPIRIT ZONE

day four

Walk by the Spirit

Read, write and mark Galatians 5:16–21.

_____

_____

_____

_____

_____

_____

_____

_____

_____

_____

_____

_____

_____

_____

_____

_____

_____

_____

A long, long time ago, to an ancient people uniquely chosen and gathered on the plains of Moab before a land full of promise, Moses expounded the commandments and instructions of God's law, to "keep the commands of the LORD . . . by walking in his ways" (Deut 8:6). Moses commanded God's miraculously delivered people not to turn to the left or the right from the words of the law, to live long in the land (Deut 28:14).

Many centuries after Moses, Paul from Tarsus, a Jewish man profoundly steeped in that same law, exhorted a group of Gentiles called out of their godlessness and into an unwavering trust and commitment to the crucified, resurrected Jewish Messiah: "Walk by the Spirit" (v.16).

What will guide the new Gentile Christians' ethics if not the revered, time-tested Law of Moses? This was the question of the hour for our Galatians. And Paul's answer was—the Holy Spirit. As Gordon Fee puts it, "Ethical life is still a matter of 'walking in the ways of God,' but for Paul this is empowered for God's new covenant people by God's empowering presence in the person of his Holy Spirit."[1]

Just as the Galatians began in the power of the Spirit, they must continue walking in the Spirit, be led by the Spirit, and finish in the Spirit (3:3). Everything about a life in Christ happens firmly in the Spirit, from start to finish.

Walk by the Spirit.

"Walk by the Spirit" is a phrase many of us are probably too familiar with to appreciate. I have heard it so many times that I was surprised to learn it's only used once in the New Testament—right here. If you stop to think about it, "walk by the Spirit" is an interesting phrase. We receive the Spirit from God upon hearing with faith, but our relationship with the Spirit is not merely passive. Our energy and endurance are necessary. We have to rise up actively to walk in step with the Spirit.

Describe this tension between divine empowerment and human action, in your own words and from your own experiences.

_____

_____

_____

In Paul's day, a mystery had been revealed at last, and something unthinkable was happening—uncircumcised Gentiles were being welcomed by God into the family of Abraham as legitimate heirs. For these Gentile Christians,

[1] Gordon Fee, *God's Empowering Presence: The Holy Spirit in the Letters of Paul* (Grand Rapids, MI: Baker Academic, 1994), 430.

walking in the Spirit meant a life free of the Mosaic law's demands but at odds with the desire of the flesh and the ways of the world to which they had been accustomed (Eph 2:2). Life in the Spirit, as it turns out, has the same ultimate end as the law: love (Gal 5:14). We are free—to love our neighbor with the same fervency we love ourselves. As John Barclay observes, the "freedom" Paul "advocates has stringent moral obligations built into it—not the obligations of the law but the obligation of love."[2]

Read verses 16–17 and describe in a few sentences the relationship Paul describes between the flesh and the Spirit:

_____

_____

Paul describes the flesh and the Spirit as being at fundamental odds with each other; the flesh is associated with the present (evil) age and the Spirit is associated with the age to come. The flesh and the Spirit desire opposing things.

When the Spirit is in control of your life, you're not under the law but you also won't do whatever you want since the Spirit does not have an appetite for just anything. Richard Hays says brilliantly, "the Spirit provides strong leadership and direction in a world that is described as an eschatological war zone."[3]

Please read the following verses once more, circling each time "flesh" is used:

> [16] I say then, walk by the Spirit and you will certainly not carry out the desire of the flesh. [17] For the flesh desires what is against the Spirit, and the Spirit desires what is against the flesh; these are opposed to each other, so that you don't do what you want. [18] But if you are led by the Spirit, you are not under the law. [19] Now the works of the flesh are obvious: sexual immorality, moral impurity, promiscuity, [20] idolatry, sorcery, hatreds, strife, jealousy, outbursts of anger, selfish ambitions, dissensions, factions, [21] envy, drunkenness, carousing, and anything similar.

How many times is "flesh" used?   ☐ 1   ☐ 2   ☐ 3   ☐ 4

Give your best definition for "flesh" in this particular context:

_____

_____

> ## Life in the Spirit, as it turns out, has the same ultimate end as the law: love.

[2] John M. G. Barclay, *Obeying the Truth: Paul's Ethics in Galatians* (Vancouver, BC: Regent College Pub., 2005), 109.

[3] Richard B. Hays, "Galatians," in *The New Interpreter's Bible* Vol. XI (Nashville: Abingdon Press, 2000), 327. © 2000 Abingdon Press. Used by permission. All rights reserved.

The word "flesh" (σάρξ) is multifaceted. It's used about eighteen times in Galatians and, in our passage alone, no less than four times. Paul can use "flesh" to refer to a physical human being (1:16; 2:16; 4:13–14) but the word could also be associated with indulgence.[4] In the Septuagint, the Greek version(s) of the Old Testament, the same word (σάρξ) is used in Genesis 17, a significant passage about circumcision that no doubt has meaning for Paul, the Galatians, and the agitators: "You shall be circumcised in the flesh of your foreskins, and it shall be a sign of the covenant between me and you . . . So shall my covenant be in your *flesh*" (vv.11, 13; ESV).

Most enlightening for understanding the way Paul uses "flesh" in our passage is the way he sets it up in contrast to "Spirit" (πνεῦμα). The Spirit is:

> the eschatological token of the new age, the power that establishes the sovereignty of Christ in the new creation. As its opposite, σάρξ is caught up into the dualism inherent in all apocalyptic thought and is thus associated with 'the world' and 'the present age' which stand in contrast to the new creation. It is this apocalyptic dualism which gives to σάρξ its negative 'colouring': just as the present age is an evil age (1:4), so the flesh is at best inadequate and at worst thoroughly tainted with sin.[5]

> The problem is not the body but our habitual choices not to submit to the Spirit's authority . . .

In a similar vein, David A. deSilva posits that "flesh" here "carries a negative ethical nuance. It does not signify some physical aspect of human existence, but rather the sum total of the impulses, urges, and desires that lead human beings away from virtue toward self-promotion and self-gratification, often at the expense of the interests and well-being of others."[6]

Now, we would be dead wrong to conclude from all of this that our bodies are bad. Think about it: it's precisely our bodies that receive the Holy Spirit and experience the wonders of God. The problem is not the body but our habitual choices not to submit to the Spirit's authority, direction, and consolation. By the Spirit, we can experience the life of Jesus in our bodies.

If you are walking by the Spirit, you will not carry out the desire of "the flesh" (v.16), but also, if you are "led by the Spirit" you are not "under the law" (v.18). Both are true. In verse 19, Paul composes a vice list of "works of the flesh." This phrase should immediately remind us of a phrase we've seen six times in Galatians: "works of the law" (2:16, 3X; 3:2, 3:5; 3:10). While "works of the law" and "works of the flesh" are not synonymous or equally negative, Paul, using

[4] Barclay, *Obeying the Truth: Paul's Ethics in Galatians*, 203.
[5] Barclay, *Obeying the Truth: Paul's Ethics in Galatians*, 205.
[6] David A. deSilva, *Galatians: A Handbook on the Greek Text* (Waco, TX: Baylor University Press, 2014), 114–5.

wordplay, creates a link between them insofar as they are both associated with an age that is passing away. They do not represent the age that will last.

Let's look at the "works of the flesh" closely. First, we notice that there are fifteen (compared to the list of nine fruit of the Spirit coming in vv.22–23). Second, Paul is not giving us an exhaustive list. Third, they are *obvious* or "plainly to be seen."[7] Fourth, these works of the flesh are something Paul has warned the Galatians about, probably on a previous visit (v.21). This is important information since the agitators were probably claiming that Paul's gospel had no real ethics to speak of. Fifth, Paul gives these works an eschatological context; these works are typical of people who will not inherit God's kingdom (v.21).

Fee says these are works "that people do who live in keeping with their basic fallenness and that of the world around them."[8] That doesn't mean Christians won't do them, as the forthcoming lines of 6:1 make crystal clear, but that the life of a Christian who is led by the Spirit will not be characterized by works of the flesh.

How do we know Paul is not giving us an exhaustive list? (The key is in v.21)

_____

The fifteen representative "works of the flesh" fall into four categories, which Fee demarcates the following way: 1) illicit sex (sexual immorality, moral impurity, promiscuity), 2) illicit worship (idolatry, sorcery), 3) breakdowns in relationships (hatreds, strife, jealousy, outbursts of anger, selfish ambitions, dissensions, factions, envy), and 4) excesses (drunkenness, carousing).[9]

Does anything about the list come as a surprise to you?

_____

_____

We modern Christians mostly associate "the flesh" with sexual immorality and substance abuse, like drugs and alcohol. While illicit sex and excesses make the list, by far what takes up the most space is the third category: behaviors or postures of the heart that create breakdown in relationships.[10] Isn't that something? The CSB's rendering of "hatreds" is especially poignant.

[7] Walter Bauer, W. F. Arndt, F. W. Gingrich, and F. W. Danker, Editors. "φανερός" in *A Greek-English Lexicon of the New Testament and other Early Christian Literature* Third Edition (Chicago: University of Chicago Press, 2000), Accordance edition.

[8] Gordon D. Fee, *Galatians*, Pentecostal Commentary Series (Dorset: Deo Publishing, 2011), 216.

[9] Fee, *Galatians*, 212.

[10] Fee, *Galatians*, 212.

I can't think of anything more severe in our society than our innumerable hatreds and how comfortable we are at tolerating them. As for too many of our churches, dissensions and factions run rampant. People who don't agree with us politically are demonized and the tiniest theological differences spur division.

Please look up two references in our same chapter which may suggest discord was a particular problem for the Galatian churches. Fill in the blanks:

5:15 But if you bite and _____ one another, watch out, or

you will be _____ by one _____.

5:26 Let us not become conceited, provoking one

another, _____ one another.

Our list contains a mix of behaviors that were considered problematic by both Jews and Gentiles and ones that were considered sinful from a Jewish perspective. For example, the list includes a word like ἀσέλγεια ("promiscuity" in the CSB and "sensuality" in the ESV) which was used by both Jewish and pagan Greeks to denote a "lack of self-restraint which involves one in conduct that violates all bounds of what is socially acceptable."[11]

On the other hand, the mention of "idolatry" (εἰδωλολατρία) is striking (v.20). "Idolatry" is a relatively rare derogatory term used mostly by Jews to characterize Gentile worship of non-gods and shallow image-making as opposed to worship of the one true God. Idolatry was a violation of the second commandment (Exod 20:3–4). As Fee states, "pagan Greeks would never have used the word 'idol' for their deities."[12]

While Paul argues the Galatians must not observe the Law of Moses, his own ethics and expectations for Christian behavior are simultaneously deeply rooted in the Law of Moses. What verse captures this tension better than 1 Corinthians 7:19? *"Circumcision does not matter and uncircumcision does not matter. Keeping God's commands is what matters."* Gentiles do not have to become Jews to follow the Jewish Messiah, but, make no mistake, there is no Christianity without Judaism.

> ## Make no mistake, there is no Christianity without Judaism.

---

[11] Walter Bauer, W. F. Arndt, F. W. Gingrich, and F. W. Danker, Editors. "ἀσέλγεια" in *A Greek-English Lexicon of the New Testament and other Early Christian Literature* Third Edition (Chicago: University of Chicago Press, 2000), Accordance edition.

[12] Fee, *Galatians*, 214.

THE SPIRIT ZONE

day five

The Fruit of the Spirit

Read, write and mark Galatians 5:22–26.

_____

_____

_____

_____

_____

_____

_____

_____

_____

We've arrived at the most iconic section of Galatians: the fruit of the Spirit. Paul's wording in Galatians 5:22–23 is exquisite, poetic and rhythmic in much the same tenor as 1 Corinthians 13, the love chapter. This clip of Galatians is excellent in form and lyrical in feel but no more philosophical than the evidence Paul gave for the works of the flesh. In Scripture, artful words aren't just aesthetic. Resist the temptation to relegate the qualities of the fruit of the Spirit to categories like *ideals* and *goals*. The manifestations in Galatians 5:22–23 as surely signal the presence of the Holy Spirit as sexual immorality, idolatry, sorcery and fits of anger signal the gratification of the flesh. Romanticizing the nine graces as ideals rather than real and vivid outgrowths of the indwelling Spirit undermines them.

The concept of fruitfulness is one of the Bible's guiding principles. Whether the fruit is literal as in the Garden of Eden, symbolic as in Isaiah 5 or spiritual as in John 15, all fruitfulness echoes the same confession: what is nourished on the inside grows on the outside.

Read Matthew 7:15–20. Who was teaching and what were his primary points?

_____

_____

_____

In God's economy, the imagery of fruit bearing is by no means limited to trees, shrubs and vines. Matthew 3:4–8 tells a vital truth about fruit that often gets overlooked. It is one that would not only bring us considerable relief but save us considerable peril.

What is the context of fruit in Matthew 3:4–8?

_____

We sometimes panic when believers fall into a stronghold of sin as if we have no ability to discern whether or not true repentance has taken place. That's simply not the case. Our crisis is impatience, not insufficient evidence. Thankfully, our next lesson is on the priority of restoring those who have fallen into sin. The gospel is no gospel at all if there is no forgiveness of sins and no way back to fellowship. The question often causing the biggest crisis is whether or not people who have fallen into strongholds of sin should ever be restored to places of trust and positions of authority.

Some should.
Some shouldn't.
Time tells . . . because repentance bears fruit.
And fruit requires time.

> Time tells . . . because repentance bears fruit. *And fruit requires time.*

In addition to the qualities listed in the fruit of the Spirit, repentance bears fruit of sustained humility and teachability. It doesn't elbow its way back to power. The repentant divest themselves of power for the love and safety of others until they can be trusted with authority again. The repentant do not seek to be served. They serve. They don't demand to be let off the hook. They seek, where possible, to restore what they took or repair what they broke, all with God's help, and they submit to the process of earning back trust. Their lives are not marked by guilt but, make no mistake, they are marked by grace.

Use this space to express any additional thoughts you may have.

_____

_____

Take a look at Ephesians 5:8–9 for such a beautiful and unusual reference to fruit-bearing. What is the fruit bearer?

_____

Of what three things does its fruit consist (CSB) or, in ESV terminology, where can its fruit be found?

_____

_____

Focus now on the specific qualities or graces Paul names as evidence of the fruit of the Spirit in Galatians 5:22–23. Since "fruit" is singular in this section of Scripture, a cluster of grapes offers a more fitting illustration than a variety of fruits.

Now, add a quality of the fruit of the Spirit from Paul's list on each grape. I've started the first one for you.

Did it bother you to have more grapes in the diagram than you needed for the 9 qualities Paul listed? If you're nodding, know that I am, too. I love exact numbers and complete lists but Paul doesn't give us those luxuries here.

> But the fruit of the Spirit is love, joy, peace, patience, kindness, goodness, faithfulness, gentleness, and self-control. The law is not against such things.
>
> Galatians 5:22–23

We can assume his naming of nine specific graces is more illustrative than exhaustive because of two words in Galatians 5:23. "Against *such things* there is no law" (ESV, emphasis mine). The same is true for Paul's list of the works of the flesh in Galatians 5:19–21 where you noted his reference to "such things" in your previous lesson. In both cases, the words "such things" refer to similar things.

God reserves the right to withhold an exhaustive list in Scripture when He chooses. He knows our human propensity to be *exactly right. Perfectly precise.* For example, we find three lists of spiritual gifts in the New Testament (Rom 12:6–8; 1 Cor 12:8–11; 1 Pet 4:8–11) but none of them include all of them. This is a perfect time to draw a contrast between the fruit of the Spirit (*qualities* of the Spirit) and the gifts of the Spirit (*activities* of the Spirit).

Each believer possesses one or more spiritual gifts but God apportions and distributes them according to His sovereign will and eternal plan. He does this purposely so that, to function according to our design, we must be connected to others in the Body of Christ. The plan is brilliant, making fellowship a necessity rather than an alternative of convenience. You literally cannot fulfill your calling or use your giftedness to full effectiveness in autonomy. You need other believers and other believers need you.

The fruit of the Spirit operates differently. While some qualities at times may be more apparent than others, all nine are interconnected. To use the grapevine metaphor once more, a whole cluster grows out of one bloom. We could possess tremendous self-control but if we don't have love and we're utterly joyless and we're constantly in conflict and we deal harshly with others, our self-control is far more likely coming from the discipline of our flesh than from the Spirit.

Reflect on the nine qualities of the fruit of the Spirit as a whole. Offer any thoughts regarding what they have in common.

_____

_____

Do you see any connection to Paul's summation of the law in Galatians 5:14? If so, what?

_____

_____

_____

_____

F. F. Bruce writes, "If the works of the flesh as a whole be compared with the fruit of the Spirit as a whole, it will appear that the works of the flesh are disruptive of κοινωνία, whereas the fruit of the Spirit fosters it" (κοινωνία / koinonia = fellowship).[1] Each of the qualities have direct effects relationally, whether in the personal sphere, societal sphere or within the sphere of a community of faith. We can love Scripture and know our Bibles cover to cover but, if we are careless with people, we've missed a core value of the gospel. Here's freeing news: we can't force fruit. We can't make ourselves love people. Determination won't make us patient. Biting our tongues with contentious people won't produce inner peace. Plastering a smile on our faces won't give us joy. No law can make us gentle.

Each of the qualities named in Galatians 5:22-23 emerge to the surface from the fullness of the Spirit beneath. The Spirit nourished within us (a concept we'll revisit in Gal 6) bears fruit upon us. In Paul's words here in Galatians, this is tantamount to living by the Spirit, walking in the Spirit and keeping in step with the Spirit. In Christ's words in John 15, this is tantamount to the branch abiding in the Vine without obstruction. Our part is to attend to the things of Christ's Spirit. God's part is to bear the fruit of the Spirit. Each grace is meant to evidence—not our goodness but—our God.

We'll conclude with brief thoughts about each quality:

Love (ἀγάπη; *agapē*): All other qualities find their origin in this one and they each unravel without it. I love how F. F. Bruce words the connection between love and the remaining eight graces. "Where love is present, the other virtues will not be far away; it is love that binds them all together in perfect harmony (cf. Col 3:14)."[2] Bereft of love, all service to God and others and all personal sacrifice, no matter how severe, amount to nothing but noise.

Read 1 John 4:16-19—you'll be so glad you did. Record every outstanding detail about love.

_____

_____

_____

_____

_____

[1] F. F. Bruce, *The Epistle to the Galatians,* The New International Greek Testament Commentary (Grand Rapids, MI. Eerdmans, 1982), 255.

[2] Bruce, *The Epistle to the Galatians*, 255.

Joy (χαρά; *chara*): Timothy George writes, "The Greek root for joy (char-) is the same as that for 'grace,' *charis*. Obviously, there is a close connection between the two concepts."[3]

How might the two connect?

_____

_____

_____

> **Christ does not call us to joy of our own making. It is His own.**

Christ does not call us to joy of our own making. It is His own. In John 15:11, Jesus says, "I have told you these things so that my joy may be in you and your joy may be complete." We don't have to rejoice over the condition of this world or jump up and down with glee about back-breaking burdens or heart-breaking relationships. Our summons is to "rejoice in the Lord" (Phil 4:4).

Peace (εἰρήνη; *eirēnē*): To grasp the Biblical concept of peace, we rewind further than the Greek all the way back to the Hebrew term *shalom*. Shalom is no mere absence of conflict. It is the presence of wholeness and a sense of well-being that comes from being rightly related to God.

Patience (μακροθυμία; *makrothumia*): While *makrothumía* can refer to "a state of remaining tranquil while awaiting an outcome," here it likely denotes a "patience toward others" or "a state of being able to bear up under provocation."[4] Remember, we can't self-produce it.

So, what do we do in our woefully short supply of patience? Offer your thoughts.

_____

_____

_____

_____

Kindness (χρηστότης; *chrēstotēs*): The word given to Paul centuries ago meant almost exactly what it does today. Kindness is not sugary sentimentality or blindness to the facts. It is not reserved for the deserving. It is the graciousness of the graced.

---

[3] Timothy George, *Galatians*, The New American Commentary Vol. 30 (Nashville: B&H, 1994), 401.
[4] Walter Bauer, *A Greek-English Lexicon of the New Testament and Other Early Christian Literature*, rev. and ed. Frederick W. Danker, 3rd ed. (Chicago: University of Chicago Press, 2000), Electronic text.

What level of impact would you say kindness has on the witness of the Christian?

_____

_____

_____

Goodness (ἀγαθωσύνη; *agathōsynē*): Goodness is not the equivalent of niceness. The basic idea driving this term is an active disposition toward others that brings benefit.

How might this alter our impression of the good life?

_____

_____

_____

_____

Faithfulness (πίστις; *pistis*): Faithfulness is fullness of faith. It doesn't just mean to believe. It is the manifestation of a life lived believing. Of all the things Satan wants to steal from us and kill in us, our faith rates first on his list.

Gentleness (πραΰτης; *prautēs*): Timothy George offers, "As an expression of the fruit of the Spirit, gentleness is strength under control, power harnessed in loving service and respectful actions."[5] It is the furthest thing from weakness. Gentleness is strength fully submitted to God that recognizes when to sit quietly at the table and when to overturn it.

Self-control (ἐγκράτεια; *enkrateia*): Paul essentially defines this term in Galatians 5:24. Self-control is what manifests in us when we yield to what happened to us when we identified with Christ in His crucifixion.

What does Galatians 5:24 say we did?

_____

_____

_____

Galatians 5 wraps up with these words: "Let us not become conceited, provoking one another, envying one another." Ironically, being full of ourselves only makes us more insecure. The fruit of the Spirit is . . . *freedom*.

[5] George, *Galatians*, 404.

> Of all the things Satan wants to steal from us and kill in us, our faith rates first on his list.

NOTES

CROSS

zone six

CROSS

GALATIANS 6

———

Brothers and sisters, if someone is overtaken in
any wrongdoing, you who are spiritual, restore such
a person with a gentle spirit, watching out for
yourselves so that you also won't be tempted.

Galatians 6:1

VIDEO GUIDE

THE CROSS ZONE

Introduction: Our attentions now shift to the sixth and final chapter of Paul's letter to the churches of Galatia.

1 GOSPEL
2 FREEDOM
3 PROMISE
4 CHILDREN
5 SPIRIT
6

Read Galatians 6:12–15 (Acts 7:58–60, 8:1–3, 1 Cor 2:2).

This excerpt from Dr. Richard B. Hays' commentary on Galatians will provide a launching place for our introduction to our final week of study:

> "All who preach the cross, as Paul does, can expect to encounter opposition and persecution from a world offended by a gospel that proclaims the end of all _____, _____, and _____ privilege and distinction. The cross has put an _____ to all such systems (vv.14-15). By domesticating the gospel, however, and turning it into a _____ refinement of the religion of the Sinaitic Law, the *Missionaries would avoid the gospel's _____ implications and thereby fit more comfortably into recognized religious categories."[1]

> (By "Missionaries," Dr. Hays is referencing the party attempting to enslave Galatian Christians to the Mosaic Law.)

Read Galatians 3:27-29, Romans 3:27a.

1. The cross of Christ was not for _____.

Read Colossians 2:13-15.

2. The gospel's _____ implications are _____ by time.

> Theologian F. F. Bruce writes, "It might even be said that he took the document, ordinances and all, and nailed it to his cross as an act of triumphant defiance in the face of those _____ powers that were holding it over _____ and _____ in order to command their allegiance."[2]

---

[1] Richard B. Hays. "Galatians," in *The New Interpreter's Bible* Vol. XI (Nashville: Abingdon Press, 2000), 342. © 2000 Abingdon Press. Used by permission. All rights reserved.
[2] F. F. Bruce, *The Epistles to the Colossians, to Philemon, and to the Ephesians,* The New International Commentary on the New Testament (Grand Rapids, MI: Eerdmans, 1984), 110.

3. The theology of the cross does not fit comfortably into celebrated human

_____. To the human who embraces its meaning, however,

nothing compares to its _____.

Read 1 Corinthians 1:18.

NOTES

_____

_____

_____

_____

_____

_____

_____

_____

_____

_____

_____

_____

_____

_____

_____

_____

_____

_____

_____

_____

_____

CROSS

THE CROSS ZONE

day one

If Someone is Overtaken

Read, write and mark Galatians 6:1.

_____

_____

_____

We will spend today on a single verse, but, in order to retain the context, please begin your reading with Galatians 5:19 then conclude with Galatians 6:1.

When you set aside the interruption of the chapter break, how does Galatians 6:1 fit the context?

_____

_____

_____

Let's take Galatians 6:1 apart so we can put it back together with increased appreciation.

1. *"Brothers and sisters"*—Galatians 6 opens with the seventh of eight times Paul addresses his recipients of the Galatian letter with this familial touch. He does this as an endearment but also as a frequent reminder that his letter is written *to* the community of believers *for* the community of believers. It is written to *family*.

Remember, if we've grown up in a culture where individualism is a core value, our default setting is to interpret information personally and singularly before corporately or communally. Paul writes with the reverse mentality. Yes, of course, his letters apply to individual readers. But believers living day in and day out like micro islands scattered in a sea rarely, if ever, occurred to the New Testament writers. Christians' involvement with one another was assumed.

The community of saints worshipped and prayed together and heard public readings of the Scriptures together, but they also fellowshipped with one another as a way of life. They often ate together. They laughed and cried together. When one was in need, those in plenty chipped in. And, when someone fell into sin, the others, alert to their own potential for failure, helped them get back on their feet.

Interwoven living was, unquestionably, for the sake of camaraderie and mutual encouragement, but it was also for mutual accountability—and not just to holy living. The Spirit also calls saints to accountability as restorers. While we've been crucified with Christ to the passions of our flesh, the old us that died with Christ craves resurrection. Though we can no more be decrucified than Christ Himself, our old ways, thoughts and habits still tempt and try us. We will battle them and sometimes bend the knee to them as long as we inhabit this present age. No one is immune and, for this reason alongside countless others, mutual mercy and compassion are essential to the believing community. To be followers of Christ yet merciless and unforgiving betrays an absurd misunderstanding of the gospel. Grace is like oxygen to the body of Christ.

> Grace is like oxygen to the body of Christ.

2. *"if someone"*—Give me the ESV's "if *any*one" over the CSB's "if *some*one" any day in Galatians 6:1 (emphasis mine). The Greek can be translated either way, but "anyone" is among the most beautiful pronouns in the New Testament. According to the sacred pages,

anyone who has ears can hear Christ's words,
anyone who acknowledges Jesus before others will be acknowledged by Him before the angels of God,
anyone who believes in Jesus receives no condemnation,

anyone who knows the Son of God has eternal life,
anyone who serves the Son will be honored by His Father,
anyone who is in Christ is a new creation,
and, student of Scripture, "if **anyone** is caught in any transgression, you who are spiritual should restore him in a spirit of gentleness" (ESV, emphasis mine).

Do these references to *anyone* hold any particular significance to you today? If so, in what way?

_____

_____

_____

Anyone who is willing can be restored to fellowship and fruitful service to God. That includes you and me—and the one from whom we occasionally wish God would withhold restoration.

3. *"is caught in any transgression"*—"The word for 'caught' means literally to be 'detected, overtaken, surprised.' Because this word appears in the passive voice in this context, it may connote the idea of surprise: someone suddenly entrapped or discovered in an unseemly situation or heinous act."[1]

The Greek word (προλημφθῇ) can also be translated "entrapped."[2] Only those who have never been overtaken by sin tend to doubt how temptation can catch us.

Temptation can come from two different sources: our own lusts (sexual or nonsexual) and from Satan, whom Paul calls "the tempter" (1 Thess 3:5). Several elements concerning Satan's approach give weighty credibility to the potential for being caught, overtaken, surprised or entrapped by sin.

Read Ephesians 6:10–11 and list every detail suggesting the seriousness of the battle.

_____

_____

_____

_____

> Finally, be strengthened by the Lord and by his vast strength. Put on the full armor of God so that you can stand against the schemes of the devil.
>
> Ephesians 6:10-11

---

[1] Timothy George, *Galatians*, New American Commentary, Vol. 30 (Nashville: Broadman & Holman, 1994), 409.

[2] Richard N. Longenecker, *Galatians*, Word Biblical Commentary Vol. 41 (Dallas: Thomas Nelson Inc, 1990), 272. Copyright © 1990 by Richard N. Longenecker. Used by permission of Thomas Nelson. www.thomasnelson.com

The word "schemes" in Ephesians 6:11 translates the Greek term μεθοδείας. Our English word "method" is obvious in the transliteration *methodeias*.

What are the implications of Satan being methodical in his approach to Jesus followers?

_____

_____

_____

_____

Satan is systematic. He's technical. He takes good aim. He won't waste many fiery darts on the well-covered areas of your life. He knows where you're vulnerable. He knows when you're weak. He knows when you're hurt. He knows your unrequited desires and takes stock of your unmet needs.

Since we cannot rid our lives of all vulnerability, weakness or hurt nor force our every need to be met and desire to be fulfilled, what are a few things we can do when we're vulnerable?

_____

_____

_____

_____

Perhaps most chilling of all, the devil is patient. For an opportunist, timing is everything. At the conclusion of the scene where Christ is tempted in the wilderness, we find these words: "And when the devil had ended every temptation, he departed from him until an opportune time" (Luke 4:13 ESV).

Write those last two words. _____ _____

We sometimes forget the level of sophistication a satanic attack can have. Our first assumption when a well-known leader falls is that he or she was a fraud. Galatians 6:1 paints a different picture. What every Christian leader does have in common, however, is an enemy adept at numbers who continually calculates how many birds can be killed with one stone.

Our sins are our own responsibility and no one can repent for us, but Scripture illustrates again and again how temptation can catch us off guard.

Have you ever been overtaken or entrapped in sin? If so, in retrospect, what kinds of elements helped set you up for failure?

_____

_____

_____

_____

Much has been written concerning whether the instruction to restore those "overtaken in any wrongdoing" in Galatians 6:1 refers to unintentional transgressions only. I'd like to go on record saying that I certainly hope not. While the worst experience of my younger life involved being overtaken by sin, I've also, regrettably, been overtaken at times by my own foolishness. I've accidentally fallen into sin and I've also jumped into it. My guess is you have too. Thankfully, the primary prerequisite for restoration is repentance, and the catalyst of repentance is "godly sorrow" (2 Cor 7:10 NIV). Jesus never resisted the sorrowful and repentant. Regarding Galatians 6:1, James D. G. Dunn writes, "The test of spiritual maturity is dealing kindly not just with the unwitting (and regretted) mistake, but with the fellow Christian whose deliberate unacceptable conduct has come to light despite his or her attempts at concealment."[3]

4. *"you who are spiritual"*—Three possibilities are most plausible for what Paul intends by the description *"pneumatikos"* (πνευματικός). He may mean it sarcastically for those who believed themselves to be spiritually superior. Or, he may intend it as a reference to anyone who'd received the Spirit. I lean heavily toward a third possibility, which Timothy George captures well.

> It seems best, however, to understand the "spirituals" in the same kind of positive sense Paul used it in 1 Cor 2:15–3:4. There the apostle contrasted the "spiritual" believers at Corinth with those who were *sarkikoi*, "fleshly," worldly minded, that is, those who had to be fed on milk instead of meat because they were spiritually immature.[4]

5. *"restore such a person"*—*Katartizō* means "put in order," "repair," "restore," "make complete."[5]

[3] James D. G. Dunn, *The Epistle to the Galatians*, Black's New Testament Commentary (Peabody, MA: Hendrickson, 1993), 319.
[4] George, *Galatians*, 410–11.
[5] Longenecker, *Galatians*, 273.

You'll find it translated in Matthew 4:21. What was the object of restoration or repair?

_____

The main idea is to restore something (or someone) to a former condition for full use. *Katartizō* was also a term used for resetting "a fractured or dislocated bone."[6] Hebrews 12:12-13 has particular relevance when imagining restoration as a reset bone because its context is the Lord's discipline.

Read the segment and record the goal of divine discipline according to Hebrews 12:13.

_____

_____

_____

_____

> Therefore, strengthen your tired hands and weakened knees, and make straight paths for your feet, so that what is lame may not be dislocated but healed instead.
>
> Hebrews 12:12-13

Note a minute detail regarding restorers. In Galatians 6:1, the "you" is plural in "you who are spiritual" and singular in "so that you won't be tempted." Decades into ministry, I cannot emphasize enough the importance of several people being involved in the restoration process rather than leaving it to one-on-one. To be clear, I'm not talking about professional therapy that quite appropriately takes place one-on-one and can be immensely helpful in restoring the individual's crushed soul. Galatians 6:1 is primarily about restoration to loving fellowship within the faith community and returning the fallen to some form of fruitful labor for the kingdom of God. Mutual accountability and collective wisdom are essential among fellow restorers.

Can you think of any reasons why several restorers would be better than one? List them here.

_____

_____

_____

_____

6. *"with a gentle spirit"*—the ESV translates the phrase (ἐν πνεύματι πραΰτητος) "a spirit of gentleness." Paul almost certainly intends a tie between "gentleness" in Galatians 6:1 and the quality of the fruit of the Spirit four verses earlier.

[6] R. Y. K. Fung, *The Epistle to the Galatians,* The New International Commentary on the New Testament (Grand Rapids, MI: Eerdmans, 1988), 286.

Offer three reasons why gentleness would be paramount in restoration. Make sure one involves its importance to the restorers and not just to the restored.

A. _____

B. _____

C. _____

7. "*watching out for yourselves so that you also won't be tempted*"—Richard B. Hays offers the following insight into the nature of the temptation:

> The possible temptation could take either of two forms: either the admonisher could be tempted to fall into the same sin as the erring member, or the admonisher could be tempted to an attitude of pride and condescension. Paul does not specify which of these possible problems he has in view. There's no need for us to decide between them; it is sufficient to recognize that the practice of mutual correction is fraught with dangers of prideful abuse, and, at the same time, all of us share in a common human frailty. Indeed, Paul's warning here implies an astute psychological insight: we may be most harshly condemning of those failings to which we ourselves are the most susceptible.[7]

Your next lesson picks up where Hays leaves off. As God would have It, my preparation for today's lesson coincided with reading Dane Ortlund's book, *Gentle and Lowly: The Heart of Christ for Sinners and Sufferers*. This excerpt provides a fitting finish.

> In the four Gospel accounts given to us in Matthew, Mark, Luke, and John—eighty-nine chapters of biblical text—there's only one place where Jesus tells us about his own heart . . . In the one place in the Bible where the Son of God pulls back the veil and lets us peer way down into the core of who he is, we are not told that he is "austere and demanding in heart." We are not told that he is "exalted and dignified in heart." We are not even told that he is "joyful and generous in heart." Letting Jesus set the terms, his surprising claim is that he is "gentle and lowly in heart."[8]

If Jesus, the embodiment of sinless perfection, treats us with gentleness, then perhaps we are never more wholly overtaken in wrongdoing than when we harshly treat someone who desperately needs restoration. Let's be gentle out there.

> Perhaps we are never more wholly overtaken in wrongdoing than when we harshly treat someone who desperately needs restoration.

[7] Richard B. Hays, "Galatians," in *The New Interpreter's Bible* Vol. XI (Nashville: Abingdon Press, 2000), 332. © 2000 Abingdon Press. Used by permission. All rights reserved.

[8] Dane Ortlund, *Gentle and Lowly: The Heart of Christ for Sinners and Sufferers* (Wheaton, IL: Crossway, 2020), 17, Kindle edition.

NOTES

THE CROSS ZONE

day two

The Law of Christ

Read, write and mark Galatians 6:2–5.

_____

_____

_____

_____

_____

_____

_____

_____

Recently, I read this sentence in a book written by Samuel Wells, a priest in the church of England: "The Bible belongs to those who read it."[1] I yelled "amen" out loud in an empty room. Do you ever get the feeling that more of us have a "high view of the Bible" than are actually reading the Bible? We want to do more than "use" a Bible verse here and there to meet the needs of our various arguments and agendas. We want to be shaped by the whole of Scripture over an entire lifetime of reading it and being read by it. Not everything we're up to in this world matters, but I still believe immersing ourselves in Scripture does.

---

[1] Samuel Wells, *A Future that's Bigger than the Past* (Norwich: Canterbury Press, 2019), 157, Kindle edition.

Let's begin by reading verse 2 again.

Paul commands the Galatians, and us, to "carry one another's burdens." What is the outcome, according to Paul, if we do this?

_____

_____

Note carefully that Paul doesn't _command_ us to "fulfill the law of Christ." Rather, he commands us to "carry one another's burdens" and the outcome of that action fulfills "the law of Christ."[2] In Matthew 5:17, Jesus himself uses the language of fulfillment with regard to the Law: _"Don't think that I came to abolish the Law or the Prophets. I did not come to abolish but to fulfill."_

Where else have we seen the language of fulfill in Galatians? Read Galatians 5:14 and write out the whole verse below.

_____

_____

What verse from the Law does Paul quote in Galatians 5:14? (You should be able to find it in the footnotes or margins of most English Bibles.)

_____

Read Romans 13:8–10. Explain how Paul elaborates on this idea in those verses.

_____

_____

_____

_____

Finally, read 1 Corinthians 9:21–23 with particular attention to verse 21. Explain what Paul is saying there and how it relates to our present passage:

_____

_____

_____

_____

[2] John Barclay, _Obeying the Truth_ (Vancouver, BC: Regent College Publishing, 1988), 142.

The Greek word νόμος, translated as "law", is used 32 times in Galatians; this usage here in 6:2 is nothing short of the 31st time we've seen this word in the letter to the Galatians.[3] Can you believe that? The law in Galatians always refers specifically to the Law of Moses, Israel's Law, never to "law" in any kind of general sense. We've seen "the law" used in antithesis to faith in Christ (2:16, 2:21, 3:21, 3:5). We've heard Paul say that he has died to the law and been crucified with Christ (2:19). He's told us the law was temporary—a guardian for a set time period. He's declared that anyone who is led by the Spirit is not "under the law" (5:18). And now, in the final chapter, Paul connects the word "law" with "Christ," no less! This is such a classic apostle Paul move. What are we to make of it?

The "law of Christ" is one of those phrases I tremble to define because, in the process of defining it, I fear we may overload it with meaning and misunderstand it even more. But, if I had to define "law of Christ," I would point to Graham Stanton's definition: "What is the law of Christ? In Gal 6:2 it is the law of Moses redefined by Christ, with the 'love commandment' and 'carrying the burdens of others' as its essence; it is fulfilled by Christ in his own self-giving love."[4]

The agitators are urging the Galatian Christian men to be circumcised according to the Law in order to be proper sons of Abraham. But the apostle Paul urges them all instead to carry one another's burdens like Jesus carried theirs in order to fulfill the Law, according to Christ's redefinition of the Law.[5] As Richard Hays so brilliantly puts it, "The Galatians, then, are being summoned to re-enact the event by which Christ brought the Law to fulfillment . . . To fulfill the Law of Christ, then, is to play out over and over again in the life of the community the pattern of self-sacrificial love that he revealed in his death."[6] *For even the Son of Man did not come to be served, but to serve, and to give his life as a ransom for many* (Mark 10:45). Gordon Fee nicely sums up how the "law of Christ" connects to the greater context of Galatians, especially Paul's description of our life in the Spirit:

> Believers who walk by the Spirit do so because they are following where the Spirit leads; and the Spirit leads in "the law of Christ," in ways that both reflect and pattern after Christ himself—whom Paul has earlier described as "the one who loved me and gave himself for me" (2:20). This is why Torah observance is totally irrelevant; for the one led by the Spirit in "the law of Christ" the aim of Torah has been fulfilled.[7]

> ## Carry one another's burdens; in this way you will fulfill the law of Christ.
>
> Galatians 6:2

[3] J. Louis Martyn, *Galatians,* The Anchor Yale Bible (New Haven, CT: Yale University Press, 1997), 555.

[4] Graham Stanton, "What is the Law of Christ?" *Ex Auditu* 17 (2001), 47–59. Used by permission of Wipf and Stock Publishers, www.wipfandstock.com

[5] Richard B. Hays, "Galatians," in *The New Interpreter's Bible* Vol. XI (Nashville: Abingdon Press, 2000), 333. © 2000 Abingdon Press. Used by permission. All rights reserved.

[6] Hays, "Galatians," 333.

[7] Gordon Fee, *God's Empowering Presence: The Holy Spirit in the Letters of Paul* (Grand Rapids, MI: Baker Academic, 1994), 438.

Go ahead and read verse 3, a verse that feels out of place but only because our modern chapter divisions (added much, much later than the letters were written) lead us astray here. So, let's back up a little.

What does Paul say just a few verses before in Galatians 5:26? Write out the verse below:

_____

_____

> For if anyone considers himself to be something when he is nothing, he deceives himself.
>
> Galatians 6:3

Please also fill in the blanks of Galatians 6:1:

" . . . restore such a person with a _____ spirit, watching out for _____ so that you also won't be _____."

When we look upon our brother or sister who has been exposed in wrongdoing, we do not only see that we could be tempted toward the lure of that same wrongdoing, but also that we could become self-congratulatory and prideful. To derive any kind of affirmation of ourselves in the context of our brother or sister's transgression is sinister, and a sure route headed straight to the land of self deception. Christian leadership calls for both a willingness to help restore other Christians with a gentle spirit, to shoulder their heavy burdens, combined with an awareness of our own impulses to satisfy the desires of the flesh.

Have you ever been part of the complicated process of restoring a fellow Christian back to a place of wholeness after he or she had been exposed in wrongdoing? _____

What were some beautiful things about that process?

_____

_____

_____

_____

What were some things about that process that were difficult for you about it?

_____

_____

_____

Have you ever been personally exposed in a transgression? (If these questions make you feel uncomfortable, please skip them and go on ahead!)

_____

_____

_____

_____

Did any brother or sister or friend come through for you in a profound way?

_____

_____

_____

Did anyone cause you harm during that process? If so, what do you wish they had done differently?

_____

_____

_____

_____

_____

_____

The church could stand to do better at this all-around. We should be sober-minded but less squeamish about the sins of others. We could stand to be more unrelenting in the probing of our own sins. We simultaneously need more accountability and more gentleness, don't we?

One of my favorite theological writers in the world, Rowan Williams, wrote a passage in a book titled *Silence and Honey Cakes: The Wisdom of the Desert,* that has been a companion to me for over a decade now. It may seem counterintuitive on first read, but I hope it comes to mean something to you as you sit with it, too:

> Self-justification is the heavy burden, because there is no end to carrying it; there will always be some new situation where we need to establish our

We simultaneously need more accountability and more gentleness, don't we?

position, dig the trench for the ego to defend . . . Self-accusation, honesty about our failings, is a light burden because whatever we have to face in ourselves, however painful is the recognition, however hard it is to feel at times that we have to start all over again, we know that the burden is already known and accepted by God's mercy. We do not have to create, sustain, and save ourselves; God has done, is doing and will do all.[8]

Verse 4 is fascinating: *Let each person examine his own work, and then he can take pride in himself alone, and not compare himself with someone else.* We are, in fact, commanded to examine ourselves. But we are explicitly told not to prop ourselves up in reference to others, especially when they're down and we're not. We must evaluate our own *work*, but never by way of comparison with others. I just love this.

Now, we modern Protestant Christians often place our faith and work(s) in opposition to each other. We do this for a number of reasons, not least of which is a surface-level reading of Galatians. I truly hope our study over the past six weeks has at the very least toned down this habit.

One of the most astonishing verses we've seen so far was back in chapter five: "what matters is faith *working* through love" (5:6). Faith in Christ expresses itself through works of love. Works are not the enemy of faith. Paul was intense about his life with God and his own faithful action even while insisting until his last breath that none of our works (of the law or otherwise) save us, in the end. I often think of Paul's words in 1 Corinthians 9: *"Run in such a way to win the prize . . . I discipline my body and bring it under strict control, so that after preaching to others, I myself will not be disqualified"* (vv.24–27). This is not a person who is passive about, what he calls, "the obedience of faith."

In the end, *each person will have to carry his own load.* I have come to believe that verse 5 is an eschatological allusion, which I have never seen in this verse in the past. These verses we've looked at today express a mysterious paradox: we are deeply responsible to each other, but ultimately, we are each responsible for ourselves and will stand before God alone in the future. Many scholars point out in their commentaries on this verse that 4 Ezra 7 (a Jewish apocalyptic text written a little later than Galatians) expresses a similar idea with the day of judgment clearly in view.[9] We examine our work alone before God, because in the end, on that great day of judgment still to come, we will be examined on

---

[8] Rowan Williams, *Silence and Honey Cakes: The Wisdom of the Desert* (Oxford: A Lion Book, 2003), 47-8. Copyright © 2003 Medio Media. Reproduced with permission of the Licensor through PLSclear.
[9] Hays, "Galatians," 335.

our own, alone before God. This is a sobering thought, of course. And yet, because of Jesus, I also take comfort. Ben Myers' breathtaking words about the judgment have been filed somewhere deep in my heart since I first read them:

> Jesus will come to judge the living and the dead. That will be the best thing that ever happens to us. On that day the weeds in each of us will be separated from the wheat. It will hurt—no doubt it will hurt—when our self-deceptions are burned away. But the pain of truth heals; it does not destroy. On our judgment day we will be able for the first time to see the truth of our lives, when we see ourselves as loved.[10]

Jesus saved us, is saving us, and will save us still. May we walk in the Spirit faster today than we did yesterday. And may our works here on the earth, in between these two ages, be rooted in and energized by the One who loved us and gave Himself for us (Gal 2:20). Thanks be to God.

Jesus saved us, is saving us, and will save us still.

[10] Ben Myers, *The Apostles' Creed: A Guide to the Ancient Catechism* (Bellingham, WA: Lexham Press, 2018), 61–2, Kindle edition.

NOTES

THE CROSS ZONE

day three

If You Don't Give Up

Read, write and mark Galatians 6:6–10.

_____

_____

_____

_____

_____

_____

_____

_____

_____

Nothing seems flashy about Galatians 6:6 at first blush but, within those words, Paul signals a remarkable development in the New Testament church. Remember, Galatians is believed to be among his earliest letters. Yet, this verse informs us that some degree of formal instruction was already underway in the churches of Galatia. In a few moments, we'll discover what Paul means by "the word."

For now, fill in the two representative people in Galatians 6:6 whose lives were connected through "the word."

_____ "the word" _____

Take a look below at the Greek transliteration of "one who is taught the word" and "the one who teaches" in Galatians 6:6. Search the segment for hints of a word commonly used for religious instruction. Consider sounding out the syllables phonetically to catch the association:

ho katēchoumenos ton logon tō katechounti
(one who is taught)   (the word)   (the one who teaches)

Depending upon your background and whether or not the term is familiar to you, hints of "catechism" may have caught your eye. The English words "catechist" (meaning teacher/instructor) and "catechumen" (meaning one who is taught) are each derived from those Greek terms. Teaching is as crucial to Christ's body as food is to ours. A community of faith can exist without it but it cannot mature and bear its intended fruit. Learning is the identifying marker of any "disciple."

Christ's final instructions to the Eleven and beyond were these: "Go . . . *make disciples* of all nations, baptizing them in the name of the Father and of the Son and of the Holy Spirit, *teaching them . . .*" (emphasis mine). The apostles took Jesus at His word and taught those early churches to teach. They did not just evangelize. They *discipled*. Within several centuries, formalized creeds and catechisms were emerging.

> We know from the history of the early church in the second and third centuries that a well-developed system of catechetical instruction did emerge as a standard feature of church life with teachers (who were often opposed by the bishops!) playing a major role in the formation of Christian doctrine. Origen, for example, began his ecclesiastical career as a teacher in the catechetical school at Alexandria.[1]

Galatians 6:6 doesn't indicate a fully developed catechism like those that took shape several centuries later. It does, however, reveal that teaching and studying were immediately implemented as core disciplines within local churches. The text, in fact, goes further than that. It conveys that in-depth discipleship of new converts was of sufficient priority to require some teachers in the early church to take on the tasks heavily enough to hinder their income. Paul calls those with whom these teachers share the word to share all good things with them in return.

New Testament scholar C. K. Barrett writes, "It is interesting to note here what may be the earliest reference to any kind of paid Christian ministry . . . They

---

Teaching is as crucial to Christ's body as food is to ours.

---

[1] Timothy George, *Galatians*, New American Commentary Vol. 30 (Nashville: Broadman & Holman, 1994), 420.

were rewarded for their work, though not, it seems, with a regular salary but by spontaneous sharing on the part of the person being instructed."[2]

The range of "good things" that can be shared is river-wide. The one with nothing to give financially could offer other encouragements and consolations immeasurably beneficial to the teacher. With all the abuses we've seen and heard about, some squirming over an imperative for learners and disciples to help support their teachers is more than understandable.

What are some of the abuses that give you pause in dialogues like these?

_____

_____

Until Christ's kingdom comes, opportunists, manipulators, liars and thieves will be drawn like moths to a flame to try to defraud people who are taught to give. If they are not held accountable in this life, we need not wonder if God will call them to account at the judgment. But, notice how far removed abuses are from Paul's idea of mutuality in Galatians 6:6.

What could help reduce abuses in communities of faith?

_____

_____

_____

Glance back at Galatians 6:6. What exactly was taught?

_____

No matter where scholars land in the window of possibilities for the dating of Galatians, the letter was unquestionably written before the canon was complete. John's Gospel, his three letters and the book of Revelation, for example, were written several decades after Paul was martyred. So, what did Paul mean when he referenced the teaching of "the word"? Paul's letter to the Colossians helps answer the question. If you're up for a treasure hunt, you'll find it interesting.

What does Paul identify as "the word of truth" in Colossians 1:5–6?

_____

_____

> Let the one who is taught the word share all his good things with the teacher.
>
> Galatians 6:6

---

[2] C. K. Barrett, *Freedom and Obligation: A Study of the Epistle to the Galatians* (Philadelphia, PA: Westminster John Knox Press, 1985), 82.

How does Paul define "the word" in Colossians 4:3?

_____

What does Paul say God commissioned him to do in Colossians 1:25?

_____

_____

_____

What does Paul describe as "the word of God fully known" according to Colossians 1:26–27?

_____

_____

_____

Based on these discoveries, what do you think Paul meant by "the word"?

_____

_____

In Galatians 6:6, "the word" refers to neither the entire canon as we know it nor a two-minute synopsis of salvation detached from the Old Testament. When Paul speaks of "the word" taught to the churches, he means the gospel of Jesus Christ and (here, at least) in no short form. Otherwise, extended efforts of teachers would be unnecessary.

"The word" is Paul's reference to the gospel in long hand. Converts were taught about the coming of Jesus, the God-man, who gave His sinless life on the cross for us, was buried and rose again, is now seated at God's right hand and will come again in glory. But that wasn't all. They were taught the backstory of Jesus, rolling the scroll to Genesis 12 where God first called Abram and Scripture preached the gospel beforehand that all nations would be blessed through him.

They were discipled in the teachings and ways of Christ according to the apostles who followed Him closely. They were taught the implications of His gospel for the world and for believers in this life and in the next. They were taught about the kingdom of God and the indwelling Spirit. They were told of demonic powers and principalities and taught how to withstand temptation and turn away from evil. These kinds of elements were and will remain basic essentials to the thriving church.

I love how Gordon Fee captures the gospel in his book *Listening to the Spirit in the Text*:

> The gospel is Paul's singular passion, and the gospel has to do with salvation—not simply salvation from sin, in the classical fundamentalist sense, but in the more profound biblical sense of God's purposes that began with creation and that will be consummated at Christ's coming— namely creating a people for his name, who will live in close relationship with him and will bear his likeness, and thus be for his glory.[3]

In the next several verses of Galatians, Paul draws on a maxim with a long history both in the Hebrew world and the Greco-Roman world.

Review Galatians 6:7–10. Write a one-sentence synopsis of Paul's teaching in these four verses.

_____

_____

Behold the laws of the harvest:

1. Sow what you want to reap.
2. Plant what you want to grow.

Conversely, if you don't want something to grow, don't plant it. Small seeds sprout into larger things by divine order. This is both a beautiful truth and terrifying truth. God took the agricultural dynamics He designed for this terrestrial soil and displayed them as a visible life principle for humankind. In Galatians 6:8, the law of the harvest is cast in terms of eschatological inheritance. Those who have sown to their flesh alone will, in the end, reap corruption. Those who have sown to the Spirit will, in the end, reap eternal life.

Elsewhere in the Bible, the principle of sowing and reaping is set within the framework of earthly existence and not always limited to the individual lifetime. One generation could sow idolatry and another generation reap captivity. What makes the concept of sowing and reaping somewhat unique in Galatians 6:7 is the positive overall tenor. While Paul makes clear what the end will be for those who sow their life efforts and energies to the flesh, take stock of all he says to those who sow to the Spirit.

The divine principle of sowing and reaping is good news for all except the mocker who thinks God is either make-believe or gullible enough to be deceived. It says to those who believe, what we do *now* matters *then*. Seed

> The divine principle of sowing and reaping is good news for . . . those who believe: what we do *now* matters *then*.

3 Gordon D. Fee, *Listening to the Spirit in the Text* (Grand Rapids, MI: Eerdmans, 2000), 25.

that does not spring up in the soil of earth is sown in the soil of heaven. There, it cannot fail to sprout. There, no bird of prey can snatch it from the ground before it takes root. There, no pestilence can devour it and no enemy can trample it.

Little debilitates the human spirit like a feeling of futility. Futile is defined as "serving no useful purpose: completely ineffective . . . Futile may connote completeness of failure or unwisdom of undertaking."[4] Ever felt like you've invested tremendous time, emotion and energy into something or someone that, from all outward appearances, proved "completely ineffective"? Paul feared the same (Gal 4:11; 1 Thess 3:5).

Has something you believed to be good—something you believed to be of God—resulted in what appears to be "completeness of failure"? Expound on it as a way of bringing it before the Lord.

_____

_____

_____

Feelings of futility are inextricably tied to the temptation to give up. Since Satan is deeply invested in Spirit-empowered people giving up, imagine how he fans the flame of futility. Here are some things Galatians 6:9–10 would have us know: no effort we have sown into the things of the Spirit is in vain. No prayer, no time in Scripture, no fasting, no serving nor sacrifice, no help to our neighbor, no aid to the poor, no word on behalf of the unheard is bereft of effect. Any work we have done for the good of others—even what did not seem to "work" at all—is seed sown in eternal soil.

It cannot fail to matter. If it doesn't matter to them, you can be certain it matters to God and He will see to it that it matters to you, whether in this lifetime or the next. Paul writes in 1 Corinthians 13:8 that "love never fails" (NIV) but we've each experienced times when love seemed to fail miserably. The gospel truth is that we, for now, see only in part (1 Cor 13:12). One day we will see the whole. We will discover that our human definitions of failure were far removed from God's. So many things we thought were successes will turn out to mean shockingly little, and the seeds we thought we'd sown in vain will turn into harvests shockingly large.

In due season, Loved of God, we will reap. When God seems to be taking His own sweet time, He's only taking time for the sake of eternity.

⁴ _Merriam-Webster's Collegiate Dictionary,_ Tenth Ed. (Springfield, MA: Merriam-Webster, Incorporated, 1997), 475.

THE CROSS ZONE

day four

New Creation

Read, write and mark Galatians 6:11–16.

_____

_____

_____

_____

_____

_____

_____

_____

_____

_____

_____

_____

_____

_____

_____

_____

_____

We have arrived, too soon if you ask me, at the apostle's conclusion of his letter. Spoiler alert: Paul does not wind down. He winds up and spins off into the horizon of a flaming red, apocalyptic sunset. Mom will wrap it up tomorrow with a lesson that is decidedly my favorite so far—I smiled the whole time I read it and then I cried. I am, every single day I have the opportunity, honored to partner with my Mom, who has gifts I simply have not been given and skills I could not contrive on my most lucid day.

Working under her leadership, I've learned that accepting the reality of the body of Christ can be liberating if we find a way to get over ourselves and the absurd ideal of needing to be Everything. We have only to show up with the gifts the Spirit allotted to each of us and never the ones the Spirit didn't. God gave those gifts to other people for a reason. We are responsible for stewarding our own gifts and honoring the gifts we don't have—even the gifts we wish we had—in brothers and sisters who do, for the glory of Christ.

As Paul began to dictate this most impassioned and scathing of all his extant letters without any delicacy of diplomacy, so also, he ends it without exchange of warm greetings to or from dear co-laborers either with him or in Galatia. But, in verse 11, he picks up the pen to authenticate the words of his letter with a few lines of his own. Letters and documents in the ancient world were often written by professionals trained in both dictation and penmanship.

Look up Romans 16:22. Who wrote Paul's long letter to the Romans? Check the correct answer:

☐ Phoebe   ☐ Junia   ☐ Andronicus   ☐ Tertius

Paul greets his recipients explicitly in several of the letters we have in the New Testament. My personal favorite is the colorful one at the end of 1 Corinthians where he greets the church "in his own hand" and then inserts: *"If anyone does not love the Lord, a curse be on him. Our Lord, come!"* (16:21–22)

I've always assumed that verse 11 was a reference to the length of Galatians itself but, instead, "large letters" almost certainly refers to the size of the alphabetic symbols and not the size or length of the epistle itself.[1] The REB makes this obvious in their translation: *"Look how big the letters are, now that I am writing to you in my own hand."* It's hard to know what significance the size of Paul's script would have carried for the Galatians and if it would have conveyed something unique about Paul that they recognized. Since his handwriting was larger than his scribe's, it may have been used merely for distinction or emphasis. The eight verses he chose to write are an incredible summary of Galatians, in fact. A stunning end.

> We have only to show up with the gifts the Spirit allotted to each of us and never the ones the Spirit didn't.

[1] Craig S. Keener, *Galatians: A Commentary* (Grand Rapids, MI: Baker Academic, 2019), 558–561.

Glance through the six verses in front of us today and list as many ideas as you can that you've already seen in Galatians, now repeated here by way of conclusion:

_____

_____

_____

_____

In verses 12–13, Paul makes his final claims about the agitators; here they are "the ones who would compel you to be circumcised" (v.12). We've seen this verb two other important times in the letter. First, when Paul gives the prime example of Titus, a Greek, who was not "compelled" to be circumcised, while at a private meeting with the leaders in Jerusalem (2:3). Second, when Paul opposes Peter's double standard at the table in Antioch: *"If you, who are a Jew, live like a Gentile and not like a Jew, how can you compel Gentiles to live like Jews?"* (2:14)

These agitators want to make a good impression "in the flesh" (v.12). We've seen how Paul uses "the flesh" in opposition to the Spirit in the last few chapters of Galatians. Thus, as David deSilva concludes, "The area of concern to the rival teachers is unambiguously presented as negative and inferior to the realm of concern for Paul."[2]

Not only this, but from Paul's perspective, the agitators are driven by a desire to dodge persecution. Whatever the nature of the persecution is, Paul associates it with the offensive cross of Christ, the only thing in the world Paul has left to "boast" about. The agitators resist being persecuted for precisely what Paul deems the one remaining thing to find any glory in: Christ's cross.

I appreciate Richard Hays pointing out that this does not mean the agitators did not acknowledge or confess the crucifixion of Jesus as significant, but simply that they did not "interpret the cross, in Paul's fashion."[3] These are Jews who are preaching some kind of "gospel" and awfully involved with the Gentile Christian community (1:6). Certainly, the cross of Jesus would have held import to them. They likely made a different kind of theological sense of it entirely. For Paul, the cross "proclaims the end of all ethnic, social, and religious privilege and distinction" and is not merely "a minor refinement of the religion of the Sinaitic Law."[4] Paul's radical gospel was prone to be persecuted

---

[2] David A. deSilva, *Galatians: A Handbook on the Greek Text* (Waco, TX: Baylor University Press, 2014), 140.
[3] Richard B. Hays, "Galatians," in *The New Interpreter's Bible* Vol. XI (Nashville: Abingdon Press, 2000), 346. © 2000 Abingdon Press. Used by permission. All rights reserved.
[4] Hays, "Galatians," 342.

in the complex world he inhabited, while the far more tame, domesticated version of the agitators, in Paul's view, evaded persecution.

In verse 13, I understand "the circumcised" as a reference to the agitators, the group of Jewish Christians causing trouble in Gentile Galatia, rather than a reference to all Jews in general. Paul suggests their persuasion is motivated by self-interest (v.13b) and he adds an even more savage claim: they "don't keep the law themselves" (v.13a). We have to keep Paul's biography in mind. He had been a Pharisee, blameless with regard to the Law's righteousness (Phil 3:6). In Galatians, he has described his former life in Judaism as highly successful and extremely zealous. From the other side, Paul accuses the agitators of creating unnecessary problems for Gentiles and, even worse, for emptying the death of Jesus of its significance (Gal 2:21). And the greatest irony is that they themselves are Law-observant-lite. Hays puts it this way:

> Paul is saying that the circumcision advocates are only dabblers in the Law, not really carrying out its comprehensive requirements. This accusation reflects Paul's rigoristic interpretation of the total demand of the Law. In the eyes of Paul, the former zealous Pharisee, those who merely practice circumcision and observe some of the feasts cannot claim to be living fully in accord with everything the Law requires. There can be no partial or selective observance of the Law.[5]

Successfully persuading the Galatians to adhere to circumcision would be grounds for the agitators to boast, while Paul can now only boast in the cross of Jesus (vv.13–14). Jeanette Hagen Pifer, in her monograph titled *Faith as Participation,* writes beautifully on the paradoxical nature of Paul's boasting:

> In contrast to his opponents, Paul's boast, his dependence upon and identification with Christ are the basis of his own life . . . By boasting in the cross, Paul counters all other systems of value and focuses on something he himself has not done. Paul boasts in a work that was entirely accomplished by Christ and which completely altered his own existence. Through boasting only in the cross of Christ, Paul draws together the central focus of this letter—faith relativises all things under Christ.[6]

What does it mean to "boast" in the cross of Jesus?

_____

_____

_____

[5] Hays, "Galatians," 343.
[6] Jeanette Hagen Pifer, *Faith as Participation* (Tübingen, Germany: Mohr Siebeck, 2019), 211.

In words reminiscent of 2:19–21, Paul declares, "the world has been crucified to me through the cross, and I to the world" (v.14b). The cross is at once nothing Paul himself accomplished, worked up, or chose by his own will or logic, and yet he describes his participation in Jesus's crucifixion in such a profound and intimate way. No one could articulate this better than J. Louis Martyn, a legendary interpreter of both Paul and Galatians:

> Paul preaches the cross as the foundation of his confidence, because the cross—not the advent of the Law—is the watershed event for the whole of the cosmos, affecting everything after it . . . The crucifixion of Christ (no longer an event separate from himself) was now the crucifixion of Paul's cosmos, everything he had held sacred and dependable . . . By the same token, Paul says that Christ's cross brought about his own crucifixion to the cosmos. He thus uses the image of crucifixion to emphasize his own lethal separation from his previous, cherished and acknowledged identity. With this event, that is to say, Paul ceased to be known by others on the basis of his place in that old cosmos of the Law (1:13–16).[7]

Verse 15, to my mind, is the heart of the entire letter. If you haven't paid a bit of attention so far, all is not lost, because here it is: "For both circumcision and uncircumcision mean nothing."

What does Paul say matters instead?

_____

_____

Galatians isn't about something as small as circumcision being bad and uncircumcision being good or vice versa. It's far more revolutionary than that. Neither matters, because the world in which those categories held such weight has been, is being and will be utterly replaced by a new one. And in that new world, we are new, too. Paul had been caught up into the crucifixion of Christ and was already living in and from a new world as a brand-new person but doing it all right in the midst of the same, present evil age. No wonder he's difficult to follow sometimes!

I don't know about you, but God is often up to bigger things in my life than I want Him to be. I'd be happy with one little desire being fulfilled. While I believe God cares about my dreams and desires, I have come to suspect that God is also after the birth of totally different dreams and desires in me, ones that are generated from and fulfilled in another, better world.

> God is often up to bigger things in my life than I want Him to be.

[7] J. Louis Martyn, *Galatians,* The Anchor Yale Bible (New Haven, CT: Yale University Press, 1997), 564.

Our final verse ends with a blessing composed of two parts: (a) peace for those who follow "this standard" and, (b) mercy to "the Israel of God." The standard Paul refers to is not a rule of law, new or old, but New Creation. Abraham's family lives into, for lack of better terms, this new creation when they walk by the Spirit of God's Son, crucified and made alive forevermore. As for the second part of this blessing, well, I'm going to leave this one in your good hands.

What does Paul mean by "Israel of God"? To whom is he referring? Use everything you have learned about Galatians to give this answer your very best attempt. Don't worry, no one is looking over your shoulder.

_____

_____

_____

_____

_____

_____

_____

_____

Our week is not quite over, but my time with you has come to its end. My mind spins with all I've learned but even more with all I still don't know about Paul's letter to the Galatians. Case in point, what Paul means by "the Israel of God." By the way, do you know that in 2019 someone published a gigantic 848-page commentary on just these six chapters of Galatians alone?[8] Eight hundred and forty-eight pages on six chapters!

I hope you have learned a few things over the past six weeks. Most of all, I hope you walk away with questions that intrigue you and draw you back to this ancient letter for a lifetime. The more we learn about Scripture, the more we still have to learn about Scripture. We will not reach the end of this rich pursuit in our lifetimes. Perhaps we will only keep making our way around wider and wider circles.

[8] Craig S. Keener, *Galatians: A Commentary* (Grand Rapids, MI: Baker Academic, 2019).

THE CROSS ZONE

day five

Bearing the Marks

Read, write and mark Galatians 6:17–18.

_____

_____

_____

_____

_____

How does it feel to write the final two verses?

_____

_____

_____

_____

Life doesn't go on hold during a Bible study series. Bills, rentals and mortgages still have to be paid. Loved ones still get sick, cars break down and sinks stop up. Crises don't have the decency to wait until we're done. And this is as it should be. We weren't meant to keep our focused pursuit of God in a stratosphere detached from the topsoil clinging to the soles of our shoes. Holiness is not unhooked from all this earthiness. The kingdom of heaven invades the globe with blades of grass between human toes. This is the way God planned it. For these very reasons and more, you are commendable—dare

I say exceptional—for making it to a final lesson in a multi-week series. In an increasingly unfocused world, you've fought distractions, temptations, deadlines and demons to finish. God bless you.

Not only does my world look different than it did when I began this journey well over a year ago, the entire world looks different. We both know, however, that it doesn't take a year for our worlds to change. It can happen overnight.

Have you had to navigate your way through any unforeseen changes while working your way through this Bible study? If so, what were they?

_____

_____

_____

_____

_____

_____

_____

_____

> I love great endings, especially if they are a bit unpredictable.

Were there times you thought you wouldn't finish? Me, too. Melissa, too. But, by the grace of God, here we are. Hopefully you'll get a chance to view the final session since it adds nuance to these final verses but, either way, we've officially held out for Paul's last words to the churches of Galatia. I love great endings, especially if they are a bit unpredictable. Paul's ending in his letter to the Galatians is perfection. The closing two verses combine the moxie, the poignancy and the affection we've found braided like colorful cords throughout the whole letter.

"From now on, let no one cause me trouble . . . " Galatians begins with a reference to trouble, remember? Paul writes in 1:7, "there are some who are troubling you and want to distort the gospel of Christ." Those very troublers were used by God to dip the quill of Paul in the boldest of ink. Having responded with 147 no-holds-barred verses, he says, in effect, in the 148th, "Now, back off. If you've got a problem with my service, see my Boss."

"Because I bear on my body . . . " God gave His words and the gospel of His Son to souls clothed in mortality. No act of God in creation was haphazard, least of all the incarnational aspect of His image bearers. Our hearts and minds are not just emotion and thought. They are also muscle and organ. God fashioned our frames to have form and substance, skull, spine and ribs. The wear-and-tear-ability of the human body after the fall of man was most intentional. How would God become man and purchase our redemption through His blood without a body to bleed? "Therefore, as [Jesus] was coming into the world, He said: 'You did not desire sacrifice and offering, but you prepared a body for me'" (Hebrews 10:5).

Jesus took on a body like ours, vulnerable to the elements both within and without. Vulnerability is built into our bodies like sand is built into glass. We can practice mind-over-matter all we want but we cannot keep these bodies from being worn and torn.

When was the last reminder of your own physical vulnerability?

_____

_____

_____

_____

_____

_____

_____

_____

We are not made of rubber. We don't always bounce back. We humans made "a little lower than the angels and crowned . . . with glory and honor" (Ps 8:5 NIV) are subject to the perils of life on a rock carpeted by thistle and thorn.

Paul's sufferings took their toll but their toll was no disgrace. They were marks of grace. Jacob wrestled with the angel of God and walked forward with a limp. No human encounters the heavenly things without earth becoming less hospitable. Faith stirs up a longing for a place we've never been. We don't walk the same after journeying in close company with God. The world views the effects of walking with God as liabilities. Detriments. Humiliations. Disloyalties. To the world, our sufferings despite our faith make us look weak. Pitiable. Paul saw it a whole different way.

What does Paul say he bears on his body in Galatians 6:17?

_____

> Faith stirs up a longing for a place we've never been.

In Greek, τὰ στίγματα τοῦ Ἰησοῦ (ta stigmata tou Iēsou), in English, the marks—or stigmata—of Jesus. The apostle's reference is to the scars on his body.

Read 2 Corinthians 11:23–25. Which of these sufferings were likely to have permanently marked the body? _____

David deSilva explains,

> Paul wrote this catalog sometime between 54 and 57 CE. There would have been considerably fewer items on it at the time he wrote Galatians in 49 or early 50 CE.
>
> Nevertheless, Paul's South Galatian mission gave ample opportunity for scars (Acts 13–14; 2 Tim 3:11) . . . Paul pointed to his scars as "brand marks" (stigmata). The term may refer to the custom of fugitives taking refuge in a temple and receiving the marks of the local god (and with these marks of belonging, amnesty from further molestation); it may also refer to the custom of branding slaves with the mark of their owner or (less frequently) soldiers with the mark of their general.[1]

Considering the theme of slavery versus freedom in Galatians, and the frequency with which Paul calls himself Christ's bondservant in his writings, Paul is almost certainly referencing his scars as the permanent branding of his servitude to Jesus. His scars were the physical results of his repeated unwillingness to forsake his master. He would not change his story to lessen his punishment. He would not cater to those with the power to hurt him by compromising the gospel. He did nothing to soften the blow if doing so would soften the truth.

The credibility of Paul's testimony was engraved in his skin. He wore it everywhere he went. Remarkably, every smack of a stone or slash of a whip became a signature of Christ that his detractors could not erase. Paul intended to make a red-hot point to the troublers who'd tried to force Gentile converts to be circumcised: he bore something beyond the mark of circumcision on his flesh. With Christ had come a new covenant and, with this new covenant, a new eschatological sign: the marks of Jesus.

Contemplate this fascinating excerpt by scholar Richard B. Hays:

> Paul interprets these bodily scars as signs of his identification with his crucified Lord. Indeed, his battered body becomes for him a visible

[1] David A. deSilva, *The Letter to the Galatians,* The New International Commentary on the New Testament (Grand Rapids, MI: Eerdmans, 2018), 514.

depiction of the gospel of the cross. This is probably what he has in mind when he describes himself as "carrying in the body the putting to death of Jesus, so that the life of Jesus may also be made visible in our bodies" (2 Cor 4:10). The wounded apostle becomes a walking exhibit of the message of "Jesus Christ, and him crucified." In all likelihood this conviction explains what Paul means when he says that in his original preaching to the Galatians "Jesus Christ was publicly exhibited as crucified" (3:1 NRSV).[2]

Paul's identity *in* Christ and his identification *with* Christ meant everything to him. Whatever the flash of burning light from heaven did or did not do to Paul's physical eyes, that noonday revelation of Jesus on the road to Damascus succeeded in giving the former persecutor a lifelong lens transplant. He viewed everything in his life through the lens of Christ crucified and raised from the dead. Every wound was an opportunity to enter into his afflictions.

How did this lens shape his perspective in Colossians 1:24?

_____

_____

_____

_____

I have known people, most of them missionaries in nations opposed to the gospel, who bore the marks of Jesus in their flesh. I stood at the hospital bedside of a young woman with multiple gunshot wounds, the sole survivor of a targeted attack on the car she occupied with her husband and coworkers. The majority of us will never bear physical scars for the sake of Christ's gospel. But, to be sure, we do endure sufferings and some of those will come as direct results of faithfulness to Jesus. In those sufferings, we have the same opportunity as Paul to fellowship with Jesus—to know Him intimately *right* there in our sufferings.

To rely on Him fully *right there,*
receive of His consolations *right there,*
take Him at his word *right there,*
remember His cross *right there,*
long for His glorious return *right there*
and place our hope in the resurrection *right there.*

[2] Richard B. Hays, "Galatians," in *The New Interpreter's Bible* Vol. XI (Nashville: Abingdon Press, 2000), 346. © 2000 Abingdon Press. Used by permission. All rights reserved.

These are the things that keep our afflictions, losses and pain from being sentenced to an echoing void. When we're tempted to limit Paul's identification with Jesus to His sufferings, let's hasten to remember Galatians 2:20. Paul's desire to identify with the death of Jesus was in order to also identify with His risen life. In Christ, dying always leads to living.

Reflecting on what you've learned in a series of this kind is not just a sentimental gesture though, like me, you may be tenderhearted about seeing it end. Reflection helps us store what we've studied. We've amassed treasures over these six weeks. We don't want to lose what we've gained or forget what we've learned. We want Galatians to be more than dear to us for the remainder of our lives. We want it to be active and operative and alive in our bones. We want God to use what we've learned to guard us in our freedom and in our understanding of the gospel. We want the words inspired by the Holy Spirit to continue to challenge, encourage, strengthen, inspire, empower and bless us and, when necessary, rebuke us.

I've gained courage from Galatians that I don't want to surrender. Have you? In what way?

_____

_____

_____

_____

During my last 48 hours of writing this series, I circled back around in my Scripture memory work to Galatians in my morning walk. Walking through the woods near our home, I choked back the tears as I recited verses to Jesus that will no doubt move me for the rest of my days. I'm not sure I've ever said these two verses aloud without emotion:

For I would have you know, brothers, that the gospel that was preached by me is not man's gospel. For I did not receive it from any man, nor was I taught it, but I received it through a revelation of Jesus.
Galatians 1:11–12 ESV

The Holy Spirit may have used entirely different verses to captivate you, so I'd like to ask you to stir up the embers of the entire letter again before we say goodbye. Go to your Bible, glance at each chapter and record the verse, phrase or truth that has held you most in this season and series.

Galatians 1

_____

_____

_____

Galatians 2

_____

_____

_____

Galatians 3

_____

_____

_____

Galatians 4

_____

_____

_____

_____

Galatians 5

_____

_____

_____

Galatians 6

_____

_____

_____

_____

What is your biggest takeaway as you reflect on the letter as a whole?

_____

_____

_____

_____

_____

_____

_____

Let's believe big and love big, then let's all go home.

I'd like to call to mind one of the most powerful takeaways for me. It is found in Galatians 2:18.

"For if I rebuild what I tore down, I prove myself to be a transgressor." (ESV)

All that has bound, enslaved, and stolen so much life, joy and fruitfulness from us was torn down by Christ on the cross. Oh, that we would take the greatest care not to rebuild what He has torn down. Let no one and nothing drag you back into slavery, whether to the passions of the flesh or to confidence in the flesh. "For you were called to be free, brothers and sisters" (Gal 5:13). Bind yourself to your master, Jesus, whose yoke is easy, whose burden is light.

And a few final Galatian exhortations! Resist the temptation to finish in the flesh what you started in the Spirit. Walk by the Spirit, be led by the Spirit and sow to the Spirit. Remember when life gets so complicated and convoluted that, at the end of the day for the follower of Christ, what matters is faith working through love. Let's believe big and love big, then let's all go home.

It is the greatest privilege of my serving life to pore over the pages of Scripture with you. Thank you. I can't think of a better way to conclude our series than with Paul's closing words to the churches of Galatia.

Brothers and sisters, the grace of our Lord Jesus Christ be with your spirit. Amen.

Galatians 6:18

GALATIANS
WRAP UP

––––

From now on, let no one cause me trouble,
because I bear on my body the marks of Jesus.
Brothers and sisters, the grace of our Lord
Jesus Christ be with your spirit. Amen.

Galatians 6:17–18

VIDEO GUIDE

WRAP UP

Introduction: In today's session we conclude our 6-week study of the book of Galatians. Our hope in this wrap-up is to be irreversibly marked by the message that had indelibly marked the apostle Paul.

Read Galatians 6:11–18.

In keeping with the closing of Paul's letter to the Galatians, let's end our series...

1. Marveling over a _____ so sturdy, it could not be _____ out of him.

Galatians 6:17—Paul saw the marks as _____.

2. _____ toward brothers and sisters with whom we strongly _____.

ἡ χάρις τοῦ κυρίου ἡμῶν Ἰησοῦ Χριστοῦ μετὰ τοῦ πνεύματος ὑμῶν, ἀδελφοί· ἀμήν

The NET translates it in this exact arrangement: (6:18) The grace of our Lord Jesus Christ be with your spirit, brothers and sisters. Amen.

3. Committed to be able to say in regard to anyone, no matter how _____,

respected or _____, who tries to drag us into slavery, "to them we did

not yield in submission even for a moment, so that the _____ of the gospel

might be _____ for you" (Gal 2:5 ESV).

Read Galatians 2:18 and 6:18 one last time. Paul ended it the way he started it: GRACE.

NOTES

_____

_____

_____

_____

_____

_____

_____

_____

_____

_____

_____

_____

_____

_____

_____

_____

_____

_____

_____

_____

_____

_____

GALATIANS CROSSWORD

All answers are words found in the CSB translation of Galatians.

An asterisk (*) beside any clue indicates an answer of more than one word.

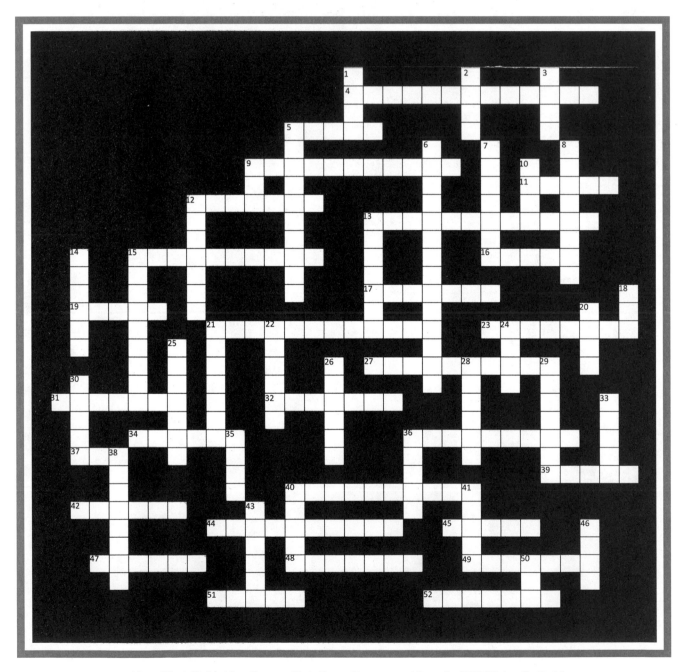

Now That Faith Has Come: Galatians Crossword Puzzle ©2020 by Beth Moore

(Answers are located on page 271)

ACROSS:

4   Eagerly awaiting this hope

5   There is no Jew or this

9   Chirography

11   Child of promise

12   This, not from men or by man

13   *What people did who heard the news that the former persecutor was preaching

15   *Christ's Spirit quoted

16   These according to the promise

17   Share all good things with this person

19   Let us not get this

21   *The women represent this

23   Barren

27   *Paul suffered these

31   That for which Christ set us free

32   Cephas came there

34   Some want to distort it

36   The world had been this to Paul

37   Not a slave

39   Hagar

40   Give the right hand

42   Through these the law was put into effect

44   Paul did this and was this

45   Those of Jesus were on Paul

47   God is not this

48   A wife has this

49   Test

51   About nothing but the cross

52   They were doing this well

DOWN:

1   Jerusalem above

2   Paul wished to change this of his

3   We will do this if we don't give up

5   A quality of the fruit of the Spirit

6   Doesn't accomplish anything

7   A description of the Galatians

8   A work of the flesh

9   Faith _____ come

10   It was unthinkable to Paul that Christ did this in vain

12   Seed of

13   You can find Galatians there

14   Not a brother

15   Separated

18   All in Christ

20   By the Spirit

21   Don't cause Paul this

22   Peter

24   This present age

25   The Law could not cancel this

26   Received by believing what we heard

28   Paul did not _____ circumcision

29   If Paul and his companions were found to be these, Christ was not the promoter

30   Paul's only boast

33   Paul went to this region

35   Faith works through this

36   Christ became this for us

38   Love him/her

40   Against the Spirit

41   To all who follow this standard

43   Moses, Elijah and Paul went there

46   Those in Christ are Abraham's

50   Paul was not made an apostle by them

BIBLIOGRAPHY

Adams, Marilyn McCord. *Horrendous Evils and the Goodness of God.* Ithaca, NY: Cornell University Press, 1999.

The Authorised Daily Prayer Book of the United Hebrew Congregations of the British Commonwealth of Nations Translated by S. Singer, 2nd rev. ed. London: Eyre & Spottiswoode, 1962.

Barclay, John M. G. *Obeying the Truth: Paul's Ethics in Galatians.* Vancouver, BC: Regent College Publishing, 1988.

Barrett, C.K. *Freedom and Obligation: A Study of the Epistle to the Galatians.* Philadelphia, PA: Westminster John Knox Press, 1985.

Boakye, Andrew K. *Death and Life: Resurrection, Restoration, and Rectification in Paul's Letter.* Eugene, OR: Pickwick Publications, 2017.

Boice, James Montgomery. "Galatians." In *The Expositor's Bible Commentary.* Vol. 10. Grand Rapids, MI: Zondervan, 1972.

Bruce, F. F., *The Epistle to the Galatians: A Commentary on the Greek Text.* The New International Greek Testament Commentary. Grand Rapids, MI: William B. Eerdmans Publishing Company, 1982.

Bruce, F. F., *The Epistle to the Colossians, to Philemon, and to the Ephesians.* The New International Greek Testament Commentary. Grand Rapids, MI: William B. Eerdmans Publishing Company, 1984.

Cosper, Mike. *Recapturing the Wonder: Transcendent Faith in a Disenchanted World.* IVP Books, 2017.

Cousar, Charles B. *Galatians.* Interpretation. Louisville, KY: Westminster John Knox Press, 1982.

Daniell, David. *The Bible in English: Its History and Influence.* New Haven, CT: Yale University Press, 2003.

Danker, Frederick W., Walter Bauer, and William F. Arndt. *A Greek-English Lexicon of the New Testament and Other Early Christian Literature.* Chicago: University of Chicago Press: 2000.

deSilva, David A. *Galatians: A Handbook on the Greek Text.* Waco, TX: Baylor University Press, 2014.

deSilva, David A. *The Letter to the Galatians.* The New International Commentary on the New Testament. Grand Rapids, MI: William B. Eerdmans Publishing Company, 2018.

Dunn, James D. G. *The Epistle to the Galatians.* Black's New Testament Commentary. Peabody, MA: Hendrickson, 1993.

Dunn, James D. G. *The Theology of Paul's Letter to the Galatians.* Cambridge: Cambridge University Press, 1993.

Emerson, Michael O. and Christian Smith. *Divided by Faith: Evangelical Religion and the Problem of Race in America*. Oxford: Oxford University Press, 2000.

Fee, Gordon D. *Galatians*. Pentecostal Commentary Series. Dorset: Deo Publishing, 2007.

Fee, Gordon D. *God's Empowering Presence: The Holy Spirit in the Letters of Paul*. Grand Rapids, MI: Baker Academic, 1994.

Fee, Gordon D. *Listening to the Spirit in the Text*. Grand Rapids, MI: William B. Eerdmans Publishing Company, 2000.

Fretheim, Terence E. "Genesis." In *The New Interpreter's Bible*. Vol. 1. Nashville: Abingdon Press, 1994.

Fung, R. Y. K. *The Epistle to the Galatians*. The New International Commentary on the New Testament. Grand Rapids, MI: William B. Eerdmans Publishing Company, 1988.

Gaventa, Beverly Roberts. *Our Mother Saint Paul*. Louisville, KY: Westminster John Knox Press, 2007.

George, Timothy. *Galatians*. The New American Commentary. Vol. 30. Nashville: Broadman & Holman, 1994.

Gupta, Nijay. *Paul and the Language of Faith*. Grand Rapids, MI: William B. Eerdmans Publishing Company, 2020.

Harris, W. Hall, ed. *The NET Bible Notes*. Richardson: Biblical Studies Press, 2005.

Hays, Richard B. "The Letter to the Galatians." In *The New Interpreter's Bible*. Vol. 11. Nashville: Abingdon Press, 2000.

Hays, Richard B. *Echoes of Scripture in the Letters of Paul*. New Haven, CT: Yale University Press, 1989.

Heim, Erin M. *Adoption in Galatians and Romans: Contemporary Metaphor Theories and the Pauline Huiothesia Metaphors*. Leiden; Boston: Brill, 2017.

Holman Illustrated Bible Dictionary. Nashville: Holman Bible Publishers, 2003.

Imes, Carmen Joy. *Bearing God's Name: Why Sinai Still Matters*. Downers Grove, IL: IVP Academic, 2019.

James, Carolyn Custis. "Lost in Translation," HuffPost Blog, September 19, 2016, https://www.huffpost.com/entry/lost-in-translation_5_b_12019892.

Jervis, L. Ann. *Galatians*. Understanding the Bible Commentary Series. Grand Rapids, MI: Baker Books, 1999.

Junior, Nyasha. *Reimagining Hagar: Blackness and Bible*. Oxford: Oxford University Press, 2019.

Keener, Craig S. *Galatians: A Commentary*. Grand Rapids, MI: Baker Academic, 2019.

Longenecker, Bruce W. *The Triumph of Abraham's God: The Transformation of Identity in Galatians.* Nashville: Abingdon Press, 1998.

Longenecker, Richard N. *Galatians.* Word Biblical Commentary. Vol. 41. Dallas: Word Books, 1990.

Luther, Martin. *Commentary on the Epistle to the Galatians* (1535). Translated by Theodore Graebner. Reprint n.d., Project Gutenberg, 2013.

Manning, Brennan. *All Is Grace: A Ragamuffin Memoir.* Colorado Springs: David C Cook, 2011.

Martyn, J. Louis. *Galatians.* The Anchor Yale Bible Commentaries. Vol 33A. New Haven, CT: Yale University Press, 1997.

Mason, Eric. *Woke Church: An Urgent Call for Christians in America to Confront Racism and Injustice.* Chicago: Moody Publishers, 2018.

McKnight, Scot. *Galatians.* NIV Application Commentary Series. Grand Rapids: Zondervan, 1995.

Merriam-Webster's Collegiate Dictionary, Tenth Ed. Springfield, MA: Merriam-Webster, Incorporated, 1997.

Moo, Douglas J. *Galatians.* Baker Exegetical Commentary on the New Testament. Grand Rapids, MI: Baker Academic, 2013.

Myers, Ben. *The Apostles' Creed: A Guide to the Ancient Catechism.* Bellingham, WA: Lexham Press, 2018.

Ortlund, Dane. *Gentle and Lowly: The Heart of Christ for Sinners and Sufferers.* Wheaton, IL:Crossway, 2020.

Peterson, Eugene. *Eat This Book: A Conversation in the Art of Spiritual Reading.* Grand Rapids, MI: William B. Eerdmans Publishing Company, 2006.

Peterson, Eugene. *Traveling Light: Modern Meditations on St. Paul's Letter of Freedom.* Colorado Springs: Helmers and Howard, 1988.

Pifer, Jeanette Hagen. *Faith as Participation.* Tübingen, Germany: Mohr Siebeck, 2019.

Pinnock, Clark H. *Truth on Fire: The Message of Galatians.* Eugene, OR: Wipf and Stock, 1998.

Pitre, Brant, Michael Barber, and John A. Kincaid. *Paul, A New Covenant Jew: Rethinking Pauline Theology.* Grand Rapids, MI: William B. Eerdmans Publishing Company, 2019.

Richter, Sandra L. *The Epic of Eden: A Christian Entry into the Old Testament.* Downers Grove, IL: IVP Academic, 2008.

Robertson, A.T. *Word Pictures in the New Testament.* Nashville, TN: Broadman Press, 1933.

Saner, Andrea D. "Of Bottles and Wells: Hagar's Christian Legacy," *The Journal of Theological Studies* 11.2 (2017): 199–215.

Schreiner, Thomas R. *Galatians*. Zondervan Exegetical Commentary on the New Testament Grand Rapids, MI: Zondervan, 2010.

Soards, Marion L. and Darrell J. Pursiful, *Galatians*. Smyth & Helwys Bible Commentary Series. Macon, GA: Smyth & Helwys Publishing, 2015.

Stanton, Graham. "What is the Law of Christ?" *Ex Auditu* 17 (2001): 47–59.

Steiner, George. *After Babel*. New York: Oxford University Press, 1975.

Scott, I. W. *Implicit Epistemology in the Letters of Paul: Story, Experience and the Spirit*. Tubingen: Mohr Siebeck, 2006.

Stott, John. *The Contemporary Christian: Applying God's Word to Today's World*. Downers Grove, IL: InterVarsity Press, 1992.

Stott, John R. W. *The Message of Galatians*. The Bible Speaks Today. Downers Grove, IL: InterVarsity Press, 1968.

Taylor, John W. "The Eschatological Interdependence of Jews and Gentiles in Galatians," *Tyndale Bulletin* 63.2 (2012): 291–316.

Thielman, Frank. *The Law and the New Testament: The Question of Continuity*. New York: The Crossroad Publishing Company, 1999.

Wells, Samuel. *A Future that's Bigger than the Past*. Norwich: Canterbury Press, 2019.

Williams, Rowan. *Silence and Honey Cakes: The Wisdom of the Desert*. Oxford: A Lion Book, 2003.

Wilson, Todd A. "Under Law," *The Journal of Theological Studies* 56 (2005): 362–392.

Wright, N. T. "Paul, Arabia, and Elijah," *Journal of Biblical Literature* 115, no. 4 (1996): 683–692.

Zodhiates, Spiros. *The Complete Word Study Dictionary*. Chattanooga, TN: AMG Publishers.

LEADER GUIDE

Participants, we are thrilled that Jesus has entrusted you to lead your community of women in this in-depth study of Scripture. We believe there are so many hidden treasures He will reveal through His word during your meeting time.

We've provided a few suggestions that we hope are simple and functional to help you get started.

Pray

PRAY, PRAY, PRAY before each week, and ask the Holy Spirit to guide you as you prepare to lead your group.

Time

Start on time. This is an essential component. You want to honor the time allotted for your weekly gathering.

How to Use the Study

- Each week you will gather and welcome the participants, watch the video for that week's session, discuss the previous week's homework.
- At the end of day three in Weeks 1-6, you will share that week's podcast.
- Session 7 is the wrap up.
- Close in prayer.

Get to Know You

An ice-breaker is optional, but it's a great way to get to know your sisters.

Nametags

Depending on your group size, we encourage you to have name tags to help facilitate community.

Discussion Time

Discussion time is essential and it allows everyone to share what they have learned and how they were impacted. As the leader, you have full freedom to choose a question from Beth and Melissa's lesson each week to discuss with your group from the prior week's homework. We have made suggestions, but please follow the Lord's leadership for your group.

Follow Up

Follow up with your participants throughout the week. Be sure to gather emails and phone numbers to send texts during the week to check-in.

WEEKS 1-6
Leader Information

Videos Times, Discussion Questions, Closing Suggestions

WEEK 1
THE GOSPEL ZONE

WATCH: Video 1 (31:21)

DISCUSS: What has brought you to the group and the Study of Galatians?

CLOSING: Inform the class you will be sharing the podcast after day 3 each week.

WEEK 2
THE FREEDOM ZONE

WATCH: Video 2 (27:05)

DISCUSS: Leader (and members) share their story

CLOSING: Members share their contact with another in the group and commit to praying for each other this week.

WEEK 3
THE PROMISE ZONE

WATCH: Video 3 (30:56)

DISCUSS: Discuss the concepts of promises and Beth's point about only God keeping promises

CLOSING: Encourage the group to continue on with their homework, even if they are a little behind

WEEK 4
THE CHILDREN ZONE

WATCH: Video 4 (36:48)

DISCUSS: Share your take away from week 3 podcast

CLOSING: Invite the women to look back at verses from this week's study and share them with the group.

WEEK 5
THE SPIRIT ZONE

WATCH: Video 5 (37:03)

DISCUSS: Does your relationship with your earthly father impact your relationship with your Heavenly Father?

CLOSING: Divide into groups, take prayer requests and ask a member to volunteer and pray over the requests mentioned.

WEEK 6
THE CROSS ZONE

WATCH: Video 6 (30:55)

DISCUSS: Revisit the question: Can you lose your salvation and how would you explain that to someone?

CLOSING: Pray as a group for lost friends or family members.

WRAP UP

WATCH: Video 7 (40:26)

DISCUSS: What is your biggest takeaway from the letter to the Galatians as a whole?

CLOSING: Ask your members to partner with another member and read Galatians 6:18 together.

GALATIANS CROSSWORD ANSWERS

All answers are words found in the CSB translation of Galatians.
An asterisk (*) beside any clue indicates an answer of more than one word.

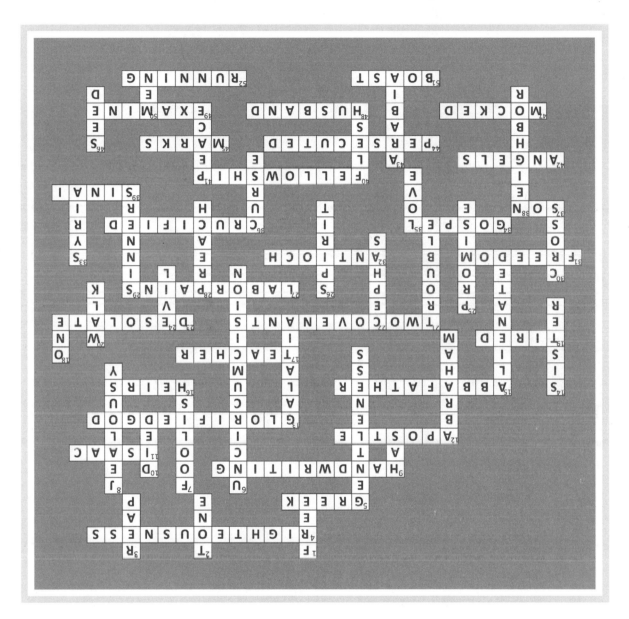

Now That Faith Has Come: Galatians Crossword Puzzle ©2020 by Beth Moore

ACROSS:

4 righteousness, **5** greek, **9** handwriting, **11** isaac, **12** apostle, **13** glorifiedgod, **15** abbafather, **16** heirs, **17** teacher, **19** tired, **21** twocovenants, **23** desolate, **27** laborpains, **31** freedom, **32** antioch, **34** gospel, **36** crucified, **37** son, **39** sinai, **40** fellowship, **42** angels, **44** persecuted, **45** marks, **47** mocked, **48** husband, **49** examine, **51** boast, **52** running

DOWN:

1 free, **2** tone, **3** reap, **5** gentleness, **6** uncircumcision, **7** foolish, **8** jealousy, **9** has, **10** died, **12** abraham, **13** galatia, **14** sister, **15** alienated, **18** one, **20** walk, **21** trouble, **22** cephas, **24** evil, **25** promise, **26** spirit, **28** preach, **29** sinners, **30** cross, **33** syria, **35** love, **36** curse, **38** neighbor, **40** flesh, **41** peace, **43** arabia, **46** seed, **50** men